Fear of Crime in the
United States

Fear of Crime in the United States
Causes, Consequences, and Contradictions

Jodi Lane

Nicole E. Rader

Billy Henson

Bonnie S. Fisher

David C. May

CAROLINA ACADEMIC PRESS

Durham, North Carolina

Library of Congress Cataloging-in-Publication Data

Lane, Jodi, 1967-
  Fear of crime in the United States : causes, consequences, and contradictions
/ Jodi Lane, Nicole Rader, David C. May, Bonnie S. Fisher, Billy Henson.
     pages cm
  Includes bibliographical references and index.
  ISBN 978-1-61163-066-4 (alk. paper)
  1. Fear of crime--United States. 2. Fear of crime--United States--Public
opinion. 3. Crime--United States. I. Title.

  HV6250.3.U5L357 2014
  364.97301'9--dc23

                       2014006968

CAROLINA ACADEMIC PRESS
700 Kent Street
Durham, North Carolina 27701
Telephone (919) 489-7486
Fax (919) 493-5668
www.cap-press.com

Printed in the United States of America

For Our Patient and Supportive Families
Chris and Cooper Wilson
Cody, Lucas, and Kate Rader
Sally Paulson
Nicolas, Olivia, and Camille Williams
Natalie, James, Will, and Grace May

For Our Students Who Listened Attentively and
Then Asked Insightful Questions

Contents

Acknowledgments

All of us were able to work on this book because we had the help of others, throughout our careers and during the writing process. We are especially grateful to Beth Hall at Carolina Academic Press for her patience and helpful advice while we developed and wrote this manuscript. Graduate students Caitlin Henriksen at the University of Cincinnati and Ethan Stokes at Mississippi State University provided countless hours of help at the end of the writing process by carefully reviewing, formatting, and proofreading each chapter. We also thank all of our academic and practitioner colleagues who influenced the development our ideas about fear of crime over the years.

Jodi especially thanks the University of Florida for allowing her to take a sabbatical leave during the 2013–2014 school year (a break from teaching and service to focus on research), which facilitated the completion of this book. She also thanks her family, Chris and Cooper, for their patience and understanding during the writing process as well as the fun diversions they provided. She also thanks Cooper's grandparents—Jackie, Lou, and Jo—for regularly keeping Cooper entertained while she works on research.

Nicole would like to thank Cody, Lucas, and Kate for their support, for keeping her grounded, and for making life more fun than she ever expected. She would also like to thank her colleagues at Mississippi State University who have been amazingly supportive and wonderful to her over the years. Finally, she'd like to thank Michelle Hughes Miller (University of South Florida) for believing in her in the beginning and fostering her fear of crime scholarship.

Billy would like to thank his fellow authors for their guidance during the process of writing this book. As this was his first experience writing a book, he is very thankful for their patience and leadership. He would also like to give a special thanks to Bonnie Fisher for introducing him to the world of fear of crime and for her mentoring and friendship over the years. Finally, he would like to thank his fiancée Sally for the support she gives him everyday.

Bonnie expresses her gratitude to Wesley Skogan who showed her how fascinating the study of fear of crime could be, especially its measurement, while she was his graduate student years ago. That interest remains with her today. Thanks to her students who have endured years of fear of crime discussions in and outside the classroom, especially Billy who listened! Most of all, she thanks her family—Nick, Olivia and Camille—for their years of love, support and sense of humor every day.

David would like to thank his family, Natalie, James, Will, and Grace May, for their understanding for those times when he couldn't do whatever they requested because he was "writing a book." He would also like to thank the coauthors of this book and his colleagues in the Mississippi State University Department of Sociology for their patience, prayers, thoughts, generosity, and kindness in the journey through Natalie's cancer that occurred concurrently with the writing of this book.

Fear of Crime in the United States

Chapter 1

The Current State of Fear of Crime in America: A Broad Overview

What people want is that crime and criminals be brought under control so that we can be safe on the streets and in our homes and for our children to be safe in schools and at play, today that safety is very, very fragile.... Crime and the fear of crime have permeated the fabric of American life....

Burger, February 9, 1981

Crime is a real threat, but at least some of the tremendous fear Americans have is the product of a variety of factors that have little or nothing to do with crime itself.... The failure to build criminal justice policy from facts rather than fear helps explain why our policies fail in their mission to make Americans safe.

Donziger, 1996, p. 63

On June 11, 2013, media outlets reported that the Newtown, Connecticut, schools were placed in lockdown after someone made a threatening phone call to Hawley Elementary School (Associated Press, 2013). Although these sorts of threats and lockdowns occur relatively frequently throughout the United States, this reaction is important because of the significance of the location of the school that received the threat. Hawley Elementary School is located less than two miles from Sandy Hook Elementary School, where a gunman killed 20 first-graders and six teachers and staff in December, 2012. This tragic mass murder sparked a wide variety of media coverage and legislative proposals to reduce the availability of guns and increase school safety throughout the United States. From a researcher's standpoint, these initiatives vary widely from strategies that are research-based (e.g., background checks of those purchasing firearms to prevent criminogenic individuals from purchasing guns) to some that can best be described as "knee-jerk reactions to an incredibly rare event" (e.g., arming teachers in elementary schools). No matter what the proposal, much of its foundation can be traced to the public's fear that a tragic event like the shootings at Sandy Hook will not only happen again but happen to them or their loved ones.

These legislative and public reactions to Sandy Hook are certainly not new; similar reactions have occurred after events such as the mass shootings that occurred at a theater in Aurora, Colorado, in 2012 and on the Virginia Tech University campus in 2007. Tragic events such as these may spur an emotional response of fear among those who are aware of these events, especially among people who live near the places where they occur.

In addition, events such as these often prompt policymakers to feel they must "do something" to lessen fear of crime and crime itself, in the immediate aftermath of the violence. For example, since the Newtown, Connecticut, shootings, policymakers have once again hotly debated the importance of gun control (The White House, 2013). Even more commonly, however, policymakers use fear of crime among the public as a rallying cry to get support for their broader "get tough" crime policies focused on reducing street violence and other offenses. For example, the public's fear of crime was a convenient justification for legislators' push for laws such as Three Strikes and You're Out, Truth in Sentencing (which required offenders to serve 85% of their sentence), and sex offender notification laws during the 1990s, as well as for anti-terrorism laws in the 2000s (Glassner, 1999). Yet, research shows that the public rarely knows what the crime and punishment statistics are. They often *overestimate* the amount of crime that is violent and *underestimate* the amount of punishment people receive (Donziger, 1996). That is, as a group, citizens are not well-informed on the criminal justice system or its workings. The causes and consequences of fear of crime are more complex and intricate than can be addressed simply by focusing on crime reduction. Consequently, while attempting to reduce the public's fear of crime is a lofty and important goal, the use of fear as a justification for tough policies can be problematic (Potter & Kappeler, 2006).

In this book, we explore a number of dimensions of individual's fear of crime, a term we use interchangeably with fear of victimization and fear of criminal victimization. We examine the causes, contextual cues, and consequences of fear of crime and the implications that fear has for society at-large. Although sensationalized events such as those described above have a short-term impact on individual's fear of crime, immediate fear after a major event and fear of crime generally have a real impact for both individuals who experience it and society, especially when fear is used to promote criminal justice strategies, such as policing approaches and tough punishment policies. Thus, it is important that we understand how fear of crime develops, what makes some humans more fearful of crime than others, and what implications this fear has for the larger society. We begin that discussion with a brief review of the emotion of fear and how it develops over time.

Fear Is an Emotion

Fear has been the subject of more scientific investigation than any other emotion and affects every human being in some fashion (Izard, 1977). Fear is a typical and often rational response to a current or perceived threat and can serve as a coping function to allow both animals and humans to increase their chances of survival (Lazarus, Kanner, & Folkman, 1980; Marks 1978). Fear allows people to avoid danger by sending a warning signal that allows both humans and animals to avoid or resist the presence of the source of fear (Kemper, 1978). In dangerous situations, small levels of fear induce caution, while more fear allows individuals to flee in the face of danger, thus increasing their chances of survival. Fear thus can serve an adaptive function (Marks, 1987), although abnormal anxiety or fear can be extremely harmful, resulting in changes to one's lifestyle that prevent that person from experiencing the most out of their daily lives.

Some people may even experience phobias. When one's fear becomes disproportionate to the fear-inducing situation and cannot be justified or reasoned away, that fear can become a phobia (Marks, 1987; Wolman, 1993). Phobias are considered abnormal due to their terrifying intensity and can cause people to engage in behavior that to others may seem irrational (Cole, 1964). More than 1 in 10 individuals have some type of phobia (Lindeman, 1993), including agoraphobia (fear of going into public places), social phobias (fear of social occasions that involve dealing with other people), and simple phobias (which can include fear of particular objects or situations, such as heights or spiders). Simple phobias are the most common (Lindeman, 1993). One could imagine people who have a phobia related to crime (e.g., an extreme fear of rape or murder). Crime-related phobias might even prompt people to take extreme behavioral precautions to avoid victimization. Although not a typical response, some may completely avoid large cities due to extreme fear of street crime or completely shun commercial airplanes due to intense fear of terrorist activity.

With this broader discussion of fear to set the context, we focus in this book on fear of crime (or victimization). Over time, researchers have defined this concept in many ways, but as we note in more detail in Chapter 3, there are three common elements to most scholars' definitions of fear of crime. It is considered to be (1) an emotional response (2) to a danger or threat (3) of a criminal incident.

Development of Fear over the Life Course

All humans are born with a "fear potential," but fear is typically a learned emotion (Scruton, 1986). People are taught when and what to fear as well as what not to fear. For example, parents often teach their children to fear strangers, novelty, snakes, spiders, thunder and lightning, parking lots, etc. (Marks, 1978). Thus, over time, human beings develop fear of certain situations, objects, or people through socialization. There is a fairly stable pattern of common fears that develop, plateau, and decline throughout the course of one's life. Infants demonstrate few signs of fear during the first six months of life (Marks, 1987). As children become older, however, they use hints from their parents or other caregivers to evaluate situations and determine if they should be fearful. Children often share the fears of their parents (Emmelkamp & Scholing, 1993). As a person matures, fears change. Some of these fears learned in childhood, however, may persist throughout adulthood (fear of doctors, snakes, heights, etc.).

Moreover, parents and others also teach people what they should not fear. For example, parents often tell their children to trust, not fear, policeman, teachers, etc. Parents and others may also discourage children from showing fear, even if they feel it. For example, they may tell them not to "act like a baby" or that there is "no reason to cry." Shame which is associated with fear in early life may serve as a regulator of fear or the expression of fear later on. As we discuss later in the book, shared messages about when and how to express fear may be especially relevant to explaining why some people (e.g., women) are more willing to express fear than others are (e.g., men).

Interestingly, sometimes, both children and adults are taught not only to tolerate the experience of fear, but to find the courage to face it head on. That is, they can "feel the fear and do it anyway." For example, children may be told that it is ok to be afraid of an academic test, but that they must still take it. Or, they may be told that it is normal to be afraid before a big game or performance. Likewise, in adulthood, people may be expected to express emotions, even if they are afraid to do so. Even in the face of violence, some must proceed. For example, soldiers must crawl forward while shots are being fired just above their heads. Confrontations with bullies, going to the dentist, and uncomfortable interactions with persons of authority are all methods of learning to counteract fear by going forward rather than retreating (Izard, 1977).

The subject of this book is fear of crime, and it is one of the fears that individuals can develop over their life course. As we discuss in future chapters, socialization is considered an important component in the development of crime-related fear. For example, women may be told by their parents to stay inside, away from certain boys, or to avoid certain types of clothing to avoid victimization. Or, some children may be told to stay away from people of other ethnicities and races, because they are not to be trusted. Chapter 4 discusses gender socialization, and Chapter 5 briefly discusses what has been termed racial socialization.

The Prevalence of Fear of Crime

Most analysts and scholars admit that many people are fearful of crime. However, fear of crime scholars and policymakers disagree on what proportion of the population experiences fear. Estimates regarding the prevalence of fear of crime come from a number of sources.

Fear of Crime Levels

One common way to estimate the amount and levels of crime-related fear is to ask regular citizens through national surveys. A number of polling agencies regularly provide estimates of fear of criminal victimization among the public. One of the most well-known estimates of the prevalence of fear of crime comes from the National Opinion Research Center's (NORC) General Social Survey (GSS). Each year, the GSS asks a series of questions to approximately 2,000 randomly selected adults in the United States to uncover social trends, including trends in fear of crime. The GSS asks respondents, "Is there any area around here—that is, within a mile—where you would be afraid to walk alone at night?" Table 1.1 shows responses to that question since 2000. In 2010, one in three respondents (32.7%) agreed that they were afraid to walk alone in their neighborhood at night (National Opinion Research Center, 2012). This proportion is the same as the proportion in 2008 and the third lowest percentage of fearful respondents since 1973 (30.2% in 2004 and in 31.0% in 2002). In general, over the past decade, one in three respondents agreed that they were afraid. This percentage has decreased markedly since 1974, when 43.6% of respondents to the GSS responded that they were afraid (National Opinion Research Center, 2012).

For several decades, analysts employed by Gallup have also asked a similar question: "Is there any area near where you live—that is, within a mile—where you would be afraid to walk alone at night?" Annual responses to that question are presented in Table 1.2.

Since 2000, approximately a third of those respondents interviewed (35.4%) have responded that there was an area where they were afraid to walk alone at

Table 1.1 Proportion of Respondents Responding to
"Is there any area around here—that is, within a mile—where you would
be afraid to walk alone at night?" from Biannual General Social Survey

Year	Yes, afraid (%)	No, not afraid (%)
2000	37.7	62.3
2002	31.0	69.0
2004	30.2	69.8
2006	35.1	64.9
2008	32.7	67.3
2010	32.7	67.3
Decade Average	33.2	66.8

Adapted from analyses conducted by authors through GSS data analysis tool available at
http://sda.berkeley.edu/cgi-bin/hsda?harcsda+gss10.

night. In 2011, a similar proportion (38%) agreed with that statement. As with
the GSS results, this percentage is smaller than that proportion reported in the
1980s and 1990s (Gallup, 2012).

The Pew Research Center also asks about citizens' perceptions regarding
what issues should be most important on the presidential agenda. In 2011,
more than two in five (44%) respondents felt that reducing crime was a top priority for the presidential agenda. This is the smallest percentage responding
affirmatively since 2001, when 76% felt that reducing crime should be considered a top presidential priority (Pew Research Center, 2011).

Finally, the findings presented above are not unique to the United States.
Hummelsheim, Hirtenlehner, Jackson, and Oberwittler (2011) examined data
about the fear of crime from 43,000 respondents in 23 industrialized countries from the European Social Survey. Respondents in these countries were
asked, "How safe do you—or would you—feel walking alone in this area after
dark?" Across the entire sample, 51% of the respondents felt safe and 25% felt
very safe. Only 19 percent felt unsafe and five percent felt very unsafe. These
feelings of safety varied greatly by country; less than 1 in 10 (9.7%) respondents
in Slovenia felt unsafe or very unsafe, while almost two in five respondents in
Slovakia (39.7%) and Estonia (40.0%) felt unsafe or very unsafe. In sum, poll
data indicate that the majority of people do not generally admit feeling fear, but
about ⅓ to ½ do depending on the year and place.

Table 1.2 Proportion of Respondents Responding to
"Is there any area near where you live—that is, within a mile—where you
would be afraid to walk alone at night?" from Annual Gallup Poll

Year	Yes, afraid (%)	No, not afraid (%)
2000	34	66
2001	30	69
2002	35	64
2003	36	64
2004	32	67
2005	38	62
2006	37	63
2007	37	62
2008	37	63
2009	34	66
2010	37	63
2011	38	61
Decade Average	35.4%	64.2%

Adapted from Table 2.37.2011 from the *Sourcebook of Criminal Justice Statistics Online* available at *http://www.albany.edu/sourcebook/pdf/t2372011.pdf.* The "don't know" and "refused" categories have been omitted; thus, percentages do not always equal 100%.

Fear of crime scholars have also conducted surveys to examine fear of crime, often in one geographical area. However, in 1995, Kenneth Ferraro published what remains a seminal work in the field of fear of crime.[1] In that book, Ferraro analyzed data from one of the first in-depth fear of crime surveys of people across the United States. Using a multistage cluster sample, Ferraro conducted telephone interviews of 1,101 adult respondents regarding their levels of fear

---

1. Ferraro's 1995 book was certainly not the first effort to examine fear of criminal victimization but is the most frequently cited work from that decade. For example, Skogan and Maxfield (1981) and work by Ferraro and LaGrange (e.g., Ferraro & LaGrange, 1987; LaGrange, Ferraro, & Supancic, 1992) and Warr (1984) were published prior to this work. Nevertheless, we refer to Ferraro's 1995 work as a seminal work because he tied previous work with his own individual research to inform fear of crime research for years to come.

of crime and perceptions of risk. This important book by Ferraro (1995) set the stage for much of the fear of crime research agenda that has grown dramatically over the past two decades.

Although Ferraro's work made a number of contributions and prompted many others as discussed throughout this book, one of the most important contributions he made was the distinction he highlighted between fear of crime and perceptions of risk. Similar to the research on fear generally that we discussed earlier, Ferraro defined fear of crime as "… an emotional response of dread or anxiety to crime or symbols that a person associates with crime" (Ferraro 1995, p. 4). While there are certainly many more definitions of fear of crime that have been developed since his work, Ferraro's definition highlighted two elements: (1) fear is an emotional response and (2) fear results from both personal crime victimization and symbols of crime. Thus, Ferraro's definition was one of the first to note that the emotional response of fear of crime can be evoked by symbols of crime, including problems such as neighborhood disorder (e.g., graffiti, litter, youths hanging out, or gang members). This argument had important consequences for other scholars whose work is discussed throughout this book.

Ferraro also was among the first to clearly distinguish between perceptions of risk and fear of crime (see also Ferraro & LaGrange, 1988; LaGrange & Ferraro, 1989; Warr, 1984; Warr & Stafford, 1983). Ferraro defined perceived risk as "… recognition of a situation as possessing at least potential danger, real or imagined …" (Ferraro, 1995, p. 4). Fear of crime research prior to Ferraro's book—except some he co-authored with LaGrange and Mark Warr's work—had largely either (1) ignored perceptions of risk altogether, or (2) used measures of fear of crime that blended perceptions of risk and fear of crime in such a way that it was difficult to separate the two. Ferraro (1995) conceptualized fear of crime as a distinct phenomenon from perceived risk and estimated the impact of perceived risk on fear of crime in the United States. Ferraro determined that while a number of factors affected perceptions of victimization risk, perceived risk was the strongest predictor of fear of crime, regardless of the other variables included in the model. This finding profoundly influenced the fear of criminal victimization research by stressing the importance of treating fear of crime as a conceptually distinct phenomenon from perceived risk of crime.

Nevertheless, as we highlight throughout this book, not all pollsters (or even all researchers in the United States) paid attention to this distinction. One of the most evident areas where this distinction was and still is ignored is national polling of levels of fear of crime in the U.S. (including those discussed above). Despite the measurement shortcomings of many of these polls and our calls for improvement, which we discuss later, these national polls are an important source of general estimates of fear of crime in society and have allowed scholars and policymakers to examine trends in this emotion over time.

The United States is not the only hotbed of crime-related fear research, however. A number of researchers in Great Britain also have spent several years examining crime-related fear, and they have made some important contributions to how researchers think about and measure fear of crime. We discuss these measurement contributions later, but here focus on what they have found about the prevalence of fear in Great Britain. Farrall, Jackson, and Gray (2009) found that 11% of the respondents to the 2003/2004 British Crime Survey were very worried about robbery, while 24% were fairly worried. Respondents also were asked "In the past 12 months, have you actually worried about being robbed?" (Farrall et al., 2009, p. 169). Only 15% of the respondents indicated that they were actually worried about being robbed. Only 8% were "very" or "quite" worried about being robbed (Farrall et al., 2009). Over half of the respondents were worried about burglary (40% were quite worried and 13% were very worried). One in three (31%) had worried once or more in the past 12 months about being burglarized. That is, their findings are similar to findings in the U.S.

Implications of Fear of Crime in Society

We discuss in later chapters important implications of fear of crime for individuals' quality of life as well as how it affects their behaviors, because this is where the bulk of fear of crime research lies. Before delving into the predictors and consequences of fear of crime for individuals; however, we first pause to take a broader look at how fear of crime affects society more generally.

Fear of Crime and Race Relations

One of the most significant areas influenced by fear of crime is race relations. Blalock (1967) and Liska (1992) have suggested that one of the greatest impacts that fear of crime has in society is through what is called the "racial threat hypothesis." This hypothesis suggests that Blacks present a threat to Whites, who then take political, social, and economic steps to prevent Blacks from achieving equality. One of the ways that Whites prevent Blacks from achieving equality is by promoting fear of crime. In particular, media focus on the "racialization of crime," where race and crime are merged with one another to lead the general public to believe that most criminals are black and most Blacks are criminals (Mears, Mancini, & Stewart, 2009), despite statistics to the contrary (Federal Bureau of Investigation, 2012).

This racialization of crime has serious implications for race relations. Skogan (1995) suggests that Whites attribute violent crime to Blacks and, because Whites are so fearful of criminal victimization, that fear of crime translates into a fear of Blacks, which creates a divisive impact for race relations, particularly in the United States. Skogan suggests that White politicians often have much to gain by "playing the race card" (p. 60) and preying on Whites' fear of Blacks to win votes in a get tough on crime platform. Skogan substantiated this argument by using responses to a general fear of crime measure from the National Crime Victimization Survey (NCVS), coupled with a measure of prejudice created from examining respondents' agreement with measures examining their views about "... the acceptability of white and black children's going to school together under the circumstance of varying racial composition of the school" and white people's "... right to a racially segregated neighborhood" (Skogan, 1995, p. 63). Skogan found that Whites who were most fearful and who lived in closest proximity to Blacks were also most prejudiced, even after controlling for demographic factors. Thus, research indicates fear of crime has at least an indirect association with racial prejudice in society.

Fear of Crime's Impact on Residential Housing

The study of the spatial nature of the fear of crime has garnered quite a bit of attention over the past three decades (Pain, 1997, 2000). Typically, people report greater levels of fear in certain types of places, particularly those that are dark, disorganized, or in disrepair (Warr, 1984). Although the examination of the relationship between place and fear of crime is relatively new, the theoretical perspective used to make sense of the relationship is now four decades old. Newman (1972) coined the term "defensible space" and argued that poor place design can increase the fear of the residents inhabiting that place (and conversely, well-designed spaces can reduce the fear of residents of those places). He argued that both residential and commercial locations could be designed (or modified) to increase the territoriality of the residents by increasing surveillance, establishing ownership of the location among its residents, limiting access, and improving the appearance of the area. Newman argued that well-designed and well-maintained spaces could reduce both crime and fear of crime by (1) creating natural surveillance (designing spaces so that residents have the greatest visibility of those spaces), (2) reducing opportunity for crime by making spaces more visible and thus more easy to defend, and (3) increasing the likelihood that residents would (or could) use or protect their space.

A number of researchers have demonstrated that fear of crime has detrimental effects for residential neighborhoods. Skogan (2006) argued that:

> Fear is a key "quality of life" issue for many people. Research also indicates that concern about crime has bad consequences for the neighborhoods in which we live. Fear leads to withdrawal from public life, and it undermines informal and organized efforts by the community to control crime and delinquency. It is difficult to organize activities in the neighborhoods where people fear their own neighbors. Fear undermines the value of residential property and thus the willingness of owners to maintain it properly (p. 255).

Cordner (2010) suggested that fear of crime has been a key factor that has pushed residents from central city neighborhoods to suburbs and this "flight" has assisted race and class residential segregation in cities throughout the United States. Over two decades ago, (Skogan 1986, 1989) argued that fear of crime was an important accelerant of neighborhood decline, causing individuals to withdraw from their social networks and community life. This withdrawal thus weakens community ties by reducing the amount of informal social control, which, in turn, leads to increased delinquency/crime and increased levels of fear. In fact, Skogan (1986) argued that changes in the composition of residential neighborhoods can often be stimulated by fear of crime and exacerbated by other factors. A number of researchers have supported these arguments over the past two decades (see Hinkle, 2009, for review). Consequently, the impact of fear of crime on neighborhoods can be both extremely negative and pervasive.

Policymakers have used this knowledge of both defensible space and place-based fear to attempt to reduce crime through situational crime prevention. According to Clarke (1997), situational crime prevention consists of measures that are directed at specific forms of crime and manage an environment to make it more difficult for offenders to successfully commit crime in those places. Examples of situational crime prevention measures designed to reduce fear include removing signs of physical incivility such as graffiti and litter (Skogan & Maxfield, 1981), increasing street lighting (Painter, 1993), and using closed circuit television and security cameras to reduce fear of users in certain areas (Short & Ditton, 1998). Spinks (2001) suggested that these efforts to reduce fear by design can be traced all the way back to Bentham's classic panopticon prison design, whose design allowed all prisoners to be under constant surveillance, thus reducing the fear of the officers that supervised them. Evaluations of these efforts suggest that, at least in some situations, these measures successfully reduce the fear of crime among residents in these areas (Lab, 2010).

Nevertheless, even the strongest advocates of situational crime prevention admit that these measures designed to reduce fear are both (1) likely to be short-lived, and (2) difficult to isolate as the only cause of reduced fear of crime among residents in these areas (Pain, 2000).

The use of situational crime prevention and defensible space, and their respective success in reducing residents' fear of crime, has been one of the strongest reasons that planners have designed neighborhoods to reduce fear of crime among residents in these areas. Nevertheless, this residential planning to reduce fear has had negative consequences. Ellin (2001) argued that fear of crime is one of the causes of the increased move toward both "retribalisation" (efforts by individuals to emphasize cultural differences between their own culture and the culture of other groups) and "escapism" (extreme forms of retreat from larger communities by certain residents of those communities). Ellin argued that one of the consequences of both retribalisation and escapism has been the building of segregated, gated communities. While these communities are not "officially" exclusive, they often become racially/ethnically segregated, exclusive communities that only individuals of higher socioeconomic status can afford. She argued that there are over 20,000 gated communities in the United States alone (housing over 8 million residents) and suggested that these gated (and often segregated) communities increase the perceptions of security from crime of the residents living in those communities but also heighten an "us against them" mentality that is immensely harmful to race relations in those areas.

Ellin (2001) also argued that these changes are not limited to residential neighborhoods. She argued that fear of crime has been a key component in transforming public places, particularly in urban areas, into spaces that are controlled and guarded in an effort to reduce fear of crime of those citizens passing through those areas. She cites examples of barrel-shaped, "bum-proof" benches and invisible, randomly activated sprinkler systems installed in Los Angeles parks to discourage homeless people from using those parks (Ellin, 2001).

Fear of Crime and Its Transformation of Democracy

Jonathan Simon (2009) has argued that fear of crime has not only transformed criminal justice policy in the United States, it has also significantly impacted its core democratic principles. Simon argued that fear of crime became a nationally visible topic of discussion after a decade of increasing crime rates and media attention about crime at the end of the 1960s. In 1968, President Nixon openly accused the Supreme Court (which had made a number of landmark decisions throughout the 1960s that provided increased due process protections for individuals accused of crime) of lacking concern about the safety of citizens. According to Simon, this and similar criticisms of judicial decisions designed to protect individual rights helped to "... turn the crime wave into an axis for critical scrutiny of government" (Simon, 2009, p. 115). This scrutiny was particularly acute in the judicial realm, as conservative legislators openly criticized judicial decisions as an influential factor in increasing crime rates. Simon asserted that this scrutiny had long-lasting impacts on the democratic process.

First, Simon contended that fear of crime and the media attention given to crime caused each judicial decision to be openly examined and routinely criticized. Critics argued that any decision that protected the individual rights of citizens necessarily decreased the abilities of criminal justice agents to provide public safety; thus, judicial decisions became a "zero-sum" game around whose rights would receive protection (the criminal or the public). In general, after 1968, the individual that allegedly committed the crime lost this game. Thus, a move to protect individual rights by the Supreme Court throughout the 1960s came to a screeching halt in the 1970s, at least in part because of the public's heightened fear of crime.

Second, Simon maintained that these critics suggested that each judicial decision about criminal procedure that extended protection of individual rights was a tradeoff in the area of crime control and that any decision protecting individual rights inevitably produced more crime victims. This rationale merged the discussions of individual rights of criminals with the discussion of fear of crime. In the end, the public's fear of crime hampered judicial efforts to protect individual rights of citizens.

Finally, Simon suggested that the controversy about judicial decisions related to criminal procedure brought about by the public's fear of crime extended into criticism of judicial decisions in other areas of democracy. Two of these areas include defending state-instituted racial segregation and continuing support of capital punishment. He reasoned that the public's fear of crime (which is often equated with fear of black people) has allowed institutional racism to continue in many areas (e.g., residential segregation and social network exclusion) that hampers the upward mobility of non-Whites, particularly Blacks. Additionally, he suggested that the public opinion in support of capital punishment (partially based on that fear of criminal victimization) was influential in both the speed with which state legislatures revamped their death penalty statutes in response to *Furman v. Georgia* from 1972 to 1976 and the subsequent increased usage of the death penalty throughout the 1980s and early 1990s.

In sum, Simon established that fear of crime has important consequences for the larger democratic society and the social agencies (e.g., family, school, church, and police) that function in society. Of all the social agencies, police agencies probably have the greatest impact on fear of crime among the citizenry. The research regarding the relationship between policing agencies and fear of crime is discussed below.

Fear of Crime and Policing

As Cordner (2010) and Lab (2010) highlight, while the most evident goal of law enforcement throughout the world is to prevent the actual occurrence of criminal activity, preventing or reducing fear of criminal victimization also is a critical role of law enforcement. Cordner (2010) contended that police departments should actively seek to reduce fear of crime as part of their mission. In other words, as part of their daily law enforcement activities, police officers and supervisors should work to inform citizens about their risk of crime victimization and strategies they can use to reduce that risk. In turn, this should reduce their fear of crime as well.

A wide variety of policing efforts have been designed to reduce the public's fear of crime. For example, one of the goals of the classic Kansas City preventive patrol experiment (Kelling, Pate, Dieckman, & Brown, 1974) was to measure the impact of preventive patrol on fear of crime. Although Kelling and his associates did not find any impact of preventive patrol on fear of victimization, this research highlighted the importance of the relationship between policing strategies and fear of crime among community residents. Cordner (2010) suggested that, with the exception of the Kansas City experiment, " ... no major studies have specifically tested whether rapid police response or solving crime helps reduce fear" (p. 16). Thus, it appears that "common knowledge" continues to be that rapid response time, increased crime solving capabilities, and increased police presence in neighborhoods may be necessary law enforcement strategies, but these factors have little to do with the levels of fear of crime in that neighborhood (Cordner, 2010).

Nevertheless, there is some evidence that suggests that police strategies and operations can reduce fear of crime. While the results are mixed, in Chapter 6 we review a number of studies that have examined the impact of community policing on fear of crime. As we point out in that chapter, a number of questions about this relationship remain unanswered, but it continues to be a promising area of research.

Fear of Crime and the Media

Unlike the limited number of studies regarding the impact of policing strategies on fear of crime, the relationship between the media and fear of crime has been thoroughly examined over the last three decades. The broad theoretical ideas about relationship between the media and fear of crime (and the nuances of that relationship) are explored below, while Chapter 6 discusses specific research on media effects in more detail.

Although estimates vary widely regarding the proportion of the media devoted to crime, it is safe to say that "crime sells" and thus all forms of media promote crime as a salient issue. As Sacco (1995, p. 143) highlights, media coverage of crime often "… provides a map of the world of criminal events that differs in many ways from the one provided by official crime statistics." In fact, the amount and type of crime presented by the media, and often the types of victims and offenders, bear little resemblance to the reality of crime. Media coverage primarily focuses on violent crime and criminals (while most crime is nonviolent) and the media typically present victims as older Whites (when, in reality, both victims and offenders are disproportionately younger and non-White) (Sacco, 1995). Thus, the media portrayal of crime may cultivate fear among certain groups and is best described through the lens of crime cultivation theory.

Crime cultivation theorists argue that people who are avid media consumers often adopt perspectives similar to those presented in the mainstream media (Gerbner & Gross, 1976). According to this theory, if the media devote an inordinate (or even disproportionate) amount of coverage to crime, then regular media users will perceive that crime is as pervasive as portrayed by the media. Despite the intuitiveness of this argument, findings regarding the validity of crime cultivation theory are mixed at best. After controlling for demographic factors, some researchers find no positive correlation between the amount of television an individual watches and his or her fear of crime while others find only a moderate positive relationship (at best) and these relationships are often contingent on the gender, age, class, and race/ethnicity of the television viewer (Callahan, 2012; Morgan & Shanahan, 1997).

In response to these findings, Gerbner, Gross, Morgan, & Signorelli (1980) offered the resonance hypothesis, which argues that the impact of the media on fear of crime is stronger when it corresponds well with the viewer's own experiences and circumstances. Consequently, those individuals at highest risk of victimization by crime (e.g., residents of high-crime neighborhoods, non-Whites, and individuals of lower socioeconomic status) will become even more fearful when viewing crime-related media. The counter-argument to the resonance hypothesis is the substitution hypothesis (Adoni & Mane, 1984), which suggests that the media has a stronger impact on individuals with lower rates of crime victimization (e.g., elderly, wealthy, and Whites). While both hypotheses receive some support, as Callahan (2012) suggests, audience characteristics moderate the influence of crime media on fear of crime, but the direction of the moderation appears to vary by sampling design and methodology, by race, and by socioeconomic factors.

Sacco (1995) argued that recent changes in technology, particularly the 24-hour news channels and the Internet, have allowed media to cover larger numbers of news stories and to expand the "net" of the media to capture stories that only 20 years ago would not have been newsworthy. This expansion of the news media "... has been to raise to national prominence stories with no real national significance. Crime stories that would have been a purely local affair in an earlier period now attract much wider attention because a videotape of the incident is available for broadcast" (Sacco, p. 145). This expanded coverage of crime-related news has led to the creation of a number of media-generated "crime waves" that have little basis in fact yet often increase fear of crime among those viewing these news stories. Sacco cites the concerns about the increasing number of serial killers and the "rise" in freeway shootings in California in the 1980s as evidence of this phenomenon. Recent news coverage of school shootings at Newtown, Connecticut and other schools (e.g., Columbine, Colorado, Jonesboro, Arkansas, and Red Lake, Minnesota) is further evidence that, no matter what the crime reality, media stories of crime have significant impacts on the levels of fear in society. In Chapters 6 and 8, we discuss these issues in more detail.

In this chapter, we have examined explanations for why individuals are fearful of crime, discussed what scholars understand about fear of crime, and presented a broad overview of how fear of crime influences different aspects of life particularly in the United States. We have discussed the importance of fear for both individual quality of life and crime policy. We have also defined fear of crime, focusing on the common elements across the many definitions provided in the literature. We also have established that there is an important distinction between fear of crime and perceived risk of victimization; fear is primarily an emotional response to crime while perceived risk is more of a cognitive assessment about the likelihood of being victimized (this distinction will be explored in greater detail in later chapters). We have shown that polls generally show that about one in three residents in the United States indicates that they are afraid of crime.

We also have established that fear of crime has important implications for society as a whole, affecting race relations, residential mobility and segregation, and policing. Importantly, we have discussed the argument that fear of criminal victimization may have an important association with the core democratic principles in our society. Each of these relationships is fueled (often to a large extent) by media depictions of who is committing crime and who the crime victims are.

In the following chapters, we provide an in-depth analysis of fear of criminal victimization from a scholarly perspective. This book is designed so that each chapter builds upon the previous chapters yet, if necessary, can stand alone to serve as an additional reading for a class or for a policy brief. In Chapters 2 through 7, we review the current research around the topic addressed in that chapter, then offer a number of recommendations for research at the conclusion of the chapter. Our hope is that the reader can digest each chapter in one setting and then consider the implications of the chapter prior to delving further into the book. Before we close this chapter, we provide a brief summary of each chapter so the reader can have an idea about the journey to come.

In Chapter 2, we trace the birth and progress of fear of crime as a field of study. We begin by reviewing the social and political climate that brought about focus on fear of crime research, and discuss the important role of the Commission on Law Enforcement and Administration of Justice in prompting fear of crime research. We categorize fear of crime research into three eras—its infancy (1971 to 1985), its adolescence (1986 to 2000), and its current, mature era (studies produced since 2001). For each time period, we discuss the major trends in fear of crime research during that era, and highlight many of the most significant studies produced as part of that era.

In Chapter 3, we discuss the measurement of fear of crime. We highlight the important debate around exactly what definition should be used for fear of crime, and then discuss the various methods through which fear of crime has been conceptualized and operationalized over the five decades since fear of crime research began. We propose that a good definition of fear of crime involves three elements common to most definitions: (1) an emotional response (2) to a danger or threat (3) of a criminal incident. We also review how operationalization of fear of crime measures have evolved in the wording and structure of the measures (e.g., feel safe v. afraid), the temporal reference used in those measures (e.g., at night v. other times during the day), and the reference to place of the measures (e.g., at school or at home v. general measures that do not mention place). We suggest that the best measures of fear of crime (1) ask respondents if they are fearful of specific crimes or people in specific places (e.g., are you afraid of being robbed while at school v. how worried are you about walking alone in your neighborhood at night; or how afraid are you of intimates v. strangers v. specific perpetrators, such as gang members or terrorists); (2) are scored on a metric that allows a wide range of agreement (e.g., Likert-type measure v. dichotomous measure of agreement); and (3) distinguish between fear of crime and perceived risk of crime by using measures that ask respondents how "afraid" they are of specific crimes and how "likely" they are to be victimized by specific crimes.

In Chapter 4, we examine one of the most well-documented, oldest relationships in the fear of crime literature: the impact of gender on fear of crime. Numerous studies over the five decades of research (using a wide variety of measures) have demonstrated that females are more fearful of crime than males, even though they are far less likely to be victimized by street crime than their male counterparts. We then summarize seven explanations for these gender differences and provide insight into why each of those explanations is relevant. These explanations include (1) demographic explanations (e.g., race, social class, and marital status); (2) the irrationality explanation (which argues that women's fears are irrational given their likelihood of victimization); (3) the vulnerability explanation (that argues women feel more vulnerable to victimization than men because of physical or environmental differences); (4) the socialization explanation (that argues women are socialized to both experience and express fear in different ways than men); (5) the patriarchy and social control of women explanation (which argues that women are socially controlled to behave in ways that restrict their mobility and increase their fear of crime); (6) the shadow of sexual assault explanation (which argues that women's higher levels of fear are due to their increased risk of sexual assault); and (7) the hidden victimization explanation (which argues that women's likelihood of victimization by crime is actually much higher than commonly believed because of their tendency to underreport crime victimization, especially in the home or by intimates). We also discuss two explanations for men's lower fear of crime levels. These explanations include (1) the "boys don't cry" perspective (which argues that men are as fearful of crime as women but neutralize this emotion in various ways) (see Goodey, 1997) and (2) the location specific explanation, which argues that men are as fearful as women in some specific locations (e.g., large cities) but not others. We discuss the strengths and weaknesses of each explanation and close by suggesting specific areas of research to help examine these explanations.

In Chapter 5, we examine the impact of age, race/ethnicity, and social class on fear of crime. We provide a detailed discussion around the theoretical and methodological reasons why these variables affect fear of crime and note that differences in fear of crime among these groups may be due to social and physical vulnerability explanations. These explanations argue that older persons, non-Whites, and poor people have greater levels of both social and physical vulnerability, which leads them to be more fearful of crime. We also discuss additional explanations for fear of crime for each group and close by discussing the importance of considering intersections of these demographic variables with each other and with gender when explaining fear of crime.

In Chapter 6, we discuss contextual differences in fear of crime. We divide this chapter into four contextual situations then discuss the current research and theoretical explanations regarding how these contexts impact fear of crime. We begin by examining how an individual's direct personal experience with crime (e.g., their personal victimization experience, witnessing the victimization of others, and their participation in criminal activities) affects their fear of criminal victimization. We highlight the fact that there is no consensus on the impact of personal victimization experience on fear of crime. Additionally, there is also no consensus regarding the impact of either witnessing criminal victimization or engaging in crime on one's fear of criminal victimization. In fact, both of these relationships remain relatively unexplored. We then examine the impact of an individual's indirect experience with crime on their levels of fear of crime. As with direct victimization experience, there is no consensus regarding the relationship between indirect experience with crime and levels of fear of crime either. It appears that the strength of the relationship between fear of crime and the media—television and newspapers—is influenced by personal characteristics of the reader or watcher but there is not yet enough research to demonstrate a causal relationship between indirect experience with crime and fear of crime. It also appears that learning or hearing about crime from one's friends, family, neighbors, and police officers may increase fear of crime rather than decrease it. The research reviewed in Chapter 6 also suggests that individuals living in disorderly neighborhoods are more fearful of crime, as are those that live in more racially heterogeneous neighborhoods. This relationship can be at least partially explained through social disorganization theory and through environmental cues that indicate one's likelihood of victimization is greater in one neighborhood than another.

In Chapter 7, we examine the research regarding behavioral responses to fear of crime. We categorize behavioral responses into three categories and then review the research around these behaviors. The first type of behavioral response to fear of crime is avoidance behaviors. Avoidance behaviors restrict where individuals go and what they do (e.g., not going out at night, avoiding parking decks, or avoiding stores or neighborhoods). The second type of behaviors is termed protective behaviors. Protective behaviors are those that individuals engage in to reduce their fear of crime and risk of criminal victimization. Examples of these behaviors include adding lighting or locks to a house, taking a self-defense class, or purchasing a guard dog for protection.

The final category involves weapons behaviors, where individuals secure or purchase a weapon (whether a firearm or some other type of weapon) for protection. We provide a detailed discussion of the "fear of victimization" hypothesis that argues people purchase and carry weapons because of their fear of crime and highlight the fact that little empirical research exists to support this hypothesis. Additionally, we add to the extant literature by discussing environmental design decisions that have focused on reducing fear of crime, including the principles of defensible space and crime prevention through environmental design, in the context of avoidance behaviors designed to reduce fear of crime.

We close this book in Chapter 8 by presenting a concluding chapter written in a "lessons learned" format. We begin that chapter by reviewing the findings from each chapter of the book and then use that knowledge to make policy recommendations to the reader on how to more effectively control fear of crime. We close the book with a discussion of important tracks for future research and attempt to lay out a proposed agenda for fear of crime research in the next decade.

This book is a compilation of work from five authors that have approached fear of crime from a number of perspectives over our careers. Some of us have been working in the exploration of fear of crime for two decades while one of us is much "newer" to the topic. Our hope is that our varied backgrounds, experiences, and perspectives allow us to explore fear of crime in a way that heretofore has been neglected. By the end of this book, we hope you share our opinion that, despite over four decades of research in fear of crime, we still have much to learn and many research paths to explore. Our hope is that this book will provide a solid "launch pad" for that exploration.

References

Adoni, H., & Mane, S. (1984). Media and the social construction of reality: Toward an integration of theory and research. *Communication Research*, *11*(3), 323–340.

Associated Press. (June 10, 2013). Threat prompts lockdown of Newtown, CT schools. Accessed June 11, 2013 at http://abcnews.go.com/U.S./wireStory/threat-prompts-lockdown-newtown-conn-schools-19367410#.UbcnpJy3GF8.

Blalock, H.M. (1967). *Toward a theory of minority group relations*. New York: Wiley.

Burger, W.E. (February 9, 1981). Excerpts from Chief Justice Warren Burger's Address Before the American Bar Association. *New York Times*, Accessed November 26, 2013 at http://www.nytimes.com/1981/02/09/us/excerpts-from-address.html.

Callahan, V.J. (2012). Media consumption, perceptions of crime risk and fear of crime: Explaining race/ethnic differences. *Sociological Perspectives, 55*(1), 93–115.

Clarke, R.V. (1997). *Situational crime prevention: Successful case studies.* Monsey, NY: Criminal Justice Press.

Cole, L. (1964). *Psychology of adolescence (6th ed.).* New York: Holt, Rinehart, and Winston, Inc.

Cordner, G. (2010). *Reducing fear of crime: Strategies for police.* Washington D.C.: United States Department of Justice, Community Oriented Policing Services.

Donziger, S.R. (1996). *The real war on crime: The report of the national criminal justice commission.* New York: Harper Collins.

Ellin, N. (2001). Thresholds of fear: Embracing the urban shadow. *Urban Studies, 38* (5–6), 869–883.

Emmelkamp, P., & Scholin, A. (1993). Behavioral Interpretations, pp. 30–56 in *Anxiety and related disorders: A handbook,* B.B. Wolman & G. Stricker (eds.). New York: John Wiley and Sons, Inc.

Farrall, S., Jackson, J., & Gray, E. (2009). *Social order and the fear of crime in contemporary times.* New York: Oxford University Press.

Federal Bureau of Investigation. (2012). *Arrests by Race, 2012.* Accessed November 26, 2013. http://www.fbi.gov/about-us/cjis/ucr/crime-in-the-u.s/2012/crime-in-the-u.s.-2012/tables/43tabledatadecoverviewpdf.

Ferraro, K.F. (1995). *Fear of crime: Interpreting victimization risk.* Albany, NY: State University of New York Press.

Ferraro, K.F., & LaGrange, R.L. (1987). The measurement of fear of crime. *Sociological Inquiry, 57*(1), 70–97.

Ferraro, K.F., & LaGrange, R.L. (1988). Are older people afraid of crime? *Journal of Aging Studies, 2*(3), 277–287.

Gallup. (2012). *Crime.* Available at http://www.gallup.com/poll/1603/Crime.aspx.

Gerbner, G., & Gross, L. (1976). Living with television: The violence profile. *Journal of Communication, 26*(2), 172–194.

Gerbner, G., Gross, L., Morgan, M., & Signorielli, N. (1980). The 'mainstreaming' of America: Violence profile no. 11. *Journal of Communication, 30*(3), 10–29.

Glassner, B. (1999). *The culture of fear: Why Americans are afraid of the wrong things.* New York: Basic Books.

Goodey, J. (1997). Boys don't cry: Masculinities, fear of crime, and fearlessness. *British Journal of Criminology, 37*(3), 401–418.

Hinkle, J. (2009). *Making sense of broken windows: The relationship between perceptions of disorder, fear of crime, collective efficacy and perceptions of crime.* Ann Arbor, MI: Proquest, University of Michigan Dissertations Publishing.

Hummelsheim, D., Hirtenlehner, H., Jackson, J., & Oberwittler, D. (2011). Social insecurities and fear of crime: A cross-national study on the impact of welfare state policies on crime-related anxieties. *European Sociological Review, 27*(3), 327–345.

Izard, C.E. (1977). *Human emotions.* New York: Plenum Press.

Kelling, G., Pate, T., Dieckman, D., & Brown, C.E. (1974). *The Kansas City preventive patrol experiment: A summary report.* Washington D.C.: Police Foundation.

Kemper, T.D. (1978). *A social interactional theory of emotions.* New York: John Wiley and Sons, Inc.

Lab, S.P. (2010). *Crime prevention: Approaches, practices, and evaluations (7th ed.).* New Providence, NJ: Lexis Nexis Group.

LaGrange, R.L., & Ferraro, K.F. (1989). Assessing age and gender differences in perceived risk and fear of crime. *Criminology, 27(4),* 697–720.

LaGrange, R.L., Ferraro, K.F., & Supancic, M. (1992). Perceived risk and fear of crime: Role of social and physical incivilities. *Journal of Research in Crime and Delinquency, 29*(3), 311–334.

Lazarus, R.S., Kanner, A.D., & Folkman, S. (1980). Emotions: A cognitive-phenomenological analysis, pp. 189–217 in *Emotion, Theory, Research and Experience. Volume 1. Theories of Emotion,* R. Plutchik and H. Kellerman (eds.). New York: Academic Press.

Lindeman, C. (1993). Phobias, pp. 161–176 in *Anxiety and Related Disorders: A Handbook,* B.B. Wolman & G. Stricker (eds.). New York: John Wiley and Sons, Inc.

Liska, A.E. (1992). *Social threat and social control.* Albany, NY: State University of New York Press.

Marks, I.M. (1978). *Living with fear: Understanding and coping with anxiety.* New York: McGraw Hill Book Company.

Marks, I.M. (1987). *Fears, phobias, and rituals: Panic, anxiety, and their disorders.* New York: Oxford University Press.

Mears, D.P., Mancini, C., & Stewart, E.A. (2009). Whites' concern about crime: The effect of interracial contact. *Journal of Research in Crime and Delinquency, 46*(4), 524–552.

Morgan, M., & Shanahan, J. (1997). Two decades of cultivation research: An appraisal and meta-analysis. pp. 1–45 in *Communication Yearbook, 20,* B.R. Burleson (ed.). New York: Routledge.

National Opinion Research Center. (2012). *General Social Survey, 2010 Data*. Author analyses of data available at http://sda.berkeley.edu/archive.htm.

Newman, O. (1972). *Defensible space: Crime prevention through urban design*. New York: McMillan.

Pain, R. (2000). Place, social relations and the fear of crime: A review. *Progress in Human Geography, 24*(3), 365–387.

Pain, R. (1997). Social geographies of women's fear of crime. *Transactions, Institute of British Geographers, 22*(2), 231–244.

Painter, K. (1996). The influence of street lighting improvements on crime, fear and pedestrian street use, after dark. *Landscape and Urban Planning, 35*(2), 193–201.

Parkin, D. (1986). Toward an apprehension of fear, pp. 158–172 in *Sociophobics: The Anthropology of Fear*, D.L. Scruton (ed). Boulder, CO: Westview Press.

Pew Research Center. (2011). *Economy dominates public's agenda, dims hopes for the future; Less optimism about America's long-term prospects*. Available at http://www.people-press.org/2011/01/20/section-1-publics-policy-priorities/.

Potter, G.W., & Kappeler, V.E. (2006). *Constructing crime: Perspective on making news and social problems (2nd ed.)*. Prospect Heights, IL: Waveland.

Sacco, V.F. (1995). Media constructions of crime. *Annals of the American Academy of Political and Social Science, 539*, 141–154.

Scruton, D.L. (1986). The anthropology of an emotion, pp. 7–49 in *Sociophobics: The Anthropology of Fear*, D.L. Scruton (ed). Boulder, CO: Westview Press.

Short, E., & Ditton, J. (1998). Seen and now heard: Talking to the targets of open street CCTV. *British Journal of Criminology, 38*(3), 404–428.

Simon, J. (2009). *Governing through crime: How the war on crime transformed American democracy and created a culture of fear*. New York: Oxford University Press.

Skogan, W. (1989). Communities, crime, and neighborhood organization. *Crime and Delinquency, 35*(3), 437–457.

Skogan, W. (1995). Crime and the racial fears of White Americans. *Annals of the American Academy of Political and Social Science, 539*(1), 59–71.

Skogan, W. (1986). Fear of crime and neighborhood change. *Crime and Justice, 8*(8), 203–229.

Skogan, W. (2006). *Police and the community in Chicago: A tale of three cities*. New York: Oxford University Press.

Skogan, W.G., & Maxfield, M.G. (1981). *Coping with crime: Individual and neighborhood reactions*. Beverly Hills, CA: Sage.

Spinks, C. (2001). *A new Apartheid? Urban spatiality, (fear of) crime, and segregation in Capetown, South Africa.* London: Destin Working Paper No. 20, London School of Economics.

Warr, M. (1984). Fear of victimization: Why are women and the elderly more afraid? *Social Science Quarterly, 65*(3), 681–702.

Warr, M., & Stafford, M.C. (1983). Fear of victimization: A look at the proximate causes. *Social Forces, 61*(4), 1033–1043.

The White House. (2013). *Now is the time: The president's plan to protect our children and our communities by reducing gun violence.* Accessed September 25, 2013. http://www.whitehouse.gov/sites/default/files/docs/wh_now_is_the_time_full.pdf.

Wolman, B.B. (1993). Defining anxiety, pp. 3–10 in *Anxiety and Related Disorders: A Handbook,* edited by B.B. Wolman & G. Stricker. New York: John Wiley and Sons, Inc.

Chapter 2

Reviewing the Fear of Crime Literature: What Has Been Learned from 45 Years of Research?

The most damaging of the effects of violent crime is fear, and that fear must not be belittled.

Katzenbach et al., 1967, p. 3

From a purely scientific standpoint, research on the fear of crime can continue indefinitely. There is no critical experiment that will answer all the questions, so there will always be hypotheses to test and new paths of inquiry to follow. However ... it is useful periodically to take stock of where we are....

Garofalo, 1981, p. 1

Crime is truly a unique phenomenon in modern culture. It is often the topic of everyday conversation. It is regularly the central premise of entertainment, including many movies, television shows, books, and video games. With the news media, accounts of criminal events often serve as the lead stories and are frequently rated as the most viewed. Without a doubt, crime truly fascinates the public. According to Warr (2000), "As condensed and emblematic accounts of human conflict, [criminal events] raise profound questions about the nature and sources of human motivation, the misfortune of fellow humans, the ability of the state to maintain social order, and, ultimately, the presence or absence of justice in human affairs" (p. 452). Interestingly, while crime fascinates us, it also frequently terrifies us. While it keeps us glued to our televisions and computers, crime also makes us afraid to leave our homes.

Given the impact and unique role of crime in society, many are often surprised to find that fear of crime is a relatively new topic among scholars. Fear of crime has only become a topic of criminology and victimology research in the last few decades. The purpose of this chapter is to outline the progression of fear of crime as a field of study from its birth to the modern day. In doing so, the fear of crime timeline will be divided into three separate time periods. Beginning after the birth of fear of crime research, we characterize studies produced between 1971 and 1985 as the infancy era of fear of crime research. We categorize studies produced between 1986 and 2000 as the adolescence era of fear of crime research. Finally, we group studies produced since 2001 into the current, mature era of fear of crime research. For each time period, we discuss the major trends in fear of crime research, along with several of the most significant studies produced. Please note that the dates chosen as the beginning and ending of each time period are in essence arbitrary. For example, while there are substantial differences in the studies produced during the infancy and adolescence eras, there is no substantive difference between fear of crime research performed in 1985 and 1986. The dates are used merely as a guide to distinguish between the different developmental eras of the fear of crime field of research.

Birth of Fear of Crime Research

The 1960s marked an important time in U.S. history, especially in regards to crime and public perception of crime. From the era of the Great Depression in the early 1930s through the early 1960s, crime rates in the U.S. remained relatively stable and low. During the early 1960s, the U.S. began to experience its first rapidly growing crime rate in decades. From 1960 to 1969, the rate of reported crime almost doubled. In addition to, or possibly in conjunction with the rising crime rate, the 1960s saw widespread civil unrest in urban areas throughout the U.S., as the civil rights movement spread across the nation. Almost every news outlet in the country presented viewers with images of protesters and police battling in the streets. These factors combined to have a dramatic impact on the general public's perceptions. Public opinion polls, which had traditionally reported that people were most worried about the economy or war, began identifying crime as the nation's biggest problem (Hilbink, 2006).

It was clear that the general public saw crime as a major concern and warranted attention from all levels of government. Capitalizing on that demand, candidates in the 1964 presidential election made law and order one of their central topics of debate. After winning the election, President Lyndon B. Johnson pledged that the federal government would take on the growing crime problem gripping America. On July 23, 1965, he authorized the development of the Commission on Law Enforcement and Administration of Justice, the goal of which was to "deepen our understanding of the causes of crime and of how our society should respond to the challenge of our present levels of crime" (Katzenbach et al., 1967). The Commission included over a dozen attorneys, scholars, and advisors, including several previous and future state and U.S. attorneys (e.g., Nicholas Katzenbach, Thomas Lynch, and William Rogers).

The Commission on Law Enforcement and Administration of Justice

The main task of the Commission was to evaluate the current state of knowledge of crime and law enforcement in the United States and make suggestions for potential crime prevention and reduction processes and programs. The main report produced by the Commission was entitled "The Challenge of Crime in a Free Society," and it contained information from dozens of small- and large-scale studies performed in various cities all over the U.S., including Chicago, Boston, and New York City. The report provided information on topics such as general crime prevalence, juvenile delinquency, drug abuse, police actions, and science and technology. In addition, though not its central premise, the Commission's report was one of the first research-based documents to stress the importance and consequences of fear of crime. As stated in the report (Katzenbach et al., 1967):

> The most damaging of the effects of violent crime is fear, and that fear must not be belittled. Suddenly becoming the object of a stranger's violent hostility is as frightening as any class of experience. A citizen who hears rapid footsteps behind him as he walks down a dark and otherwise deserted street cannot be expected to calculate that the chance of those footsteps having a sinister meaning is only one in a hundred or in a thousand or, if he does make such a calculation to be calmed by its results. Any chance at all is frightening (p. 3).

Though important, the Commission's report went beyond simply stating that fear of crime was a topic worthy of study. It also reported findings from several studies that specifically measured fear of crime. Such findings helped illuminate several issues that were either unknown or simply overlooked by criminologists and policy makers up to that point. First, the general public is more afraid of those crimes they perceive as most serious (i.e., violent crimes), even though they occur much less frequently than the least serious crimes (i.e., propoerty crimes). In essence, individuals were most afraid of crimes that they had the least likelihood of experiencing, such as murder or robbery. Secondly, many individuals' fear of crime directly influenced their habits and behaviors. Because of their fear of crime, many people indicated that they began locking their doors, staying home at night rather than going out, and even thought about moving to a new neighborhood. Third, the neighborhoods whose residents had the highest reported fear of crime did not necessarily have the highest rates of crime. For example, in examining two comparable neighborhoods, researchers revealed that the residents who lived in neighborhoods with the lower crime rate actually reported higher levels of concern about crime. Finally, fear of crime is not limited solely to individuals who have been criminally victimized but can also occur in individuals who have never been victims (Katzenbach et al., 1967). This finding was in direct opposition to the beliefs of many early criminologists who thought that fear of crime was only a consequence of actually experiencing victimization.

Development of Victimization Surveys

While the Commission on Law Enforcement and Administration of Justice's report was instrumental in the birth of fear of crime research, there was also a very important secondary consequence. Both the methodologies of the studies described and the recommendations made in the Commission's report provided strong support for the use of self-report surveys to measure the extent and nature of criminal victimization. Before the 1960s, the use of self-report victimization surveys had never been attempted at the national level. The Commission report helped to show that self-report surveys could be administered on a large scale and, importantly, could provide valuable information on victimization. It was the report's description of large-scale studies and recommendations for improved methods of victimization measurement that lead to the creation of many of today's most commonly utilized victimization surveys (Rand, 2005).

First administered in 1972, the General Social Survey (GSS) is a self-report survey administered to a nationally representative sample of individuals. As mentioned in Chapter 1, the central focus of the GSS is measuring social change and public opinion. Second only to the U.S. Census, the GSS is one of the most commonly used sources of social sciences information in the U.S. (National Opinion Research Center, 2011). The National Crime Survey (NCS)— now known as the National Crime Victimization Survey (NCVS)—is also a self-report survey administered to a nationally representative sample of respondents; however, it focuses on measuring victimization. First administered in 1973, the NCS was not only one of the first large-scale victimization surveys, it is currently the principal source of national-level victimization statistics in the U.S. (Bureau of Justice Statistics, 2011). Each survey was inspired in part by the methodologies and recommendations of the Commission on Law Enforcement and Administration of Justice. Further, as we will discuss in more detail in Chapter 3, each survey contains measures that have been frequently utilized to examine fear of crime over the last 40 years.

1971–1985: The Infancy Era of Fear of Crime Research

One of the many recommendations of the Commission on Law Enforcement and Administration of Justice's report was the continued examination of the nature of fear of crime. Armed with data, it took relatively little time for scholars to begin examining the extent and correlates of fear of crime. Throughout the 1970s and early 1980s, fear of crime articles began to appear in academic journals. Researchers published dozens of fear of crime studies between 1971 and 1985. Although the fear of crime research was rather prolific during that time, there was very little variation in the research questions or correlates that researchers examined. As a result, we describe that era as the infancy of fear of crime research, as there was little theoretical development and limited variation in the studies produced.

Trends in Fear of Crime Research

In the fear of crime research published between 1971 and 1985, several trends are apparent. As often occurs in academic research, the trends developed as a result of the large number of studies that focused on the same or a similar topic. During the infancy era of fear of crime research, key topics examined by researchers included the relationship between demographic characteristics and fear of crime and fear of crime among vulnerable populations, specifically the elderly. In addition, there was also a clear commonality in terms of the methodology used to measure fear of crime, with many researchers using similar types of survey questions to measure fear of crime (for more explanation, see Chapter 3). Each of these trends will be discussed in more detail below.

The influence of demographic correlates on fear of crime. As stated above, a large number of studies published between 1971 and 1985 focused principally on the relationship between individuals' demographic characteristics (e.g., sex, race, and age) and fear of crime. For example, Clemente and Kleiman (1977) examined the relationship between demographic characteristic (i.e., sex, age, race, and socioeconomic status) and fear of crime. Similarly, with his examination of the link between fear of crime and gun ownership, DeFronzo (1979) included mostly measures of demographic information (i.e., religion, marital status, income, race, political orientation, and/or age). While several demographic characteristics were often significantly related to fear of crime across various studies, the effect of gender was consistently significant. Women typically reported higher levels of fear of crime than men (e.g., Braungart, Braungart, & Hoyer, 1980; Clemente & Kleiman, 1977; Erskine, 1974).

Fear of crime among vulnerable populations. It also was common for fear of crime researchers to limit their focus to specific populations that they considered especially vulnerable rather than examining fear of crime in general (Warr, 2000). One group that received considerable attention from researchers during that era was the elderly. A large number of fear of crime studies published between 1971 and 1985 focused specifically on senior citizens. For some time, scholars and policymakers just generally accepted that the elderly was more afraid of crime than any other age group, and many fear of crime researchers provided empirical support for that argument (e.g., Kennedy & Silverman, 1985; Lebowitz, 1975; Toseland, 1982). For example, Toseland (1982) found that the percentage of individuals who reported being afraid of crime increased across age categories, with individuals in higher age groups reporting they were more fearful of crime. While many researchers simply showed that the elderly were more fearful of crime than other age groups, some went one step further by providing evidence that increased fear among the elderly was actually influenced by other factors. For example, Warr (1984) reported that while fear of crime is higher among older individuals, it is partially driven by their perceived risk of being victimized. As we mentioned in Chapter 1 and we will discuss more in the next chapter, perceived risk of crime is a term used to describe how likely an individual thinks he/she is to be a victim of crime. In addition, Yin (1980, 1982) argued in the early 1980s that the elderly were not as afraid as some researchers thought (see Ferraro, 1995). A selection of similar studies is displayed in Table 2.1. As will be demonstrated later in this chapter, the focus on vulnerable populations (e.g., women and the elderly) remains a key area of interest among researchers in the next era of the fear of crime timeline.

Common fear of crime measures. A final trend during the infancy era of fear of crime research was the lack of variation in the constructs used to measure fear of crime. The majority of studies performed between 1971 and 1985 utilized measures of fear of crime similar to those used by the National Crime Survey (NCS) and the General Social Survey (GSS). With the NCS, fear of

Table 2.1 Selected Influential Fear of Crime Studies Focusing on the Elderly: 1971–1985

Date	Author(s)	Focus	Findings
1975	Lebowitz	Relationship between fear of crime and demographic characteristics	Age magnified fear of crime for individuals who had low income, lived alone, and were in large cities
1976	Clemente & Kleiman	Relationship between fear of crime and demographic characteristics	Age magnified fear of crime for female, Black, and urban individuals
1980	Yin	Review of literature on fear of crime among elderly	Several issues with fear of crime research, including scarcity of research and lack of information on consequences of fear
1982	Clarke & Lewis	Correlates of fear of crime among the elderly	Residents of non-sheltered housing were more fearful than residents of sheltered housing
1983	Jeffords	Relationship between age and fear of crime inside and outside the home	Elderly were more fearful of crime outside the home
1984	Warr	Relationship between fear of crime, age, gender, and risk	Women and elderly had higher perceived risk and fear of crime

crime was measured with the question, "How safe do you feel or would you feel being out alone in your neighborhood at night?" A number of researchers utilized this measure. Similar to the NCS survey question, the GSS measured fear of crime by asking, "Is there any place right around here—that is, within a mile—where you would be afraid to walk alone at night?" (see Ferraro, 1995). Many other studies also utilized the GSS measure. Further, a small number of researchers utilized both measures to examine fear of crime. For example, Erskine (1974) asked respondents 12 different questions about their fear of crime, including both the GSS and NCS questions. As we will discuss in Chapter 3, while widely used on surveys, these measures were not entirely appropriate to accurately measure fear of crime. This issue is still a topic of debate among researchers today.

Key Fear of Crime Studies

DuBow, McCabe, and Kaplan (1979) Reactions to crime: A critical review of the literature. While many studies produced during the infancy era of fear of crime research were relatively rudimentary in terms of the measures and data analyses performed, there were several significant studies that pushed along the development of fear of crime research. One of the seminal works published during that era was DuBow, McCabe, and Kaplan's (1979) study, in which they outlined the current state of fear of crime research. During the first decade of fear of crime research, there were dozens of studies published, but for the most part, each focused rather narrowly on their individual topics (e.g., fear among the elderly or the link between fear and handgun ownership). DuBow et al.'s (1979) work represented one of the first attempts to summarize and evaluate the state of the fear of crime research. The authors wrote that their goal was to provide "a set of conceptions around which existing research findings can be organized and compared. Emphasis is given to the consistency or inconsistency of findings and to an identification of variables, areas of research, and methodologies which have received insufficient attention" (DuBow et al., 1979, p. vii). That work, along with Garofalo's (1981) summary study, greatly focused the development of the fear of crime research and gave budding scholars much needed intellectual momentum.

Skogan et al. (1982) Reactions to crime project. Another very influential study during that era in fear of crime research was Skogan et al.'s (1982) "Reactions to Crime (RTC) Project" conducted with the Center for Urban Affairs and Policy Research at Northwestern University and the National Institute of Justice (NIJ). The goal of the study was to examine how crime affected the attitudes and behaviors of individuals residing in urban areas, especially in regard to fear of crime. This particular study is significant because of its extensive research methodology—a five-year multidisciplinary study utilizing data collected across thirty neighborhoods from three major U.S. cities. It also confirmed many key findings reported only sporadically across previous research studies. Echoing the conclusions of the Commission on Law Enforcement and Administration of Justice's report from nearly a decade earlier, some of the more important findings of the project included:

- Individuals with low rates of victimization (e.g., elderly) may still have high levels of fear of crime.
- Personally experiencing victimization (i.e., direct victimization) is strongly associated with fear of crime.
- Knowing someone who was victimized (i.e., indirect victimization) explains some of the variation in fear of crime.

Skogan and colleagues' study greatly influenced much of the fear of crime research that followed, especially in terms of the examination of the influence of direct and indirect victimization on fear of crime.

Warr and Stafford (1983) Fear of victimization: A look at the proximate causes. As noted previously, the majority of studies produced between 1971 and 1985 focused predominantly on demographic measures as proximate causes of fear of crime. However, a key study performed by Warr and Stafford (1983) went beyond simply examining the demographic correlates of fear of crime (e.g., gender, race, and age). Warr and Stafford examined the relationship between fear of crime, perceived risk of crime, and perceived seriousness of crime. In addition, they went beyond using the traditional measure of fear of crime described above by asking respondents about their fear of 16 different types of crime, using a 11-point Likert-type scale (0 = not afraid at all to 10 = very afraid). Their findings showed that although some crimes were assigned a very high level of perceived seriousness (i.e., murder), respondents reported a low level of fear for those crimes. Further, the relationship was directly influenced by the low level of perceived risk respondents assigned to the crime. As we describe in Chapter 3, the methodology used by Warr and Stafford (1983) has become rather standard techniques with fear of crime research.

1986–2000: Adolescence Era of Fear of Crime Research

From the mid-1980s to the end of the century, fear of crime as a research topic grew tremendously, with the number of research studies published shadowing the number produced during the fifteen years prior. After examining the fear of crime studies performed between 1986 and 2000, we can easily argue that they represent a new and distinct era in the fear of crime research timeline. Researchers began utilizing more advanced techniques and methodologies similar to those proposed in the key articles discussed above. As a result, we describe that time period as the adolescence era of fear of crime research.

Throughout the late 1980s and 1990s, it became more conventional to develop and test comprehensive models in an effort to identify predictors that significantly explained fear of crime levels. Specifically, as suggested by Warr and Stafford (1983), researchers focused more on examining the proximate causes of fear of crime, beyond individuals' demographic characteristics. Further, rather than relying predominantly on the use of bivariate analysis to examine the fear of crime correlates, researchers more commonly estimated multivariate models (e.g., Ferraro, 1995; Smith & Hill, 1991; Wilcox Rountree, 1998). In addition, scholars began more frequently utilizing multilevel models, examining the influence of both individual- and community-level effects on individuals' fear of crime levels (e.g., Wilcox Rountree, 1998).

Trends in Fear of Crime Research

Even a brief examination of the fear of crime literature indicates that research performed between 1986 and 2000 was both more prolific and diverse than the research performed in the previous fifteen years. Specifically, several clear trends also emerged during the adolescence era. Studies produced during this era of fear of crime research often focused on the impact of gender on fear of crime, the relationship between perceived risk and fear of crime, and the role victimization plays, if any, in explaining fear of crime. We discuss each of these trends in more detail below.

Fear of crime among vulnerable populations. As discussed previously, a large portion of fear of crime studies produced between 1971 and 1985 focused on a population considered especially vulnerable — the elderly. Researchers who produced fear of crime studies between 1986 and 2000 took a similar tactic. The key difference is that the vulnerable population frequently examined in studies performed during the adolescence era of fear of crime research was women. To be clear, there were a number of research studies conducted prior to 1986 that focused specifically on women's fear of crime (e.g., Riger & Godorn, 1981; Riger, Gordon, & LeBailly, 1979; Warr, 1985). Nonetheless, it was not until the late 1980s/early 1990s that the focus on women's fear of crime became entrenched in the fear of crime literature. A sample of studies produced between 1986 and 2000 focusing on women's fear of crime can be seen in Table 2.2.

For much of the history of fear of crime research, anecdotal evidence continued to indicate that women are more afraid of crime than men. This claim is made more disconcerting when one considers that women are much less likely to be victimized than men (Craven, 1997). However, numerous studies conducted between 1986 and 2000 reported that once other factors were controlled, women were simply more fearful of being victimized than men (Ferraro, 1996; Fisher & Sloan, 2003). Further, according to a 1989 Gallup Poll, 60% of women reported they were afraid of crime, compared to 25% of men. One of the main areas of focus concerning women's fear of crime is the effect of sexual victimization on fear, which we discuss in more detail in Chapter 4. Researchers have argued that the high level of fear of crime among women may be driven by their fear of sexual victimization, which shadows their fear of other types of crime. As stated by Ferraro (1996),

Table 2.2 Selected Influential Fear of Crime Studies
Focusing on Women: 1986–2000

Date	Author(s)	Focus	Findings
1989	LaGrange & Ferraro	Age and gender differences in fear of crime	Women reported higher levels of fear of crime than men
1992	Young	Gender differences in fear of crime	Women's higher levels of fear of crime driven by victimization by non-strangers
1995	Stanko	Gender differences in fear of crime	Women's higher levels of fear of crime driven by fear of men, especially male strangers
1996	Ferraro	Gender differences in fear of crime	Women's higher levels of fear of crime driven by fear of sexual assault
1998	Gilchrist et al.	Gender differences in fear of crime	Fear driven by prior victimization, perceived risk, and perceived vulnerability, not gender

In a sense … any victimization of women may involve the possibility of sexual assault. Rape certainly qualifies as a perceptually contemporaneous offense [offenses which are associated with other types of victimization] to most crimes; but its uniqueness as a form of victimization to women probably escalates the degree of fear attending other crimes committed against women. In other words, sexual assault may "shadow" other types of victimization among women. Rape may operate like a "master offense" among women … (p. 669).

As we will discuss later in this chapter and more in Chapter 4, the impact of the threat of sexual victimization on women's fear of crime, and Ferraro's (1996) shadow of sexual assault hypothesis, spurred a substantial amount of research that continues to this day (e.g., Fisher & Sloan, 2003; Schafer, Huebner, & Bynum, 2006).

The influence of perceived risk of victimization. A second significant trend to emerge during the adolescence era of fear of crime research was the focus on the relationship between perceived risk of crime and fear of crime. Perceived risk of crime and fear of crime are closely linked, yet, as mentioned in Chapter 1 and discussed in more detail in Chapter 3, they are distinct phenomena. The importance of the relationship between perceived risk and fear and the problems deriving from the failure to distinguish between the two was not a new topic of discussion among fear of crime researchers during the adolescence era. This issue was raised by several researchers before 1986 (e.g., Janson & Ryder, 1983; Slovic, Fischhoff, & Lichtenstein, 1980; Stafford & Galle, 1984). However, as with the focus on women, the link between perceived risk and fear of crime did not garner widespread attention until the late 1980s and 1990s.

In a pioneering study, LaGrange, Ferraro, and Supancic (1992) examined the impact of physical (e.g., abandoned buildings, litter) and social incivilities (e.g., lack of social cohesion) on both perceived risk of victimization and fear of victimization. They found that both types of incivilities directly influenced individuals' levels of perceived risk and fear; however, the relationship was much more significant for perceived risk than fear. This provided empirical evidence that perceived risk and fear of crime are two distinct concepts. Table 2.3 presents a sample of other studies produced between 1986 and 2000 that discuss the importance of distinguishing between perceived risk and fear of crime. This relationship will be discussed in more detail in Chapter 3.

Table 2.3 Selected Influential Fear of Crime Studies Focused on Perceived Risk of Crime: 1986–2000

Date	Author(s)	Focus	Findings
1986	Brantingham & Brantingham	Variation between perceived risk and actual risk of victimization	Individuals in area with low actual risk had high perceived risk
1987	Ferraro & LaGrange	Comparison of perceived risk and fear of crime measures in previous research studies	Perceived risk and fear were distinct factors but were often inappropriately used as same measure
1992	LaGrange et al.	Influence of social and physical incivilities on perceived risk and fear of crime	Incivilities influenced perceived risk more than fear
1996a	Wilcox Rountree & Land	Influence of neighborhood- and individual-level factors on perceived risk and fear of crime	Both neighborhood- and individual-level factors influenced perceived risk and fear of crime differently
2000	Mesch	Relationship between perceived risk, lifestyle activities, and fear of crime	Level of perceived risk influenced both lifestyle activities and level of fear

The influence of previous victimization. Over 40 years ago, the report produced by the President's Commission on Law Enforcement and Administration of Justice reported that fear of crime was correlated with victimization, meaning individuals who were previously victimized are more likely to be fearful of crime (Katzenbach et al., 1967). Skogan et al.'s (1982) "Reactions to Crime (RTC) Project," also supported this finding, when it reported a significant positive relationship between fear of crime and both direct victimization (i.e., any type of victimization personally experienced) and indirect victimization (i.e., any type of victimization experienced by someone close to the individual). While victimization was occasionally examined, there were few studies produced before 1986 that tested whether victimization was a key predictor of fear of crime.

It was during the adolescence era of fear of crime research that the link between victimization and fear of crime became a central topic for a number of studies. Generally, studies produced during 1986–2000 reported individuals who experienced some form of victimization had higher levels of fear of crime than non-victims. For example, Ferraro (1995) stated that an individual's level of fear and/or perceived risk of victimization might be affected by both direct and indirect victimization. Similarly, with their study examining the relationship between victimization, fear of crime, and attitudes towards the justice system, Dull and Wint (1997) found that individuals who had been previously victimized reported higher levels of fear of property crime than nonvictims. A sample of other fear of crime studies produced between 1986 and 2000 that examine the role of previous victimization are displayed in Table 2.4.

Key Fear of Crime Studies

Ferraro and LaGrange (1987) The measurement of fear of crime. As with the infancy era of fear of crime research, the adolescence era was marked by several significant studies that served as seminal works that influenced subsequent fear of crime studies. One of the most influential fear of crime studies produced during that era was performed by Ferraro and LaGrange (1987). Their study focused specifically on the measurement of fear of crime. Ferraro and La-Grange's seminal study is influential for two main reasons. First, it was one of the first studies that attempted to provide a clear definition of what fear of crime means. As we discuss in more detail in Chapter 3, there are relatively few studies that actually provide a definition for fear of crime. Ferraro and LaGrange (1987, p. 73) defined fear of crime as "the negative emotional reaction generated by crime or symbols associated with crime." This definition has remained one of the mostly frequently cited in the fear of crime literature in the last 27 years.

Table 2.4 Selected Influential Studies Focusing on
Previous Victimization: 1986–2000

Date	Author(s)	Focus	Findings
1987	Skogan	The impact of previous victimization on fear of crime	Individuals who reported previous victimization were more likely to be fearful and change their behaviors
1991	Smith & Hill	The impact of previous property and violent victimization on fear of crime	Previous property victimization has more of an impact on higher levels of fear than previous violent victimization
1996	Weinrath & Gartrell	The relationship between age, gender, previous victimization, and fear of crime	Younger women who experienced assault reported higher levels of fear while older women reported lower levels of fear
1996b	Wilcox Rountree & Land	The relationship between burglary rates, perceived risk, routine activities, and fear of crime	Macro-level burglary rates and incivilities were significantly related to higher levels of perceived risk
1997	Dull & Wint	The fear of crime among victims and nonvictims	Victims reported higher levels of fear of property crime, while nonvictims reported higher levels of fear of violent crime

The second, and arguably more important, contribution of Ferraro and La-Grange's (1987) work was their meticulous examination and discussion of the measurement of fear of crime. Analyzing over 40 fear of crime studies produced during the 1970s and 1980s, Ferraro and LaGrange outlined the survey questions utilized by researchers to measure fear. In doing so, they noted that the majority of studies utilized the same few measures, such as the GSS and NCS measures. Further, they indicated that those measures "are suspect because of theoretical and methodological shortcomings" (Ferraro & LaGrange, 1987, p. 70). They argued that several studies they reviewed actually measured perceived risk of victimization but referred to it as fear of crime. Ferraro and LaGrange's examination brought to light many of the measurement issues that plagued the fear of crime literature, many of which had gone relatively unnoticed by most fear of crime researchers. In retrospect, Ferraro and LaGrange (1987) brought many of the issues to light that had served to stall any true progression in the fear of crime research.

Ferraro (1996) Women's fear of victimization: Shadow of sexual assault? Ferraro also produced another study during the adolescence era of fear of crime research that was especially influential in the development of fear of crime research. Focusing on the variation in fear of crime among males and females, Ferraro (1996) examined the potential impact that fear of sexual assault may have on fear of crime in general. He found that women's fear of sexual victimization often directly influences their fear of other crimes. The more afraid of sexual victimization women are, the more afraid of crime they are in general. In essence, women's fear of sexual assault "shadows" their fear of other types of crime, especially personal crimes (e.g., robbery or theft). Over time, this finding has received support from numerous other studies. For example, Fisher and Sloan (2003) attempted to replicate and extend the models from Ferraro's (1996) study utilizing a national sample of college students. Controlling for numerous other potential influences on fear of crime, such as the time of day, Fisher and Sloan (2003) found that college women's fear of rape accounted for a large portion of their fear of different types of personal crimes.

Ferraro's "shadow hypothesis" is significant because it provides evidence of the complexity of fear of crime. Individuals are not afraid of all types of crime equally, and their fear of one type of crime can have a meaningful impact on fear of other types of crimes (see also, Warr, 1985). Though considered rational beings, people do not always think or behave rationally. As shown by Ferraro, to truly understand the extent and impact of fear of crime, examining general fear of crime is not enough to appreciate its dimensions. Fear is a multifaceted phenomenon and incorporates a wide range of factors that need to be accounted for to fully understand and explain how it works.

Hale (1996) Fear of crime: A review of the literature. Another influential work produced during the adolescence era of fear of research was Hale's (1996) summary study, in which he reviewed the state of fear of crime literature. In the same vein as DuBow et al.'s (1979) summary study, Hale's study provided a detailed description of the growth, trends, and issues of the studies produced during the first three decades of fear of crime research's history. Hale's study described and synthesized the theoretical explanations, methodologies, and findings of over 200 empirical publications and presentations. Even today, this study serves as one of the most concise and extensive reviews of the fear of crime literature.

Hale's contribution was influential for two reasons. First, it provided a clear, yet comprehensive, picture of the thirty-year progression of the fear of crime research. Although researchers produced several other studies during the adolescence era of fear of crime research with a similar goal, including Ferraro and LaGrange's (1987) study discussed previously, for the most part, they only provided pieces of the larger picture. Hale's work provided a description of the progress of the discipline as a whole, including trends in defining, measuring, and theoretically and empirically explaining fear of crime. Second, and similarly, Hale's study was significant because it provided a clear picture of the numerous issues that had become so prolific in fear of crime research, including invalid fear of crime measures, faulty theoretical reasoning, and a lack of variation in research questions. As stated by Hale (1996, p. 94), "… theoretical casualness and empirical chaos has been the order of the day in the studies of fear of crime. Future work needs to avoid the same conceptual ambiguities and confusions if progress is to be made." As we discuss in the next section, however, there are signs of this transition beginning to appear in the current era of fear of crime research.

2001–Present: The Maturation of Fear of Crime Research

While there was some progression in fear of crime research during the adolescence era, many of these studies suffered from limitations similar to those published during the infancy era. During the infancy and adolescence eras, researchers often recycled and reused the same invalid and unreliable measures, limited theoretical models, and unsupported assumptions. As a result, the progression of fear of crime research before 2000 was relatively limited. According to Warr (2000),

> Since the days of the President's Commission, hundreds of studies of fear of crime have been conducted, and the topic regularly appears in the journals of the field. For reasons that remain elusive, however, the study of fear seems to have stalled at a rudimentary phase of development, a situation that is in danger of turning into outright stagnation. Investigators continue to revisit the same well-worn issues, and, even after three decades, the meaning of the term "fear" remains a matter of controversy (p. 453).

As stated by Warr, there was very little progress made before 2000 to develop a valid and concise definition of fear of crime that can be utilized by researchers. Further, the survey questions used to measure fear of crime remained questionable. Each of these issues played a key role in impeding the continued development of fear of crime research during the adolescence era, which we discuss in detail in Chapter 3.

Since 2000, there has been a substantial degree of maturation in fear of crime research. To be clear, there also is still much room for the field to continue to grow, as we discuss more fully in Chapter 8. The progression of fear of crime research has increased dramatically since the turn of the century. For example, criminologists have begun adopting ideals from other disciplines, such as psychology and the medical sciences, in an effort to better understand and explain fear. Scholars have extended theoretical models beyond simply using demographic characteristics to explain fear of crime. They now use advanced statistical techniques, such as multiple regression hierarchical models, and structural equation modeling in an attempt to explain variations in fear of crime. And, fear of crime measures have evolved into more valid and reliable measures.

Trends in Fear of Crime Research

As with the previous eras of fear of crime research, the present era has seen a number of trends emerge within the field. First, there has been a noticeable change in how scholars measure fear of crime. A number of researchers have begun to move away from the traditional measures that focus simply on the presence or absence of fear and have, instead, begun to utilize measures that capture the level or intensity of fear of crime. Further, researchers have shifted focus away from measuring generalized fear of crime to understanding the differences in fear across specific forms of crime. Finally, a number of studies produced in the present era of fear of crime research have focused on the importance of the victim-offender relationship in explaining variation in fear of crime. Each of these trends will be discussed briefly below and in further detail in Chapter 3.

Level of fear of crime measures. For much of the history of fear of crime research, the most commonly utilized measure of fear of crime has been the dichotomous measure of fear (Warr, 2000). This type of measure is typically used to determine whether or not an individual is fearful. As such, fear of crime is often reported as either "yes" the individual is afraid of being victimized or "no" the individual is not afraid of being victimized. For example, the GSS measure discussed previously asked "Is there any place right around here — that is, within a mile — where you would be afraid to walk alone at night?" This is a dichotomous measure, asking individuals for a yes or no response. In the last decade, there has been a growing trend with the use of intensity of fear measures (see Table 2.6 for a sample of such studies). Researchers use this type of measure to determine how fearful an individual is, and answers usually come in one of two forms — a Likert scale or 10-point scale (e.g., Farrall & Gadd, 2004; Fisher & Sloan, 2003; Wilcox et al., 2007; Woolnough, 2009).

A large number of researchers have utilized a traditional four- or five-point Likert scale, while others utilize a discrete ten or eleven-point scale. For example, Melde (2009) utilized a 5-category Likert-scale (1 = "Not At All Afraid" to 5 = "Very Afraid") to measure fear of crime, while Fisher and Sloan (2003) used a 10-point scale (1 = "Not Afraid at All" to 10 = "Very Afraid") to measure fear of crime. We list other examples of intensity measures in Table 2.5 (see also, Table 3.5 in Chapter 3). With both types of scales, responses typically range from low to high levels of fear.

The recent interest in fear of crime intensity measures is, in large part, because they are more versatile. For example, a dichotomous measure is limited in that it can only provide information indicating if individuals are afraid of crime. An intensity measure can provide information indicating if individuals are afraid of crime as well as information about how much they are afraid. With that in mind, researchers have begun utilizing intensity measures because they can provide wider variation than the traditional dichotomous measures.

Crime-specific measures of fear. Similarly, the majority of fear of crime research studies produced thus far has examined fear of crime in general, often asking individuals if they are afraid of crime or being victimized. There is a growing body of empirical evidence that suggests individuals are more afraid of certain crimes than they are of others. For example, with their work exam-

Table 2.5 Selected Fear of Crime Studies Utilizing Intensity of Fear Measures: 2001–2013

Date	Author(s)	Fear Measure
2003a	Lane & Meeker	4-Category Likert-Scale (1 = "Not Afraid" to 4 = "Very Afraid")
2003	Fisher & Sloan	10-Point Scale (1 = "Not Afraid at All" to 10 = "Very· Afraid")
2007	Moore & Shepherd	4-Category Likert-Scale (1 = "Not Worried At All" to 4 = "Very Worried")
2009	Fisher & May	4-Category Likert-Scale (1 = "Strongly Disagree" to 4 = "Strongly Agree")
2009	Melde	5-Category Likert-Scale (1 = "Not At All Afraid" to 5 = "Very Afraid")
2009	Lane, Gover, & Dahod	5-Category Likert-Scale (1 = "Not at All Afraid" to 5 = "Very Afraid")
2010	May, Rader, & Goodrum	4-Category Likert-Scale (1 = "Strongly Disagree" to 4 = "Strongly Agree")
2013	Lane & Fox	4-Category Likert-Scale (1 = "Not Afraid" to 4 = "Very Afraid")

ining the level of fear of specific types of crime, Warr and Stafford (1983) reported that individuals were more afraid of experiencing burglary than murder, although the perceived seriousness of murder was much higher. As discussed previously, both Ferraro (1996) and Fisher and Sloan (2003) reported that women are significantly more afraid of sexual assault than other types of crime, and their fear of sexual assault may directly affect their fear of other types of crime (see also Lane & Meeker, 2003b). As a result of these and similar studies, many researchers in the current era of fear of crime research have begun examining specific types of crime rather than crime in general. For example, with their analysis of the relationship between gender and fear of crime, Sutton and Farrall (2005) examined fear of burglary, assault, and vandalism. A sample of other such studies and the types of crimes examined can be seen in Table 2.6.

It should be noted that fear of crime researchers focusing on specific types of crime is not a recent phenomenon. As with many of the other trends discussed in this chapter, the intellectual seeds that have helped produce this trend were planted much earlier. In addition to the studies described above, there have been numerous studies produced during the infancy and adolescence eras of fear of crime research that focused specifically on certain types of crime (e.g., Farrall et al., 1997; Ferraro & LaGrange, 1987; Wilcox Rountree, 1998). The practice of asking about specific types of crime has become more common in

Table 2.6 Selected Influential Fear of Crime Studies Focusing on Specific Types of Crime: 2001–2013

Date	Author(s)	Types of Crime Examined
2003	Fisher & Sloan	Theft, Rape, Robbery, Simple Assault, Aggravated Assault
2005	Sutton & Farrall	Burglary, Assault, Vandalism
2007	Moore & Shepherd	Burglary, Robbery, Auto Theft, Theft from Auto, Rape, Assault, Insults, Hate Crime
2009	Fisher & May	Assault with Weapon, Robbery, Assault, Sexual Assault
2009	Melde & Esbensen	Assault (Away from School), Theft, Assault (At School)
2013	Lane & Fox	Theft, Vandalism, Burglary, Robbery, Threatened with a Weapon, Attacked without a Weapon, Stabbed, Witness Intimidation, Home Invasion, Shot At, Shot, Being Killed, Carjacking, Property Damage by Gang Graffiti, Home Invasion by a Gang Member, Gang Attack, Gang Harassment

the current era of fear of crime research. Noted above, the current era of fear of crime research is one of maturation. That maturation is marked by the willingness of scholars to utilize the best research practices from the previous eras of fear of crime research, while still striving to make progress in the understanding of the predictors of fear's effects on behavior and improving the measurement of fear rather than simply repackaging old ideals.

The role of the victim-offender relationship on fear of crime. Finally, one of the most recent trends in fear of crime research is the examination of the role of the victim-offender relationship. In criminology and victimology, researchers often consider the relationship between the victim and offender of a criminal event to be central to understanding the development of opportunities for crime. In many cases, this relationship is an especially relevant factor in understanding the crime itself. As such, fear of crime scholars also now sometimes study the victim-offender relationship. While there were a few studies produced during the earlier eras of fear of crime research that included an analysis of the relationship between the victim and offender (e.g., Keane, 1995; Warr & Stafford, 1983), the practice has only become more common in the last decade. For examples of such recent studies, see Table 2.7.

As we discuss in more detail in Chapter 3, while the inclusion of the victim-offender relationship is a growing trend in fear of crime research that is sure to continue in the future, there are currently only a handful of studies that examine the relationship. As a result, the current extent of knowledge of the role of the relationship between victims and offenders is limited. Researchers generally find that respondents, especially females, are more afraid of strangers than non-strangers, despite the fact that they are more likely to be victimized by people they know (Lauritsen & Rezey, 2013). For example, with their study examining the influence of the victim-offender relationship on fear of crime, Wilcox et al. (2006) found that respondents were more afraid of stalking, physical assault, and sexual assault by strangers than individuals they knew. As fear of crime research continues to mature, it is likely that the inclusion of the analysis of the victim-offender relationship will continue to occur.

Significant Fear of Crime Studies

Farrall and Gadd (2004) The frequency of the fear of crime. Studies produced during the current era of fear of crime research represent a general improvement over those produced during the previous infancy and adolescence eras. With that said, there are several studies that stand out as especially significant in the continuing development of fear of crime research. One of the more influential studies produced since 2001 is Farrall and Gadd's (2004) study

Table 2.7 Selected Influential Fear of Crime Studies Focusing on
Victim-Offender Relationship: 2001–2013

Date	Author(s)	Focus	Findings
2003	Scott	Relationship between gender, previous victimization, and fear of crime	Women who reported previous negative experiences with strangers were more likely to be fearful of crime
2004	Barberet et al.	Relationship between gender, previous victimization, and fear of crime	Women who reported previous negative experiences with strangers were more likely to be fearful of crime
2006	Wilcox et al.	Influence of victim-offender relationship on link between fear of sexual assault and general fear	Fear of sexual assault by stranger had most significant impact on fear of other crimes
2007	Wilcox, Jordan, & Pritchard	Influence of victim-offender relationship on link between experiences with sexual assault, physical assault, and stalking on fear of crime	Women reported experiencing victimization by acquaintances more often than strangers, but were still more fearful of strangers
2009	Hilinski	Influence of victim-offender relationship on link between fear of sexual assault and fear of nonsexual crime	Fear of sexual assault by both strangers and acquaintances was significantly related to fear of nonsexual crimes

focusing on the fear of crime among United Kingdom residents. In their work, Farrall and Gadd asked respondents if they were afraid of being victimized, how afraid they were of being victimized, and how often they were afraid of being victimized. This methodology allowed them to examine three dimensions of fear of crime: prevalence, intensity, and frequency. While the use of intensity measures has become more common among fear of crime researchers, this is one of the only published studies to date that has examined the frequency with which individuals reported being afraid.

In line with other fear of crime studies, Farrall and Gadd (2004) reported that 37% of respondents stated they were afraid of being victimized in the previous year. Further, of those respondents who reported being fearful, about 16% stated they experienced high levels of fear. Finally, of the respondents who reported being afraid of being victimized, about 69% state they were afraid on more than one occasion, with 8% stating they experienced high levels of fear frequently. With their results, Farrall and Gadd (2004) provide evidence that while many individuals may be afraid of crime, only a small percentage are frequently highly fearful of crime. By focusing on frequency of fear, this study provides researchers with a new dimension on fear of crime. In a recent book, Farrall, Jackson, and Gray (2009) expand on this contribution, arguing that "experiential" fear is that which is felt in real situations, but rarely, while "expressive" fear is that which expresses a more general anxiety about the decline of moral values in society, which may be expressed more often.

Rader (2004) The threat of victimization: A theoretical reconceptualization of fear of crime. Another significant study produced during the current era of fear of crime research is Rader's (2004) examination of what she refers to as the "threat of victimization." As described throughout this chapter, the overwhelming majority of fear of crime studies produced in the last 45 years have examined fear of crime as an outcome measure, with a range of explanatory factors (i.e., demographics, environment, and perceived risk). With her work, Rader (2004) argues that such a theoretical framework is problematic. In its place, Rader (2004) proffers a theoretical framework in which fear of crime, perceived risk of crime, and constrained behaviors (i.e., avoidance or protective behaviors) are each equal components of the threat of victimization. With this framework, fear is the emotional response to the threat of crime; perceived risk is the cognitive response; and constrained behaviors are the behavioral response.

We consider Rader's (2004) study important because it challenges other researchers to rethink the concepts that have become commonplace in fear of crime research. For example, while initially overlooked, researchers now consider the inclusion of perceived risk of victimization as necessary for any significant fear of crime study. However, few researchers have attempted to go beyond simply including measures of perceived risk in their analysis. It has generally been accepted that an individual's perceived risk of victimization directly influences his/her fear of crime. Conversely, Rader (2004) proposed that while the two concepts are linked, their occurrence is simultaneous rather than causal. This reconceptualization of the fear of crime theoretical framework encourages researchers to think about the traditional concepts and their relationships in novel ways, which could lead to significant redevelopments within the field.

Higgins, Ricketts, and Vegh (2008) The role of self-control in college student's perceived risk and fear of online victimization. Finally, another influential work produced in the current era of fear of crime research is Higgins, Ricketts and Vegh's (2008) study examining the relationship between self-control and perceived risk and fear of online victimization among a sample of college student Facebook users. With their study, Higgins et al. (2008) attempted to apply a traditional theoretical framework (i.e., self-control) to online victimization. While using traditional and adapted criminological theory to explain cybercrime has become a growing trend, Higgins et al.'s (2008) work was the first to focus specifically on the fear of cybercrime. As a result, this study is not only significant in the development of fear of crime research but also in the development of cybercrime research.

With their study, Higgins et al. (2008) found a positive correlation between perceived risk and fear of online victimization. While the authors do not provide information about the prevalence or intensity of fear, their results mirror the findings of many fear of crime studies that focus on traditional street crime. As this was the first study to examine fear of cybercrime, it has helped to lead to a new avenue of research. Cybercrime is a growing area of interest for criminologists, with the number of empirical studies increasing each year. It is certain that researchers will continue to follow in the footsteps of Higgins et al.'s (2008) work.

Concluding Remarks

As described in this chapter, fear of crime research has progressed dramatically over the last 45 years. As with any other research topic, there were periods of stagnation and uncertainty. In comparing studies produced today with those produced during the infancy era of fear of crime research, one can easily see that the research developed theoretically and in terms of measurement. While many of the original studies focused simply on the influence of a few demographic characteristics on fear of crime, more recent studies have examined the influence of a wide range of factors, including multilevel constructs (e.g., Wilcox Rountree & Land, 1996). Researchers are now examining the variation of fear of crime in different types of environments, such as schools (e.g., Swartz, Reyns, Henson, & Wilcox, 2011; Wallace and May, 2005; Wilcox, May, & Roberts, 2006), as well as in the virtual world of the Internet (e.g., Henson, Reyns, & Fisher, 2014; Higgins et al., 2008). In addition to the development of more refined measures and better explanatory theoretical frameworks, fear of crime has become more universally accepted among researchers as an important component of criminological understanding. Three of the most widely utilized and cited surveys in the history of social sciences—General Social Survey, National Crime Victimization Survey, and British Crime Survey—have included measures of fear of crime. It is all but certain that as fear of crime research continues to mature, so will our understanding of the impact fear of crime on human behavior. Box 2.1 provides some recommendations for future research.

Box 2.1 Recommendations for Future Research

- Expand estimating fear of crime among specific subpopulations (e.g., homeless, immigrants)
- Continue to examine the role of the victim-offender relationship in fear of crime
- Conduct more research on fear of cybercrime or other crimes committed via electronic means
- Track individuals' fear of crime over time, especially across developmental periods (e.g., adolescents to emerging adults to adults)
- Measure fear of crime in different domains (e.g., workplaces, schools, at home)

References

Barberet, B., Fisher, B.S., & Taylor, H. (2004). University student safety in the East Midlands. London: Home Office.

Brantingham, P.J., Brantingham, P.L. & Butcher, D. (1986). Perceived and actual crime risks. In R.M. Figlio, S. Hakim & G.F. Rengert, Eds., *Metropolitan Crime Patterns*. Monsey, NY: Criminal Justice Press, pp. 139–159.

Braungart, M.M., Braungart, R.G., & Hoyer, W.J. (1980). Age, sex, and social factors in fear of Crime. *Sociological Focus, 13*(1), 55–56.

Bureau of Justice Statistics. (2011). History of NCVS. Retrieved on March 15, 2011 from http://bjs.ojp.usdoj.gov.

Clarke, A.H., & Lewis, M. (1982) Fear of crime among the elderly. *British Journal of Criminology, 22*(1), 49–62.

Clemente, F., & Kleiman, M.B. (1976). Fear of crime among the aged. *Gerontologist, 16*(3), 207–210.

Clemente, F., & Kleiman, M.B. (1977) Fear of crime in the United States: A multivariate analysis. *Social Forces, 56*(2), 519–531.

Craven, D. (1997). Special report: Sex differences in violent victimization, 1994. Bureau of Justice Statistics, U.S. Dept of Justice: Washington, D.C.. NCJ-164508.

DeFronzo, J. (1979). Fear of crime and handgun ownership. *Criminology, 17*(3), 331–339.

DuBow, F., McCabe, E., & Kaplan, G. (1979). Reactions to Crime: A Critical Review of the Literature. Washington, D.C.: National Institute of Law Enforcement and Criminal Justice, U.S. Government Printing Office.

Dull, R.T. & Wint, Arthur V.N. (1997). Criminal victimization and its effect on fear of crime and justice attitudes. *Journal of Interpersonal Violence* 12(5), 748–758.

Erskine, H. (1974). The polls: Fear of violence and crime. *Public Opinion Quarterly, 38*(1), 131–145.

Farrall, S., Bannister, J., Ditton, J. & Gilchrist, E. (1997). Questioning the measurement of the 'fear of crime': Findings from a major methodological study. *British Journal of Criminology, 37*(4), 658–679.

Farrall, S., & Gadd, D. (2004). The frequency of the fear of crime. *British Journal of Criminology, 44*(1), 127–32.

Farrall, S., Jackson, J., & Gray, E. (2009). *Social order and the fear of crime in contemporary times.* Oxford: Oxford University Press.

Ferraro, K.F. (1995). *Fear of crime: Interpreting victimization risk.* Albany, NY: SUNY Press.

Ferraro, K.F. (1996). Women's fear of victimization: Shadow of sexual assault? *Social Forces, 75*(2), 667–690.

Ferraro, K.F., & LaGrange, R. (1987). The measurement of fear of crime. *Sociological Inquiry, 57*(1), 70–97.

Fisher, B.S., & May, D. (2009). College students' crime-related fears on campus: Are fear-provoking cues gendered? *Journal of Contemporary Criminal Justice, 25*(3), 300–321.

Fisher, B.S., & Sloan, J.J., III. (2003). Unraveling the fear of victimization among college women: Is the "shadow of sexual assault hypothesis" supported? *Justice Quarterly, 20*(3), 633–659.

Garofalo, J. (1981). The fear of crime: Causes and consequences. *Journal of Criminal Law and Criminology, 72*(2), 839–857.

Gilchrist, E., Bannister, J., Ditton, J., & Farrall, S. (1998) Women and the fear of crime: Challenging the accepted stereotype. *British Journal of Sociology, 38*(2), 283–298.

Hale, C. (1996). Fear of crime: A review of the literature. *International Review of Victimology, 4*(2), 79–150.

Henson, B., Reyns, B.W., & Fisher, B.S. (2013). Fear of crime online?: Examining the effects of risk, previous victimization, and exposure on fear of online interpersonal victimization. *Journal of Contemporary Criminal Justice, 29*(4): 475–497.

Higgins, G.E., Ricketts, M.L., & Vegh, D.T. (2008). The role of self-control in college student's perceived risk and fear of online victimization. *American Journal of Criminal Justice, 33*(2), 223–233.

Hilbink, T. (2006). Omnibus Crime Control and Safe Streets Act of 1968. Retrieved on February 15, 2011 from http://www.enotes.com/major-acts-congress/omnibus-crime-control-safe-streets-act.

Hilinski, C.M. (2009). Fear of crime among college students: A test of the shadow of sexual assault hypothesis. *American Journal of Criminal Justice, 34*(1), 84–102.

Home Office. (2004). *British Crime Survey.* London: HMSO.

Janson P. & Ryder L.K. (1983). Crime and the Elderly: The Relationship between Risk and Fear. *Gerontologist. 23*(2), 207–212.

Jeffords, C.R. (1983). The situational relationship between age and the fear of crime. *International Journal of Aging and Human Development, 17*(2), 103–111.

Katzenbach, N., Blatt, G., Breitel, C.D., Brewster, K., Byrne, G.H., Cahill, T.J., Youngdahl, L.W. (1967). *The challenge of crime in a free society.* Washington, D.C.: United States Government Printing Office.

Keane, C. (1995). Victimization and fear: Assessing the role of the offender and the offence. *Canadian Journal of Criminology, 37*(3), 431–455.

Kennedy, L.W., & Silverman, R.A. (1985). Perception of social diversity and fear of crime. Environment and Behavior, 17(3), 275–295.

LaGrange, R.L., & Ferraro, K.F. (1989). Assessing age and gender differences in perceived risk and fear of crime. *Criminology, 27*(4), 697–719.

LaGrange, R.L., Ferraro, K.F., & Supancic, M. (1992). Perceived risk and fear of crime: Role of social and physical incivilities. *Journal of Research in Crime and Delinquency, 29*(3), 311–334.

Lane, J., & Fox, K.A. (2013). Fear of property, violent and gang crime: Examining the shadow of sexual assault thesis among male and female offenders. *Criminal Justice and Behavior, 40*(5), 472–496.

Lane, J., Gover, A.R., & Dahod, S. (2009). Fear of violent crime among men and women on campus: The impact of perceived risk and fear of sexual assault. *Violence & Victims, 24*(2), 172–192.

Lane, J., & Meeker, J.W. (2003a). Fear of gang crime: A look at three theoretical models. *Law & Society Review, 37*(2), 425–456.

Lane, J., & Meeker, J.W. (2003b). Women's and men's fear of gang crimes: Sexual and nonsexual assault as perceptually contemporaneous offenses. *Justice Quarterly, 20*(2), 337–371.

Lauritsen, J.L., & Rezey, M.L. (2013). *Measuring the prevalence of crime with the national crime victimization survey.* Washington D.C.: Bureau of Justice Statistics.

Lebowitz, B. (1975) Age and fearfulness: Personal and situational factors. *Journal of Gerontology, 30*(6), 696–700.

May, D.C., Rader, N.E., & Goodrum, S. (2010). A gendered assessment of the 'threat of victimization': Examining gender differences in fear of crime, perceived risk, avoidance, and defensive behaviors. *Criminal Justice Review, 35*(2), 159–182.

Melde, C. (2009). Lifestyle, rational choice, and adolescent fear: A test of a risk-assessment framework. *Criminology, 47*(3), 781–811.

Melde, C., & Esbensen, F. (2009). The victim-offender overlap and fear of in-school victimization: A longitudinal examination of risk assessment models. *Crime & Delinquency, 55*(4), 499–525.

Mesch, G. (2000). Perceptions of risk, lifestyle activities, and fear of crime. *Deviant Behavior: An Interdisciplinary Journal, 21*(1), 47–62.

Moore, S., & Shepherd, J. (2007). The elements and prevalence of fear. *The British Journal of Criminology, 47*(1), 154–162.

National Opinion Research Center. (2011). General Social Survey.

Rader, N.E. (2004). The threat of victimization: A theoretical reconceptualization of fear of crime. *Sociological Spectrum, 24*(6), 689–704.

Rand, M. (2005). The National Crime Victimization Survey: 32 years of measuring crime in the United States. Paper presented to the Siena Group on Social Statistics meeting in Helsinki, February 2005.

Riger, S., & Gordon, M.T. (1981). The fear of rape: A study of social control. *Journal of Social Issues, 37*(4), 71–92.

Riger, S., Gordon, M., & LeBailly, R. (1978) Women's fear of crime: From blaming to restricting the victim. *Victimology, 3*(314), 274–284.

Schafer, J.A., Huebner, B.M., & Bynum, T.S. (2006). Fear of crime and criminal victimization: Gender-based contrasts. *Journal of Criminal Justice, 34*(3), 285–301.

Scott, II. (2003) Stranger danger: Explaining women's fear of crime. *Western Criminology Review, 4*(3), 203–214.

Skogan, W.G. (1987). The impact of victimization on fear. *Crime & Deliquency, 33*(1), 135–154.

Skogan, W.G., Lewis, D.A., Podolefsky, A., DuBow, F., Gordon, M.T., Hunter, A., Maxfield, M.G., & Salem, G. (1982). *Reactions to crime project: Executive summary.* Washington, D.C.: U.S. Department of Justice, National Institute of Justice.

Slovic, P., Fischhoff, B., & Lichtenstein, S. (1980). Facts and fears: Understanding perceived Risk. In *Societal risk assessment: How safe is safe enough?,* edited by Richard C. Schwing and Walter A. Albers, Jr. New York: Plenum Press.

Smith, L.N., & Hill, G.D. (1991). Victimization and fear of crime. *Criminal Justice and Behavior, 18*(2), 217–39.

Stafford, M.C., & Galle, O.R. (1984). Victimization rates, exposure to risk, and fear of crime. *Criminology, 22*(2), 173–185.

Stanko, E.A. (1995). Women, crime and fear. *Annals of the American Academy of Political and Social Science, 539*(1), 46–58.

Sutton, R.M., & Farrall, S. (2005). Gender, socially desirable responding and the fear of crime: Are women really more anxious about crime? *The British Journal of Criminology, 45*(2), 212–224.

Swartz, K., Reyns, B.W., Henson, B., & Wilcox, P. (2011). Fear of in-school victimization: Contextual, gendered, and developmental considerations. *Youth Violence and Juvenile Justice, 9*(1), 59–78.

Toseland, R.W. (1982). Fear of crime: Who is most vulnerable? *Journal of Criminal Justice, 10*(3), 199–209.

Wallace, L.H., & May, D.C. (2005). The impact of parental attachment and feelings of isolation on adolescent fear of crime at school. *Adolescence, 40*(159), 457–474.

Warr, M. (1984). Fear of victimization: Why are women and the elderly more afraid? *Social Science Quarterly, 65*(3), 681–702.

Warr, M. (1985). Fear of rape among urban women. *Social Problems, 32*(3), 238–250.

Warr, M. (2000). Fear of crime in the United States: Avenues for research and policy. In D. Duffee (Ed.), *Measurement and analysis of crime and justice* (Vol. 4, pp. 452–489). Washington, D.C.: National Institute of Justice.

Warr, M., & Stafford, M.C. (1983). Fear of victimization: A look at the proximate causes. *Social Forces, 61*(4), 1033–1043.

Weinrath, M., & Gartrell, J. (1996). Victimization and fear of crime. *Journal of Research in Childhood Education, 11*(3), 187–197.

Wilcox, P., May, D.C., & Roberts, S.D. (2006). Student weapon possession and the "fear and victimization hypothesis": Unraveling the temporal order. *Justice Quarterly, 23*(4), 502–529.

Wilcox, P., Jordan, C.E., & Pritchard, A.J. (2007). A multidimensional examination of campus safety: Victimization, perceptions of danger, worry about crime, and precautionary behavior among college women in the post-Clery era. *Crime & Delinquency, 53*(2), 219–254.

Wilcox Rountree, P. (1998). A reexamination of the crime-fear linkage. *Journal of Research in Crime and Delinquency, 35*(3), 341–372.

Wilcox Rountree, P., & Land, K.C. (1996b). Burglary victimization, perceptions of crime risk, and routine activities: A multilevel analysis across Seattle neighborhoods and census tracts. *Journal of Research in Crime and Delinquency, 33*(2), 147–180.

Wilcox Rountree, P. & Land, K.C. (1996a). Perceived risk versus fear of crime: Empirical evidence of conceptually distinct reactions in survey data. *Social Forces, 74*(4), 1353–1376.

Woolnough, A.D. (2009). Fear of crime on campus: Gender differences in use of self-protective behaviors at an urban university. *Security Journal,* *22*(1), 40–55.

Yin, P. (1980). Fear of crime among the elderly: Some issues and suggestions. *Social Problems, 27,* 492–504.

Yin, P. (1982). Fear of crime as a problem for the elderly. *Social Problems, 20*(2), 240–245.

Young, V. (1992). Fear of victimization and victimization rates among women: A paradox. *Justice Quarterly, 9*(3), 419–441.

Chapter 3

Measuring Fear of Crime over the Years: Sundry Methods Muddle the Validity

From our review of the literature it is evident that the fear of crime is only partially understood at best. This has led to a 'vicious circle' where poor conceptualization of the fear of crime ... has created methodological insensitivity, which has perpetuated poor operationalization. This poor operationalization is beset by technical inaccuracies, which only serve ultimately to muddy the conceptual waters.

Farrall, Bannister, Ditton & Gilchrist, 1997, p. 662

We are not suggesting here that emotions cannot be measured. We believe, however, that such measurement is difficult when the emotion is fear, the object is crime, and the method is survey.

Gibbs & Hanrahan, 1993, p. 387

Experiencing Fear

Picture yourself walking alone down a dimly lit street after dark and no one else is in sight. Suddenly, you see a strange shadow or hear a loud noise. Your heart begins to pound and you feel the warmth of your blood pressure rising. You begin to breathe more heavily; the inside of your mouth becomes dry. Your pupils dilate as your eyes vigilantly scan your surroundings. You feel anxious yet more alert. What you are feeling is fear—an apprehensive expectation that something bad could happen or is going to happen—that was triggered by perceived or audible cues in the immediate physical environment. As we note in Chapter 2, this is "experiential" fear (see Farrall, Jackson, & Gray, 2009, p.2).

Fear is one of our most basic and most primal emotions. One can become fearful when cognitively perceiving a personal threat or risk of loss, danger, harm, or negative consequences. Almost every living creature is united in the ability to feel fear. Perhaps not too surprising, none experience fear exactly the same. Fear has the capacity to petrify individuals by keeping them in a perpetual state of panic and terror—to create phobias, as we discuss in Chapter 1. Fear also has the capacity to protect by making individuals behave more prudently or defensively while experiencing potentially dangerous situations that threaten one's personal wellbeing, as we discuss in more detail in Chapter 7. According to Fanselow and Gale (2003, p. 125), "Fear represents a complex functional behavior system, and widely distributed neural circuitry contributes to the perception and recognition of danger, the learning and remembering about dangerous experiences, and the coordination of defensive behaviors to environmental threat." As such, the origins of fear lie within one's cognitive structure, the brain.

The Neuroanatomical Location of Fear: It Is All in Your Head

The process of learning fear is controlled by a "fear network" in the brain that is centered in the amygdalae and involves the interaction of several regions of the brain—neocortex, thalamus, and hippocampus. Studies have shown that the amygdalae play a critical role in conditioned fear and other emotions such as pleasure and anger. Many experts, however, acknowledge that the amygdalae's exact role in generating emotions, including fear, is still unclear (Fanselow & Gale, 2003). As we show in Diagram 3.1, the amygdalae are two small, almond-shaped masses of nuclei located deep within the temporal lobes away from the side of the hypothalamus and adjacent to the hippocampus in the brain.

With a healthy brain, learning occurs primarily through the process of conditioning. Conditioning happens when a neutral stimulus and an aversive stimulus are presented together repeatedly, a person becomes conditioned to experience the behavioral effect produced by the aversive stimulus. This effect happens even if the initially neutral stimulus is presented by itself (Davis, 1992). To illustrate, if researchers present a lab rat with a mild audio tone (neutral stimulus) and a slight electronic shock (aversive stimulus) at the same time repeatedly, the rat will continue to feel the surprise caused by the shock when only a mild tone is presented. In terms of conditioned fear, when the aversive stimulus occurs, the amygdalae transmit signals through synapses to other limbic system networks, which directly influence a number of neurological functions including emotion, memory, and behavior. Over time, the brain develops conditioned behavioral responses through direct and indirect experiences and

Diagram 3.1 Appearance and Location of Amygdalae

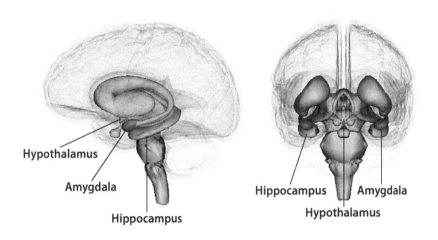

Image used with permission from BodyParts3D, © The Database Center for Life Science licensed under CC Attribution-Share Alike 2.1 Japan.

stores these responses as memories. When the same or similar stimuli are present, these memories may resurface (Adolphs, Tranel, Damasio, & Damasio, 1995; LeDoux, 1998). The conditioned responses include a wide range of neurological, physiological and/or physical reactions: increased levels of adrenaline and glucose, increased heart rate, dry mouth, nervousness, sweating, and increased alertness (LeDoux, 1998; Mayes, 1979; Ohmura & Yoshioka, 2009; Thomson, 1979).

For fear of crime, the criminal event is the aversive stimulus that leads to the fear-motivated learning process and behavioral reaction. The criminal event may be a direct personal experience, such as being robbed while walking down the street or having one's residence burgled. It also can be an indirect or vicarious experience, such as hearing a local news story about a burglary, seeing a robbery take place or knowing about an assault victim from family, friends, neighbors, or police. After either directly or indirectly experiencing a crime event, an individual's conditioned fear-response is invoked any time he/she encounters or thinks he/she encounters the same or a similar situation, even if the aversive stimulus (crime) is unlikely to occur. For example, someone who was assaulted at a bar or who has heard numerous stories of other individuals between assaulted at this bar or other bars may become fearful when patronizing a bar, even if there is no one there that is likely to assault him/her.

Muddling the Validity of Measuring Fear of Crime

As described in Chapter 2, the concept of fear of crime was neither a public policy issue nor a focus for academics' interest until the Commission on Law Enforcement and Administration of Justice stressed the importance and consequences of fear of crime on the nation's growing crime problem. With the Commission's endorsement of it as one of the outcomes of increasing crime rates, fear of crime transformed from a relatively unknown concept to one that captured the attention of social science researchers in a number of disciplines.

Labeling fear of crime as a problem in need of policy intervention or research catapulted it to the top of the respective agendas. This successful labeling turned out to be less controversial than researchers expected. In fact, attempting to define fear of crime, develop valid measures of its level and frequency, and actually measure fear using self-report surveys proved to be more challenging. Academic debates surrounding these key methodological issues have not stopped fear of crime from becoming and remaining a perennial theme in public policy, a topic of much research and embedded squarely into the public's everyday vocabulary. Thus, in the sections ahead, the importance of each of these interconnected methodological issues underlining the concept of fear of crime—its definition and measurement—will unfold.

Conceptualizing and Defining Fear of Crime

Prior to measuring the extent of fear of crime, we need a precise and clear definition, which we briefly described in Chapter 1. A definition is an important step toward both concept and theory formulation. To understand how and why fear of crime occurs and its effect on behaviors—the relationships between fear of crime and other theoretical concepts of interest—researchers must conceptualize what fear is and clearly and precisely define it. As we will discuss in the next section, both conceptualization and definition lie at the core as to how researchers operationalize and measure fear of crime (see Vanderveen, 2006).

Ferraro (1995) has defined the concept of fear of crime, or what researchers often interchangeably refer to as "fear of victimization," as an *emotional* response to crime (or the possibility of becoming a crime victim). He has distinguished it from perceived risk, which is a *cognitive* response to crime.

However, more precise definitions of fear—or this emotional response to crime—has proven difficult. In fact, Riger and Gordon (1981, p. 74) observed that "the heart of the conceptual problems in the study of fear of crime is the definition ambiguity surrounding the construct fear." This issue will be explored further in the next section.

Definitions of fear of crime. Specifically defining fear of crime is not that simple. Some researchers argue that the definition of fear of crime is obvious and therefore, do not spend much time attempting to define what it means (Ferraro, 1995). Others argue that a clear, consistent definition is necessary. Skogan (1993, p. 131) has argued that the "apparent heterogeneity of meaning simply reflects the fact that fear of crime is a general concept" suited for the public's conversation but in need of refinement for research purposes. According to Warr (1984, p. 681), "the phrase 'fear of crime' has acquired so many divergent meanings in the literature that it is in danger of losing any specificity whatsoever." It is easy to see why some might argue that the failure to utilize a universal definition of fear of crime makes the comparison of findings across studies questionable at best and unusable at worst.

What then is fear of crime? Despite much interest in fear of crime, there is no universally accepted definition. Some researchers have tried to clarify its meaning by being more precise than merely describing it as just an emotional response to crime. Garofalo (1981) was among the first researchers to offer a definition of fear of crime. Drawing from both psychological and criminological perspectives, he specified fear of crime as an "emotional reaction characterized by a sense of danger and anxiety ... produced by the threat of physical harm ... elicited by perceived cues in the environment that relates to some aspect of crime" (p. 840). Maxfield (1984) also defined fear of crime with a similar line of thinking as Garofalo by describing it as a sense of danger produced from the threat of physical injury.

One of the most commonly cited definitions of fear of crime in criminology is that proposed by Ferraro and LaGrange (1987). They defined fear of crime as "the negative emotional reaction generated by crime or symbols associated with crime" (p. 73). With more of a sociological-psychological perspective, Warr (2000) furthered reiterated and clarified the meaning of fear of crime when he offered that "fear is not itself a belief, attitude, or evaluation, but an emotion, a feeling of alarm or dread caused by an awareness or expectation of danger" (p. 453).

These definitions are obviously not identical in terms of the words their creators used. Looking at the content of each definition, however, one can see some consistencies across them. Simply put, they share key elements that characterize fear of crime and thereby, distinguish it from other crime-related constructs, such as perceived risk of crime or perceived (un)safety, which are cognitive reactions. These key elements help to conceptualize and define fear of crime as a distinct construct. First and foremost, each definition describes fear of crime as an emotional reaction. Fear is not a perception, belief, or evaluation, but rather a negative affective or emotional response—dictated by the workings of the amygdala—to perceptions, beliefs, and/or evaluations of potentially dangerous situations. Secondly, the stimuli of the emotional component of fear of crime are associated with a threat, or expectation of being harmed or victimized, which could include either one's person or property. Third, implicit in each of these definitions is the notion that fear occurs due to the immediacy, or potential immediacy, of an event, or current situation or environment. To summarize, the key elements that define fear of crime are (1) an emotional response (2) to a danger or threat (3) of a potential criminal incident.

Operationalizing fear of crime. Once researchers have defined fear of crime or at least identified its key elements, they then must translate the concept of fear of crime into something that can be observed and measured—a variable. Researchers call this process operationalization. As recommended by the Commission on Law Enforcement and Administration of Justice (Katzenbach et al., 1967), researchers have developed questions administered in self-report surveys to measure an individual's level of fear of crime. Over the last several decades, this method of measurement—questions on self-report surveys—has become the standard means to operationalize fear of crime, that is, to simply measure it (for examples see Clemente & Kleiman, 1977; Farrall & Gadd, 2004; Ferraro, 1995; Keane, 1995; Melde, 2009; Smith & Hill, 1991; Taylor & Hale, 1986; Vanderveen, 2006; Warr, 1984; Woolnough, 2009). Since there is no universally accepted definition of fear of crime, one can expect that the questions used to operationalize fear of crime also vary dramatically. What is evident across the evolution of fear of crime measures is that three aspects have changed over time: (1) the wording and structure of the measures, (2) temporal reference, (3) and reference to a specific place.

Evolution of Fear of Crime Measures

Single-item measures. Fear of crime measures have evolved over time from a single broadly worded question to more specific worded questions that include specific types of crime. Table 3.1 presents the questions used by the General Social Survey (GSS) and National Crime Survey (NCS) to measure the extent of fear of crime among individuals living in the United States. The GSS and NCS were among the first surveys to administer a fear of crime question to nationally representative samples. The National Opinion Research at the University of Chicago administers the GSS. The U.S. Census Bureau, under

Table 3.1 First Fear of Crime Questions: Single-Item Measures

Name of Survey (Year First Administered)	Fear of Crime Question
General Social Survey (1972)	Is there any area right around here—that is, within a mile—where you would be afraid to walk alone at night?
National Crime Survey/National Crime Victimization Survey (1973)	How safe do you feel or would you feel being out alone in your neighborhood at night?

the auspice of the Bureau of Justice Statistics, conducts the NCS (now called the National Crime Victimization Survey, or NCVS).

Looking at the content of these two single-item measures of fear of crime, one can easily see that they contain the same components. Each question asks about feelings of safety or fear while being out alone at night in one's immediate neighborhood. As we discuss in more length later in this chapter, neither survey question refers to a specific type of crime or even mentions crime at all. Some refer to these measures as "formless," because they ask respondents about generalized fear of crime rather than about fear of specific types of crime (Farrall, Bannister, Ditton, & Gilchrist, 1997; Ferraro & LaGrange, 1987). Both the GSS and NCVS questions proved quite popular among fear of crime researchers for much of the 1970s and 1980s, and some still frequently use them. As can be seen in Table 3.2, several researchers have used either the GSS or the NCVS question in their published studies.

Crime-specific measures. Beginning most prominently during the late 1980s when Ferraro and LaGrange (1987) first proposed their definition of fear of crime, many researchers transitioned from using *a single-item measure* of fear of crime to *crime-specific measures* of fear. As presented in Table 3.3, crime-specific measures of fear are those that focus on one specific type or several different types of crime. The use of crime-specific fear of crime measures typically takes on of two forms: one specific type of crime or multiple types of crime. First, many fear of crime researchers ask respondents about their fear of one specific type of crime. For example, Wilcox Rountree and Land (1996) asked respondents whether or not they worry about their homes being burgled. In this case, the focus was specifically on fear of burglary. Secondly, other researchers ask respondents about their fear of a series of several different types of crime. For example, LaGrange & Ferraro (1989) asked respondents to describe their level of fear of eleven different types of criminal victimization, ranging from being mugged to being murdered. In this study, the researchers wanted to ex-

Table 3.2 Use of GSS or NCVS Fear of Crime Question by Other Researchers

Author(s) (Year Study Published)	
GSS Question Is there any area right around here—that is, within a mile—where you would be afraid to walk alone at night?	NCVS Question How safe do you feel or would you feel being out alone in your neighborhood at night?
Erskine (1974)	Erskine (1974)
Clemente & Kleiman (1976, 1977)	Garofalo (1979)
Cutler (1980)	Baker, Nienstedt, Everett, & McCleary (1983)
Liska, Lawrence, & Sanchirico (1982)	Kennedy & Krahn (1984)
Stafford & Galle (1984)	Maxfield (1984)
Kennedy & Silverman (1985)	Baumer (1985)
Box, Hale, & Andrews (1988)	

amine how the level of fear of crime varied across crime types. More recently, the wording of the fear of crime questions on the British Crime Survey (BCS) was changed to include intensity of fear measures for three different types of crime (Gray, Jackson, & Farrall, 2008). In an even more recent study, Lane and Fox (2013) measured fear of twenty offenses, including property, violent and gang crimes. As time progresses, researchers continue to expand their measures of fear.

A second aspect of fear of crime measures that has changed substantially over time is the variation in temporal (i.e., time) and spatial references. As seen with the early general measures of fear of crime, these questions typically only asked respondents about their fear at night. As the GSS and NCVS measures of fear of crime highlight, early measures also focused almost solely on areas immediately surrounding the respondents' homes, either within their neighborhoods or within one mile of their homes. More recently, researchers have expanded beyond the single temporal reference by asking respondents about their fear both during the day and at night (see Covington & Taylor, 1991; Fisher & Sloan, 2003; Fox, Nobles, & Piquero, 2009; Keane, 1995). For example, Fisher and Sloan (2003) asked respondents about their level of fear of experiencing five different types of crime (i.e., theft, rape, robbery, simple assault, and aggravated assault) both during the day and at night.

Table 3.3 Crime-Specific Fear Measures: Type(s) of Crime Measured

Author(s) (Date Study Published)	Type of Crime
One Specific Type of Crime	
	Respondents asked if they worried about ...
Wilcox Rountree & Land (1996)	Home being burgled
Wilcox Rountree (1998)	Being physically attacked Home being burgled
Multiple Types of Crime	
	Respondents were asked to describe how afraid they were of becoming a victim of ...
Warr & Stafford (1983)	Burglary (while away) Rape Being hit by a drunk driver Burglary (while home) Robbery Strangers loitering near home at night Being threatened with a weapon Having noisy juveniles near home Assault (by stranger) Murder Auto theft Fraud Panhandling Obscene phone calls Contaminate food Assault (by acquaintance)
LaGrange & Ferraro (1989)	Mugging Car Theft Burglary (while away) Burglary (while home) Sexual Assault Fraud Assault Panhandling Rowdy Youth Murder Vandalism
Ferraro (1996)	Panhandling Fraud Burglary (while away)

Table 3.3 Crime-Specific Fear Measures: Type(s) of Crime Measured,
continued

Author(s) (Date Study Published)	Type of Crime
Ferraro (1996) (cont.)	Burglary (while home) Sexual Assault Murder Assault with a Weapon Auto Theft Robbery Vandalism
British Crime Survey (2004)	Car Theft Burglary Robbery
Fisher & Sloan (2003)	Theft Rape Robbery Simple Assault Aggravated Assault
Sutton & Farrall (2005)	Burglary Assault Vandalism
Moore & Shepherd (2007)	Burglary Robbery Auto Theft Theft from Auto Rape Assault Insults Hate Crime
Fisher & May (2009)	Assault with Weapon Robbery Assault Sexual Assault
Melde (2009)	Burglary (while away) Burglary (while home) Property Damage Robbery Assault with Weapon
Melde & Esbensen (2009)	Assault (away from school) Theft Assault (at school)

Table 3.3 Crime-Specific Fear Measures: Type(s) of Crime Measured,
continued

Author(s) (Date Study Published)	Type of Crime
May, Rader, & Goodrum (2010)	Burglary Sexual Assault Assault Crime at night Murder Theft
Lane & Fox (2013)	Theft without force Theft with force Burglary Property damage/vandalism Threat with a weapon Assault without a weapon Assault with a weapon Sexual Assault Stabbing Carjacking Witness intimidation Home invasion Shot at (but not hit) Shot Vandalism by gang graffiti/tagging Home invasion by a gang member Drive-by or random gang-related shooting Assault by a gang member Harassment by a gang member Murder

The third aspect of fear of crime measures that has changed is the reference to a specific location. There are a growing number of researchers who have focused on measuring the fear of crime experienced at a number of specific locations, such as schools, the workplace, and public areas. These locations go beyond the GSS or NCVS neighborhood-based reference. As seen in Table 3.4, these location-specific fear of crime questions include places such as the workplaces, primary and secondary schools, college campuses, and public areas. The goal of the location-specific questions is to examine the impact that a selected environment might have on individuals' level of reported fear.

Measuring level of fear: Variation in response sets. As we discussed in the previous section, there is variation in the wording of survey questions asking

Table 3.4 Location-Specific Fear Measures: Type(s) of Locations Measured

Author(s) (Date Study Published)	Type of Location
Fisher & Nasar (1992)	College Campus
Fisher & Sloan (2003)	College Campus
Fisher & May (2009)	College Campus
Lane, Gover, & Dahod (2009)	College Campus
Barberet, Fisher, & Taylor (2004)	College Housing
Wallace & May (2005)	Middle School, High School
Randa & Wilcox (2011)	High School
Swartz, Reyns, Henson, & Wilcox (2011)	High School
Jorgensen (2008)	Community Parks
Kish-Gephart, Detert, Trevino, & Edmondson (2009)	Workplace
Gover, Tomsich, Jennings, & Higgins (2011)	Workplace
Jenkins, Fisher, & Hartley (2012)	Workplace

respondents about their fear of crime. Similarly, there is also variation in the options offered to respondents in the response set. The metric of the response options determines how fear is measured in terms of its magnitude, that is, simply the amount of fear that someone indicates feeling. Fear of crime scholars often measure the amount of fear someone is feeling as either the presence of fear or the intensity of fear (Warr, 2000). Presence of fear measures typically determine whether or not an individual is fearful. Intensity of fear measures typically determine how fearful an individual is (Farrall & Gadd, 2004; Farrall, Jackson, & Gray, 2009; Warr, 2000). Table 3.5 displays a sample of fear of crime studies and the response options used by researchers to measure the amount of fear of crime respondents are feeling.

The presence or absence of fear is commonly measured using dichotomous response categories. Respondents indicate either "yes" they were/are afraid of being victimized or "no" they were/are not afraid of being victimized. For example, the GSS measure of fear crime that multiple studies have examined and replicated is a dichotomous measure. As shown in Table 3.5, the GSS fear of crime item asks individuals for a "yes" or "no" response after they are asked "Is there any area right around here—that is, within a mile—where you would be afraid to walk alone at night?"

Fear intensity—how afraid someone is—commonly is measured using the traditional four or five point Likert-scale response options. As can be seen in Table 3.5, researchers have adopted a variety of descriptive ordinal responses ranging from "Very Unafraid" to "Very Afraid" or "Very Unsafe" to "Very Safe" to signify categories that range from low to high levels of fear of crime. For example, May, Rader, & Goodrum (2010) asked respondents to indicate their level of agreement with six different statements about being afraid of crime using a 4-point Likert-scale ranging from "Strongly Agree" to "Strongly Disagree," while the Lane & Meeker (2003a 2003b, 2004, 2005, 2011) and Lane & Fox (2012, 2013) studies used a 4-point Likert-scale ranging from "Not Afraid" to "Very Afraid." There is also variation across in the numeric ordinal continuum. Many researchers who measure fear intensity use a ten- or eleven-point scale ranging from 0 to 10 or 1 to 10. For example, Fisher & Sloan (2003) asked respondents to rate how afraid they were of five different types of crime using a 10-point scale with 1 = "Not Afraid at All" and 10 = "Very Afraid."

Victim-offender relationship measures. One key area that has only recently received attention from fear of crime researchers is the role of victim-offender relationship and how this affects fear levels. Examining the victim-offender relationship provides valuable insights into whether individuals distinguish their fear of crime by type of offender (e.g., intimate partner, friend, stranger, gang member, or terrorist). Taking into account the victim-offender relationship when measuring fear of crime helps researchers to examine questions concerning how and why the victim-offender relationship influences levels of fear of crime. The victim-offender relationship is a critical piece of the puzzle. Several researchers have argued that most fear of crime measures implicitly only capture fear of being victimized by a stranger, thereby leaving out victimizations by intimate partners or acquaintances, which the NCVS and other studies consistently show are the primary perpetrators (see Lauritsen & Rezey, 2013; Wilcox, Jordan, & Pritchard, 2007).

There are multiple construct response types utilized to examine the victim-offender relationship by fear of crime researchers. The majority of researchers simply distinguish between strangers and non-strangers. Researchers ask respondents if they are more or less afraid of strangers than individuals they know (Jackson, 2009; Scott, 2003; Taylor & Hale, 1986; Warr, 1984; Warr & Stafford, 1983). For example, Barberet, Fisher, and Taylor (2004) examined respondents' fear of physical and sexual assault by dating/intimate partners and strangers. Similarly, Wilcox, Jordan, and Pritchard (2007) asked respondents how afraid they were of being sexually assaulted by an acquaintance and by a stranger. Other fear of crime researchers expanded upon the dichotomous stranger/non-stranger categories. In his study examining victimization and

Table 3.5 Response Options Used to Measure the Amount of Fear of Crime

Study (Date Published)	Metric of Response Options	
	Dichotomy	Likert Scale
General Social Survey (1972)	(0 = "No," 1 = "Yes")	
Clemente & Kleiman (1977)	(0 = "No," 1 = "Yes")	
DeFronzo (1979)	(0 = "No," 1 = "Yes")	
Wilcox Rountree & Land (1996)	(0 = "Not Worried," 1 = "Worried")	
Wilcox Rountree (1998)	(0 = "Not Worried," 1 = "Worried")	
Sutton & Farrall (2005)	(0 = "Don't Think About," 1 = "Think About") (0 = "Not Afraid," 1 = "Afraid")	
Warr & Stafford (1983)		11-Point Scale (0 = "Not Afraid" to 10 = "Very Afraid")
Warr (1984)		11-Point Scale (0 = "Not Afraid" to 10 = "Very Afraid")
LaGrange & Ferraro (1989)		11-Point Scale (0 = "Not Afraid" to 10 = "Very Afraid")
Smith & Hill (1991)		4-Category Likert-Scale (1 = "Strongly Disagree" to 4 = "Strongly Agree")
LaGrange, Ferraro, & Supancic (1992)		10-Point Scale (1 = "Not Afraid at All" to 10 = "Very Afraid")
Ferraro (1996)		11-Point Scale (0 = "Not Afraid" to 10 = "Very Afraid")

Table 3.5 Response Options Used to Measure the Amount of Fear of Crime, *continued*

Weinrath & Gartrell (1996)	4-Category Likert-Scale (1 = "Very Unsafe" to 4 = "Very Safe")
Fisher & Sloan (2003)	10-Point Scale (1 = "Not Afraid at All" to 10 = "Very Afraid")
Lane & Meeker (2003a, 2003b, 2004, 2005, 2011)	4-Category Likert-Scale (1= "Not Afraid" to 4 = "Very Afraid")
Moore & Shepherd (2007)	4-Category Likert-Scale (1 = "Not Worried At All" to 4 = "Very Worried")
Fisher & May (2009)	4-Category Likert-Scale (1 = "Strongly Disagree" to 4 = "Strongly Agree")
Fox, Nobles, & Piquero (2009)	4-Category Likert-Scale (1 = "Strongly Disagree" to 4 = "Strongly Agree")
Melde (2009)	5-Category Likert-Scale (1 = "Not At All Afraid" to 5 = "Very Afraid")
Melde & Esbensen (2009)	5-Category Likert-Scale (1 = "Not At All Afraid" to 5 = "Very Afraid")
May, Rader, & Goodrum (2010)	4-Category Likert-Scale (1 = "Strongly Disagree" to 4 = "Strongly Agree")
Lane & Fox (2012, 2013)	4-Category Likert-Scale (1= "Not Afraid" to 4 = "Very Afraid")

fear of crime, Keane (1995) asked respondents about their relationships with known perpetrators, specifically current/former boyfriends, spouses, and other known men versus strangers. Future fear of crime research will continue to utilize diverse offender response options, in an effort to better understand the role of the victim-offender relationship plays in assessing fear of crime levels.

Extending from the victim-offender relationship measure, another recent area of focus among fear of crime researchers is the impact of perpetrator characteristics on an individuals' fear. With such measures, researchers go beyond simply examining whether or not the criminal perpetrator, or potential criminal perpetrator, is known or unknown to the respondent. Instead, they focus on the general characteristics of the perpetrator and the impact they have on the respondent's fear of crime. For example, in a qualitative study, Lane (2002) specifically examined fear of gang crime, and studied the impact of the four key theoretical models designed to explain contextual effects on fear (which we discuss in Chapter 6). She found that when people were concerned about neighborhood diversity (i.e., undocumented Latino immigrants), they were also more concerned about neighborhood disorder (such as trash, rundown lots, and graffiti), which made them worry about neighborhood decline, leading them to more gang-related fear of crime. Lane and Meeker (2000, 2003a, 2003b, 2004, 2005, 2011) examined respondent's fear of gang members, using quantitative data. These researchers also found that perceptions of neighborhood disorder and community decline were related to more fear of gang crime (see also Katz, Webb, & Armstrong, 2003).

Nellis (2009) and Nellis and Savage (2012) also examined perpetrator characteristics, but focused on fear of terrorism in New York and Washington D.C., where the 9/11 terrorist attacks occurred. Nellis (2009) found that women were more afraid of terrorism than men were, and that women engaged in more behavioral precautions to avoid it. Nellis and Savage (2012) found that people who received more terrorism-related news felt more perceived risk of terrorism for both themselves and others, but they were only more afraid for others (not themselves). In essence, the few studies focusing on perpetrator characteristics show that they matter, too.

As this discussion shows, researchers have utilized many methods to operationalize individuals' fear of crime. Some items—such as the GSS-item, the NCVS-item or LaGrange and Ferraro's (1989) crime-specific items—are frequently used by others to measure fear of crime, and so, some response options are used more frequently. "Despite the lack of and confusion over definitions of fear of crime, one finds surprising consistency in the way it has been measured in dozens of studies" (Ferraro, 1996, p. 22). Bear in mind that consistent use of measures does not mean that all researchers agree that one valid measure of fear of crime exists. There are a lot of opinions and approaches to measuring fear, so it is important to consider the fear measures when considering what the results mean.

Measurement Issues That Muddle the Validity of Fear of Crime

As described in previous sections, conceptual ambiguity, definitional inconsistency, and a variety of operationalization characterize the fear of crime research. Almost 20 years ago, Hale (1996) concluded that "... empirical chaos has been the order of the day in the studies of fear of crime" (p. 94). A careful examination of the various measures and response options used by fear of crime researchers highlights the "empirical chaos" or in other words, measurement issues, that currently muddle the validity of fear of crime measures. These measurement issues include: the use of formless measures of fear, the use of broad measures, the limitations of dichotomous response options, and the failure to differentiate between perceived risk and fear of crime. Each issue is discussed more thoroughly in the following subsections.

Formless versus Concrete Crime-Specific Measures

Over the last 40 years, many researchers have utilized formless measures of fear of crime. Formless measures are ones that either do not even actually mention crime or refer to crime in general. For example, early measures of fear of crime did not specifically mention crime and therefore one can easily question their face validity (Ferraro & LaGrange, 1987). The original GSS measure "Is there any area right around here—that is, within a mile—where you would be afraid to walk alone at night?" asks respondents if they're afraid to walk alone, not if they're afraid of being victimized.

As other researchers so eloquently noted, the actual wording of the GSS and NCVS questions raises questions about whether this measure is actually measuring fear of crime or some other concept (Ferraro & LaGrange, 1987). Looking more closely at these words, also raise questions about whether this question captures an emotional response to harm or danger from a crime. Let us look at bit closer to decide if this measure is a valid indicator of fear of crime. Being afraid to walk alone is an ambiguous phrase. Such fear could be due to a physical condition, such as poor vision, or even something in the physical environment, such as uneven or cracked pavement or poor street lighting. As Rader (2004) and others have also pointed out, at best what these early questions were tapping into was the generalized fear individuals had about safety but not necessarily capturing fear of crime. Another example of a formless measure of fear of crime, which refers to crime, in general is Farrall and Gadd's (2004) question about the frequency of fear of crime. They asked respondents "In the past year, have you ever felt fearful about the possibility of becoming a victim of crime?" (p. 128). While this question does ask about fear of becoming a victim of crime, it does not ask about fear of specific offenses, which other researchers have argued is important (Ferraro & LaGrange, 1987; LaGrange & Ferraro, 1989; Warr, 2000).

Without a reference to a specific type of crime, respondents may often select one on their own. The type of crime selected may vary across individuals. Some may consider serious types of crime, such as murder or rape, while others may think about minor crimes, such as simple theft or vandalism. Either way, the validity of the purported fear measure is questionable at best.

Previous research has shown that individuals are more fearful of certain crimes than others. With their work examining the level of fear of 16 specific types of crime, Warr and Stafford (1983) reported that individuals were more afraid of being burglarized than being murdered, even though they perceived murder to be much more serious. Many researchers argue that rape/sexual assault is a master offense for women, meaning their fear of sexual assault drives their fear of all other crimes. Numerous studies have found that women are most fearful of being sexual victimized, which overshadows their fear of all other face-to-face crimes (Ferraro, 1995; 1996; Fisher & Sloan, 2003; Warr, 1984, 1985) (see Chapter 4). Again, when fear of crime measures do not refer to a specific type of crime, one is left wondering which type of crime the respondents are basing their response. This lack of consistency brings into question the validity of formless measures that claim to measure fear of crime (Ferraro, 1995; Ferraro & LaGrange, 1987; LaGrange & Ferraro, 1989).

Utilizing a fear of crime measure that specifies the crime type provides respondents with a clear and consistent referent. Such clarity most likely decreases the likelihood of measurement error by ensuring that each respondent reports his/her fear level for the same type of crime (e.g., burglary or rape). This train of thought influenced many researchers to argue that fear of crime research should utilize crime-specific "concrete" measures of fear of crime instead of formless ones (Warr, 2000).

Use of Broad Context Measures versus Specific Measures

Another measurement issue that has muddled the validity of fear of crime measures is the use of broad context questions. From the beginning of the study of fear of crime, researchers often worded their survey questions in a way that referenced a familiar location engaging in a routine activity during a specific time of day (Warr, 2000). For example, both the NCVS measure and the GSS measure (see Table 3.1 for wording) ask respondents if there was any area close to their home where they were afraid to walk alone at night. While these and other similar measures may seem adequate for examining fear of crime based on a precursory examination, they are actually very problematic and have received considerable criticism (Ferraro, 1995; Ferraro & LaGrange, 1987; Garofalo, 1979; Warr, 2000).

The main problem with broad context measures of fear of crime is that the generalizability of their estimates of the amount of fear (e.g., proportion fearful) is questionable. There are two inherent weaknesses that make it difficult to compare levels of fear across studies, even ones that use the GSS or NCVS fear of crime question. First, both the NCVS and GSS measures refer to walking alone at night. Many studies have reported that women are often more afraid of walking alone at night than men (Lee, 1982; Ferraro, 1995; Stanko, 1995). When using either the NCVS or GSS measure of fear of crime, a researcher may find that women are more afraid of crime than men. In actuality, it may be that women are just more afraid of crime while being out alone at night. Second, one's knowledge an area being referenced by the GSS and NCVS measures may also play a role in his/her level of fear of crime. For example, people who live in a high-crime area may not be fearful of being victimized, because they are familiar with the area and people who reside there (Ferraro & LaGrange, 1987). However, those same individuals may be very fearful of being victimized in an unfamiliar area, even if there is relatively low risk of victimization. These two examples show how broad context measures of fear of crime can undermine its validity.

To address these two limitations and enhance the validity of fear of crime measures, researchers have developed two measurement techniques that are context specific. First, some researchers worded their fear of crime measures in a way that utilizes specific contexts, which are polar opposites. In their study examining the relationship between victimization and fear of crime, Smith and Hill (1991) asked respondents to rate their fear of crime in and out of their home, within and outside of their neighborhood, and during the day and at night on a four point Likert scale. They summed the response to each of the six questions to create an overall single measure of fear of crime. Smith and Hill's

(1991) inclusion of multiple location context-specific measures allowed them to create one general measure of fear of crime. Second, as was presented in Table 3.3, some researchers use fear of crime measures that reference specific types of crime. In his work examining women's fear of victimization, Ferraro (1996) asked respondents how afraid they were of being a victim of several different types of crime, including burglary, sexual assault, and murder. With his crime-specific measures, Ferraro (1996) did not mention specific places or a time of day.

Dichotomous Response Options

Many scholars, especially in early studies, measured the presence of fear of crime. This type of fear measure captures whether or not a respondent is fearful by offering respondents a simple dichotomous response—"yes or no" or "afraid or not afraid" (Farrall & Gadd, 2004; Warr, 2000). As such, fear of crime is measured and reported as either "yes" the respondent is afraid of being victimized or "no" the respondent is not afraid of being victimized. For example, as seen in Table 3.5, Sutton and Farrall (2005) measured fear of crime using the dichotomous categories "afraid" or "not afraid." While the presence or absence of fear of crime is measured, this type of dichotomous measure does have certain limitations that muddle the measure's validity.

A dichotomous measure provides information about the existence of fear of crime. It cannot provide any information about the intensity (how much) or frequency (how often) of fear of crime. In order to capture this information, Likert-type or scale measures generally have been used in most recent studies. With that in mind, we argue that the scale measure may provide more information about an individual's fear of crime, as it can be used to examine both the presence and intensity of fear of crime. Simply, a Likert-type or scale measure of fear of crime can help determine if an individual is afraid of crime and how afraid he/she is of that crime.

Measures of Fear versus Measures of Risk

Arguably, one of the most problematic issues in early fear of crime research was the failure of researchers to distinguish between fear of crime and perceived risk of victimization. As discussed throughout this chapter, fear is an emotional response to danger or the threat of being harmed from a criminal incident. By contrast, risk is a cognitive response resulting from an assessment of the probability or likelihood of being victimized (Chadee et al., 2007; Ferraro & LaGrange, 1987). An example of a survey item used to measure perceived risk is found in The Gallup organization's surveys. The Gallup Poll annually queries the American public regarding how likely they think they are to be victimized by crime. Contrast the wording of this question with the wording of fear of crime questions discussed previously in this chapter. The difference in what is being measured, hopefully, is obvious.

Early on in the development of the definition and measurement of fear of crime, researchers did not appropriately distinguish between perceived risk and fear and produced questionable results (Brantingham, Brantingham, & Butcher, 1986; Taylor, Taub, & Peterson, 1986). Since the late 1980s with La-Grange and Ferraro's (1987) seminal work that distinguished fear of crime from perceived risk, researchers have generated considerable empirical evidence to support their notions that fear of crime and perceived risk are two separate constructs (e.g., Chadee et al., 2007; LaGrange & Ferraro, 1989; Wilcox Rountree & Land, 1996). Despite being highly correlated and thus closely linked, there appears to be a consensus among researchers to treat each as a separate construct. For example, Wilcox Rountree and Land (1996) examined the relationship between various predictors (e.g., age, gender, race, and daily activities) and perceived risk and fear of burglary. They found that there was some similarity in the effect of the predictors on both perceived risk and fear of burglary (e.g., daily activities that take individuals out of the home increases both risk and fear). However, in general, they found that the effect of many predictors was different for risk and fear (e.g., age was more strongly related to perceived risk of crime than fear of crime).

Despite researchers' consensus as to the difference between perceived risk and fear of crime, some still fail to distinguish between these two concepts. This often occurs in one of two ways. First, many researchers utilize measures that actually record risk of crime but treat them as measures of fear of crime (Ferraro & LaGrange, 1987; Warr, 2000). This typically occurs with the use of questions that ask about individuals about safety. Though intended to capture an individual's level of fear, perceptions of safety measures ask individuals to make cognitive assessments about their level of risk associated with specific situations or environments (e.g., surrounding area) (Ferraro & LaGrange, 1987; Wilcox Rountree & Land, 1996; Mesch, 2000). For example, with the NCVS, respondents are asked "How safe do you feel or would you feel being out alone in your neighborhood at night." Though this measure is frequently used to capture fear of crime, the question actually asks the respondent what risk they associate with going out at night alone. Hence, the question is capturing perceptions of safety. Second, researchers have combined measures of fear and risk and label them only as fear (Ferraro, 1995). For example, Thomas and Hyman (1977) utilized a nine-item additive index measure for fear of crime. Among the items, questions asked respondents about how afraid they were of being victimized, as well asking them to judge the risk of being victimized in their city. Similar combined measures were also used by other earlier studies (Brantingham, et al., 1986; Taylor, et al., 1986). While studies utilizing this approach focus on fear of crime, the inclusion of risk in the same measures muddle the validity of what is actually being measured. Consequently, in the last two decades, researchers have focused much energy on improving measurement.

Improvements to Measuring Fear of Crime

Methodological issues underlining the development of valid measures of fear of crime measures have been a topic of discussion among scholars since the 1960s. The conceptual, definitional and measurement issues associated with fear of crime throughout this chapter have inspired researchers to make gradual improvements in fear of crime measures. These improvements include: wording of research questions, response options, and additional fear-related measures. In addition, the complexity of information researchers have attempted to measure is steadily expanding, providing for a more in-depth understanding of fear of crime.

Changes in Question Wording

In terms of question wording, researchers have moved away from the early general fear of crime concepts and are now measuring more detailed information. This change can be seen in many of the fear of crime studies in which researchers have chosen to forgo the traditional "are you afraid of crime" approach and have adopted crime specific measures such as "are you afraid of," followed by a list of particular offenses (for examples, see Fisher & May, 2009; Lane & Fox, 2012, 2013; May et al., 2010; Melde, 2009; Melde & Esbensen, 2009; Moore & Shepherd, 2007). For example, as seen in Table 3.3, Fisher and May (2009) asked respondents about their fear of robbery, assault, assault with a weapon, and sexual assault. Others have asked about even more crimes, in an attempt to broaden the base of knowledge (e.g., Warr & Stafford, 1983; Ferraro, 1995; Lane & Fox, 2012, 2013). Such techniques reduce the likelihood that respondents will assign their own meanings to the measures and thereby add measurement error. Reducing the respondents' ambiguity as to what is being measured should help to produce a valid measure of fear of crime.

Changes in Response Options

Researchers now generally omit the traditional dichotomous response option that was used in early studies. Instead, many researchers utilize a Likert scale for a response option (see Table 3.5, for examples). As an illustration, Melde (2009) asked respondents to describe their fear of crime using a 5-point Likert scale, ranging from 1 = "Not Afraid" to 5 = "Very Afraid." By using a Likert scale, researchers are increasing the amount of information that can be obtained from a single measure. With Melde's (2009) measure, for example, one can determine if the respondent is afraid of crime (presence of fear), as well as how afraid the respondent is (intensity of fear).

Fear of Crime versus Perceived Risk

The focus on measurement has brought with it a better understanding of the role of perceived risk of victimization in fear of crime. Though seldom thought of two decades ago, it has become commonplace for researchers to include measures of perceived risk in their studies (for examples, see Chadee et al., 2007; Ferraro, 1995; Wilcox et al., 2007). Researchers have found that while fear of crime and perceived risk of victimization are highly correlated, they are two different concepts. In fact, many have argued that risk is a proximate cause of fear. As a result, researchers have begun to include perceived risk as a standard predictor in their equations predicting fear of crime.

Additional Fear-Related Measures

In addition to the prevalence and intensity of fear of crime, researchers have attempted to expand upon the understanding of fear of crime by examining various new aspects. One of the more obvious examples of this process is the work of Farrall and his colleagues (Farrall & Gadd, 2004; Farrall, Jackson, & Gray, 2009). Farrall and Gadd (2004) asked respondents if they were afraid of being victimized, how afraid they were of being victimized, and how often they were afraid of being victimized. Such measures allowed them to examine the prevalence of fear of crime (i.e., how many people are afraid of crime), the intensity of fear of crime (i.e., how afraid are those people), and also the frequency of fear of crime (i.e., how often are those people afraid of crime) (see also Farrall et al., 2009). This and similar studies have helped improve our understanding of fear of crime by continuing to expand upon the traditionally examined concepts of fear.

Concluding Remarks

This chapter has provided an in-depth discussion of issues underlying the measurement of fear of crime. Researchers have wrestled with two major issues: (1) how to best define fear of crime and (2) how to operationalize it. Throughout the 1970s and early 1980s, researchers utilized very general measures of fear of crime, most often with dichotomous response options. Throughout the late 1980s and 1990s, the use of measures with Likert-scale response options that allowed for the examination of both extent and intensity of fear of crime became more commonplace. Likewise, broad measures that focused on fear of general crime were gradually replaced with measures that examine specific types of crime and sometimes with measures focusing on specific perpetrators. Some scholars have also focused on understanding fear in context (e.g., in the neighborhood, workplace, or on campus). In the last two decades, researchers have continued to develop fear of crime measures by examining the frequency of fear of crime and comparing recent measures with those utilized in the past (Gray, Jackson, & Farrall, 2008). These methodological improvements have had a broader influence beyond pure conceptualization and operationalization. These developments have influenced the development and refinement of theories of why and how fear of crime happens and its effects on individuals' behaviors. There is little doubt that policy and research interests will continue to influence the conceptualization and operationalization of fear of crime and that over time researchers will continue to improve and refine the measurement of fear to increase understanding of this important theoretical and policy issue. Box 3.1 provides some recommendations for future research.

Box 3.1 Recommendations for Future Research

- Continue to refine fear of crime measures
- Continue to examine fear of specific types of crime (e.g., stalking, terrorism)
- Tease apart intensity (how much) and frequency (how often) of fear of crime
- Include victim-offender relationship into measurement of fear of crime
- Develop qualitative and mixed-methods research designs to more deeply probe into individuals' notion of fear of crime and their reactions

---

References

Adolphs, R., Tranel, D., Damasio, H., & Damasio, A.R. (1995). Fear and the human amygdala. *The Journal of Neuroscience, 15*(9), 5879–5891.

Baker, M.H., Nienstedt, B.C., Everett, R.S., & McCleary, R. (1983). Impact of a crime wave: Perceptions, fear and confidence in the police. *Law and Society Review, 17*(2), 319–335.

Barberet, B., B.S. Fisher, & Taylor, H. (2004). University student safety in the East Midlands. London: Home Office.

Baumer, T.L. (1985). Testing a general model of fear of crime: Data from a national sample. *Journal of Research in Crime and Delinquency, 22*(3), 239–255.

Box, S., Hale, C., & Andrews, G. (1988). Explaining fear of crime. *British Journal of Criminology, 28*(3), 340–356.

Brantingham, P.J., Brantingham, P.L., & Butcher, D. (1986). Perceived and actual crime risks, in R. Figlio, S. Hakim, G. Rengert (Eds.), *Metropolitan Crime Patterns*, Criminal Justice Press: Monsey, NY.

Chadee, D., Austen, L., & Ditton, J. (2007). The relationship between likelihood and fear of criminal victimization: Evaluating risk sensitivity as a mediating concept. *British Journal of Criminology, 47*(1), 133–53.

Clemente, F. & Kleiman, M.B. (1976). Fear of crime among the aged. *Gerontologist, 16*(3), 207–210.

Clemente, F. & Kleiman, M.B. (1977) Fear of crime in the United States: A multivariate analysis. *Social Forces, 56*(2), 519–531.

Covington, J., & Taylor, R.B. (1991). Fear of crime in urban residential neighborhoods: Implications of between- and within-neighborhood sources for current models. *Sociological Quarterly, 32*, 231–249.

Cutler, S.J. (1980) Safety on the streets: Cohort changes in fear. *International Journal of Aging and Human Development, 10*(4), 373–384.

Davis, M. (1992). The role of the amygdala in fear and anxiety. *Annual Review of Neuroscience, 15*, 353–375.

DeFronzo, J. (1979) Fear of crime and handgun ownership. *Criminology, 17*(3), 331–339.

Erskine, H. (1974) The polls: Fear of violence and crime. *Public Opinion Quarterly, 38*(1), 131–145.

Fanselow, M.S., & Gale, G.D. (2003) The amygdala, fear and memory. *Annals of the New York Academy of Sciences, 985*, 125–134.

Farrall, S., Bannister, J., Ditton, J. & Gilchrist, E. (1997). Questioning the measurement of the 'fear of crime': Findings from a major methodological study. *British Journal of Criminology, 37*(4), 658–679.

Farrall, S., & Gadd, D. (2004). The frequency of the fear of crime. *British Journal of Criminology, 44*(1), 127–32.

Farrall, S., Jackson, J. and Gray, E. (2009). *Social order and the fear of crime in contemporary times*. Oxford: Oxford University Press, Clarendon Studies in Criminology.

Ferraro, K.F. (1995). *Fear of crime: Interpreting victimization risk*. Albany, NY: SUNY Press.

Ferraro, K.F. (1996). Women's fear of victimization: Shadow of sexual assault? *Social Forces, 75*(2), 667–690.

Ferraro, K.F., & LaGrange, R. (1987). The measurement of fear of crime. *Sociological Inquiry, 57*(1), 70–97.

Fisher, B.S., & Nasar, J.L. (1992). Fear of crime in relation to three exterior site features: Prospect, refuge, and escape. *Environment and Behavior, 24*, 35–65.

Fisher, B.S., & May, D. (2009). College students' crime-related fears on campus: Are fear-provoking cues gendered? *Journal of Contemporary Criminal Justice, 25*(3), 300–321.

Fisher, B.S., & Sloan, J.J., III. (2003). Unraveling the fear of victimization among college women: Is the "shadow of sexual assault hypothesis" supported? *Justice Quarterly, 20*(3), 633–659.

Fox, K.A., Nobles, M.R., & Piquero, A.R. (2009). Gender, crime victimization, and fear of crime. *Security Journal, 22*(1), 24–39.

Garofalo, J. (1979). Victimization and the fear of crime. *Journal of Research in Crime and Delinquency, 16*(1), 80–97.

Garofalo, J. (1981). The fear of crime: Causes and consequences. *Journal of Criminal Law and Criminology, 72*(2), 839–857.

Gibbs, J. & Hanrahan, K. (1993). Safety demand and supply: An alternative to fear of crime. *Justice Quarterly, 10*, 369–394.

Gover, A., Tomsich, E., Jennings, W., & Higgins, G. (2011). An exploratory study on perceptions of safety, fear of crime, and victimization experiences among faculty and staff at an urban university: A focus on gender. *Criminal Justice Studies, 24*(1), 37–55.

Gray, E., Jackson, J., & Farrall, S. (2008). Reassessing the fear of crime. *European Journal of Criminology, 5*(3), 363–380.

Hale, C. (1996). Fear of crime: A review of the literature. *International Review of Victimology, 4*(2), 79–150.

Jackson, J. (2009). A psychological perspective on vulnerability in the fear of crime. *Psychology Crime and Law, 15*(4), 365–90.

Jenkins, E.L., Fisher, B.S., & Hartley, D. (2012) Safe and secure at work?: Findings from the 2002 Workplace Risk Supplement. *A Journal of Prevention, Assessment, and Rehabilitation, 42*(1), 57–66.

Jorgensen, L.J. (2008). *The effect of environmental cues and social cues on fear of crime in a community park setting.* Ann Arbor, MI: ProQuest LLC.

Katz, C.M., Webb, V.J., & Armstrong, T.A. (2003). Fear of gangs: A test of alternative theoretical models. *Justice Quarterly, 20*(1), 95–130.

Katzenbach, N., Blatt, G., Breitel, C.D., Brewster, K., Byrne, G.H., Cahill, T.J. ... Youngdahl, L.W. (1967). The Challenge of Crime in a Free Society. Washington, D.C.: United States Government Printing Office.

Keane, C. (1995). Victimization and fear: Assessing the role of the offender and the offence. *Canadian Journal of Criminology, 37*(3), 431–455.

Kennedy, L.W., & Krahn, H. (1984) Rural-urban origin and fear of crime: The case for "rural baggage". *Rural Sociology, 49*(2), 247–260.

Kennedy, L.W., & Silverman, R.A. (1985). Perception of social diversity and fear of crime.*Environment and Behavior, 17*(3), 275–295.

Kish-Gephart, J.J., Detert, J.R., Trevino, L.K., & Edmondson, A.C. (2009). Silenced by fear: The nature, sources and consequences of fear at work. *Research in Organizational Behavior, 29*, 163–193.

Kwon, J.T., & Choi, J.S. (2009). Cornering the fear engram: Long-term synaptic changes in the lateral nucleus of the amygdala following fear conditioning. *Journal of Neuroscience, 29*(3), 9700–9703.

LaGrange, R.L., & Ferraro, K.F. (1989). Assessing age and gender differences in perceived risk and fear of crime. *Criminology, 27*(4), 697–719.

LaGrange, R.L., Ferraro, K.F., & Supancic, M. (1992). Perceived risk and fear of crime: Role of social and physical incivilities. *Journal of Research in Crime and Delinquency, 29*(3), 311–334.

Lane, J. (2002). Fear of gang crime: A qualitative examination of the four perspectives. *Journal of Research in Crime and Delinquency, 39*(4), 437–71.

Lane, J., & Fox, K.A. (2012). Fear of crime among gang and non-gang offenders: Comparing the effects of perpetration, victimization, and neighborhood factors. *Justice Quarterly, 29*(4), 491–523.

Lane, J., & Fox, K.A. (2013). Fear of property, violent, and gang crime: Examining the shadow of sexual assault thesis among male and female offenders. *Criminal Justice and Behavior, 40*(5), 472–496.

Lane, J., Gover, A.R., & Dahod, S. (2009). Fear of violent crime among men and women on campus: The impact of perceived risk and fear of sexual assault. *Violence & Victims, 24*(2), 172–192.

Lane, J., & Meeker, J.W. (2000). Subcultural diversity and the fear of crime and gangs. *Crime & Delinquency, 46*(4), 497–521.

Lane, J., &Meeker, J.W. (2003a). Fear of gang crime: A look at three theoretical models. *Law & Society Review, 37*(2), 425–456.

Lane, J., & Meeker, J.W. (2003b). Women's and men's fear of gang crimes: Sexual and non-sexual assault as perceptually contemporaneous offenses. *Justice Quarterly, 20*(2), 337–371.

Lane, J., & Meeker, J.W. (2004). Social disorganization perceptions, fear of gang crime, and behavioral precautions among Whites, Latinos, and Vietnamese. *Journal of Criminal Justice, 32*(1), 49–62.

Lane, J., & Meeker, J.W. (2005). Theories and fear of gang crime among Whites and Latinos: A replication and extension of prior research. *Journal of Criminal Justice, 33*(6), 627–641.

Lane, J., & Meeker, J.W. (2011). Combining theoretical models of perceived risk and fear of gang crime among Whites and Latinos. *Victims and Offenders, 6*(1), 64–92.

Lauritsen, J.L., & Rezey, M.L. (2013). *Measuring the prevalence of crime with the national crime victimization survey.* Washington D.C.: Bureau of Justice Statistics.

LeDoux, J. (1998). Fear and the brain: Where have we been, and where are we going? *Biological Psychiatry, 44*(12), 1229–1238.

Lee, G.R. (1982). Sex differences in fear of crime among older people. *Research and Aging, 4*(3), 284–298.

Liska, A., Lawrence, J., & Sanchirico, A. (1982). Fear of crime as a social fact. *Social Forces, 60*(3), 760–777.

Maxfield, M.G. (1984) The limits of vulnerability in explaining fear of crime: A comparative neighborhood analysis. *Journal of Research in Crime and Delinquency, 21*(3), 233–250.

May, D.C., Rader, N.E., & Goodrum, S. (2010). A gendered assessment of the 'threat of victimization': Examining gender differences in fear of crime, perceived risk, avoidance, and defensive behaviors. *Criminal Justice Review June, 35*(2), 159–182.

Mayes, A. (1979). The physiology of fear and anxiety in *Fear in Animals and Man*, W. Sluckin (Ed.). New York: Van Nostrand Reinhold.

Melde, C. (2009). Lifestyle, rational choice, and adolescent fear: A test of a risk-assessment framework. *Criminology, 47*(3), 781–811.

Melde, C., & Esbensen, F. (2009). The victim-offender overlap and fear of in-school victimization: A longitudinal examination of risk assessment models. *Crime & Delinquency, 55*(4), 499–525.

Mesch, G. (2000). Perceptions of risk, lifestyle activities, and fear of crime. *Deviant Behavior: An Interdisciplinary Journal, 21*(1), 47–62.

Moore, S. and Shepherd, J. (2007). The elements and prevalence of fear. *The British Journal of Criminology, 47*(1), 154–162.

Nellis, A. (2009). Gender differences in fear of terrorism. *Journal of Contemporary Criminal Justice, 25*, 322–340.

Nellis, A., & Savage, J. (2012). Does watching the news affect fear of terrorism? The Importance of Media Exposure on Terrorism Fear. *Crime and Delinquency, 58*(5), 748–768.

Ohmura Y, & Yoshioka MM. (2009) The roles of corticotrophin releasing factor (CRF) in responses to emotional stress: Is CRF release a cause or result of fear/anxiety? *CNS Neurological Disorders & Drug Targets, 8*, 459–469.

Rader, N.E. (2004). The threat of victimization: A theoretical reconceptualization of fear of crime. *Sociological Spectrum, 24*(6), 689–704.

Randa, R. & Wilcox, P. (2011). Avoidance at school: Further specifying the influence of disorder, victimization, and fear. *Youth Violence and Juvenile Justice, 10*(2), 190–204.

Riger, S. & Gordon, M.T. (1981). The fear of rape: A study in social control. *Journal of Social Issues, 37*(4), 71–92.

Scott, H. (2003) Stranger danger: Explaining women's fear of crime. *Western Criminology Review, 4*(3), 203–214.

Skogan, W.G. (1993). The various meanings of fear. In W. Bilsky, C. Pfeiffer & P. Wetzels (eds.), *The Fear of Crime and Criminal Victimization.* Stuttgart: Enke.

Smith, L.N. & Hill, G.D. (1991). *Victimization and fear of crime. Criminal Justice and Behavior 18*(2), 217–39.

Stafford, M.C., & Galle, O.R. (1984). Victimization rates, exposure to risk, and fear of crime. *Criminology, 22*(2), 173–185.

Stanko, E.A. (1995). Women, crime and fear. *Annals of the American Academy of Political and Social Science, 539*(1), 46–58.

Sutton, R.M., & Farrall, S. (2005). Gender, socially desirable responding and the fear of crime: Are women really more anxious about crime? *The British Journal of Criminology, 45*(2), 212–224.

Swartz, K., Reyns, B.W., Henson, B., & Wilcox, P. (2011). Fear of in-school victimization: Contextual, gendered, and developmental considerations. *Youth Violence and Juvenile Justice, 9*(1), 59–78.

Taylor, R.B. & Hale, M. (1986). Testing alternative models of fear of crime. *Journal of Criminal Law and Criminology, 77*(1), 151–89.

Taylor, D., Taub, R., & Peterson, B. (1986). "Crime, community organization, and causes of neighborhood decline," in R. Figlio, S. Hakim and R. Renegert, eds, *Metropolitan Crime Patterns*, 161–177. New York: Criminal Justice Press.

Thomas, C.N., & Hyman, M. (1977). Perceptions of crime, fear of victimization, and public perceptions of police performance. *Journal of Police Science and Administration, 5*(3), 305–317.

Thomson, R. (1979). The concept of fear in *Fear in Animals and Man*, W. Sluckin (Ed.). New York: Van Nostrand Reinhold.

Vanderveen, G. (2006). *Interpreting Fear, Crime, and Unsafety*. Den Haag: Boon Juridische uitgevers.

Wallace, L.H. & May, D.C. (2005). The impact of parental attachment and feelings of isolation on adolescent fear of crime at school. *Adolescence, 40*(159), 457–474.

Warr, M. (1984). Fear of victimization: Why are women and the elderly more afraid? *Social Science Quarterly, 65*(3), 681–702.

Warr, M. (1985). Fear of rape among urban women. *Social Problems, 32*(3), 238–250.

Warr, M. (2000). Fear of crime in the United States: Avenues for research and policy. In D. Duffee (Ed.), *Measurement and Analysis of Crime and Justice* (Vol. 4, pp. 452–489). Washington, D.C.: National Institute of Justice.

Warr, M., & Stafford, M.C. (1983). Fear of victimization: A look at the proximate causes. *Social Forces, 61*(4), 1033–1043.

Weinrath, M. & Gatrell, J. (1996) Victimization and fear of crime. *Violence and Victims, 11*(3), 187–197.

Wilcox, P., Jordan, C.E., & Pritchard, A.J. (2007). A multidimensional examination of campus safety: Victimization, perceptions of danger, worry about crime, and precautionary behavior among college women in the post-Clery era. *Crime & Delinquency, 53*(2), 219–254.

Wilcox Rountree, P., & Land, K.C. (1996). Burglary victimization, perceptions of crime risk, and routine activities: A multilevel analysis across Seattle neighborhoods and census tracts. *Journal of Research in Crime and Delinquency, 33*(2), 147–180.

Wilcox Rountree, P. (1998). A reexamination of the crime-fear linkage. *Journal of Research in Crime and Delinquency, 35*(3), 341–372.

Woolnough, A.D. (2009). Fear of crime on campus: Gender differences in use of self-protective behaviors at an urban university. *Security Journal, 22*(1), 40–55.

Chapter 4

Gender: The Most Consistent Predictor of Fear of Crime

Fear of crime teaches women that some rights are reserved for men, such as the right to use public places, to take a walk at night, or, as one of the participants of this study said, even [to go] alone to a restaurant or to a movie. Although such places are supposed to be open to all, women's access to them is often hampered by the fear of criminal victimization....

Madriz, 1997, p. 19

Indeed, the considerably higher incidence of male victimization by strangers in the U.S. indicates that public fear among men is entirely legitimate. Ironically, and perhaps tragically, expressing this fear can be hazardous— a sign of vulnerability that may lead to greater risk of victimization.

Brownlow, 2005, p. 589

Fear of crime researchers consider gender the most consistent predictor of fear of crime (Ferraro, 1996; Rader & Haynes, 2011; Schafer, Huebner, & Bynum, 2006). Over the past 30 years, studies have demonstrated that women are more afraid of crime than men are (Ferraro, 1996; Reid & Konrad, 2004; Scarborough, Like-Haislip, Novak, Lucas, & Alarid, 2010; Smith & Torstensson, 1997). The question that most ask is why is it that women fear crime at higher levels than men? There are several plausible explanations that include women's fear of sexual assault overshadowing their fear of all other crimes (Ferraro, 1996; Fisher & Sloan, 2003; Lane & Meeker, 2003; May, 2001), women's smaller physique (Franklin & Franklin, 2009; Killias & Clerici, 2000), and that women are socialized to be afraid of crime (Gardner, 1989; Rader & Haynes, 2011; Stanko, 1995). These plausible explanations are compounded by the historical finding that men are more likely than women to be victims of both violent and non-violent, non-sexual crime (Harrell, 2012). Hence, it is not only that women fear crime, but also that women's fear of crime is often greater than their risk of street crime (but not necessarily intimate partner violence and sexual assault) (May, 2001; Rader & Haynes, 2011; Stanko, 1996).

Research has shown that men's fear of crime levels are particularly low relative to women's fear of crime levels (Beaulieu, Dube, Bergeron, & Cousineau, 2007;
Brownlow, 2005). There are several plausible explanations, including that men
are socialized to believe that fear of crime is a weak and non-masculine expression of emotion (Goodey, 1997; May, 2001), men neutralize fear of crime (e.g.,
pretending to not be afraid when they are or not expressing such fear of crime)
(Rader, 2010; Smith & Torstensson, 1997) and men only fear crime in specific
contexts (e.g., fear crime when visiting strange cities but not in the city where
they live in) (Day, Stump, & Carreon, 2003; Pain, 2000). Men's lack of fear is also
puzzling because it does not match up with their actual rate of violent non-
sexual victimization which is much higher than women's actual risk (Brownlow,
2005; Goodey, 1997). That is, consistent findings that women are more afraid
but less at risk of victimization by most crimes and men are less afraid but more
at risk are perplexing to researchers and policymakers alike (Mesch, 2000; Schafer
et al., 2006; Wilcox, Jordan, & Pritchard, 2006). This contradiction has been labeled the "gender-fear paradox" in the fear of crime literature (Ferraro, 1996).

Women and men also often respond differently to their fears of crime. For
example, women often restrict their activities more than men do due to fear
of crime (Stanko, 1995). Because of these distinctions in the causes and consequences of fear for men and women, we focus in this chapter on explaining
gender differences. Specifically, we focus on differences in victimization and fear
levels, important theoretical explanations for this gender paradox, and discuss
some of the practical ways that policymakers and practitioners might try to
reduce fear among these groups.

Women and Men Face Different
Types of Victimization Risk

Before we discuss the possible reasons that women and men's fear of crime
levels appear at odds with their victimization rates, we will set the context and
discuss differential victimization rates by gender. When researchers examine street
crime, especially violent offenses, they consistently find that men are more
likely to be victims of all types of crimes except sexual assault and intimate
partner violence (Lauritsen & Rezey, 2013). For example, studies find that
men are more likely to be victimized by homicide, assault, and robbery (Karmen, 2010). According to a 2012 Bureau of Justice Statistics report, strangers
are twice as likely to violently victimize males compared to females (Harrell,
2012). In addition, recent data from the National Crime Victimization Survey
(NCVS) echo these results (Lauritsen & Rezey, 2013).

In contrast, women are more likely than men to experience sexual assault, intimate partner violence, and stalking. For example, a 2013 Bureau of Justice Statistics Report determined that while women's rate of intimate victimization was 4.9 per 1,000 people aged 12 or older, men's rate of victimization was much smaller, only 1.1 per 1,000 (Lauritsen & Rezey, 2013). In terms of sexual assault, statistics from the 2008 National Crime Victimization Survey (NCVS) showed that while the rate of sexual assault for women was 1.4 per 1,000, the rate of sexual assault for men was only 0.3 per 1,000 (Catalano, Smith, Synder, & Rand, 2009). Studies show that sexual victimization is especially prevalent among college women, sometimes concluding that female undergraduates are four times more likely than male students to experience sexual assault (Fisher & Sloan, 2003). Moreover, a 2012 Bureau of Justice Statistics report concluded that while only about 2% of female respondents claimed to have experienced stalking, about half as many men (0.8%) did (Catalano, 2012). In summary, the type victimization people experience varies by gender. Men are more likely to experience violent victimization by street crimes, while women are more likely to experience intimate partner violence, sexual assault, and stalking.

Yet, some recent results call into question these consistent findings, finding that violent victimization risk for men and women may be converging. Specifically, a recent report released by the Bureau of Justice Statistics, using National Crime Victimization Survey data, reported that "for the first time since the NCVS began reporting on differences in victimization by sex, males (15.7 per 1,000 males age 12 or older) and females (14.2 per 1,000) had similar rates of violent victimization" (Truman, 2011, p. 11). Yet, there were still differences in victimization rates in specific categories such as robbery (men more likely to be the victim) and sexual assault (women more likely to be the victim) (Truman, 2011). In addition, these data are for one year only (2010), so it is unclear whether this is the beginning of a long-term trend or specific to one year's data. Still, over time, the general conclusion has been that women face lower risk of violent victimization overall (for all personal offenses except intimate partner violence, stalking and sexual assault), but their fear remains higher than men's.

Women and Men Differ in Their Levels of Crime-Related Fear

With this backdrop of differences in risk of victimization, we now briefly describe differences in fear of crime for men and women. Women are much more likely to report high fear of crime levels, although they are less likely to be the victim of violent street crime (excluding intimate partner violence and sexual assault) (Ferraro, 1995; Mesch, 2000; Schafer et al., 2006). This is, in fact, the most consistent finding in fear of crime research. In almost every study, women are more afraid of crime than men. This is true regardless of how fear is measured (see Lane, 2013). In addition, national polls confirm these results. For example, Gallup's 2010 Crime Survey revealed that 50% of American women said they are afraid to walk in their neighborhood alone at night, meaning they are twice as likely as male respondents to fear crime in their neighborhood (but recall the discussion of this problematic measure of fear in Chapter 3) (Saad, 2010).

Moreover, researchers find that when women and men fear crime, they do so in very different ways. From a young age, women and men learn to fear different types of people (Wallace & May, 2005), in different situations (Brownlow, 2005), and different types of crimes (Scarborough et al., 2010). For example, research has suggested that females and males are afraid of different types of crimes. In one study, Reid and Konrad (2004) argued that gender specific fear may be important to consider. They found that although women and men did not significantly differ in their fear of burglary (which they argued was a gender neutral crime), women reported a much higher level of fear of sexual assault than men (see also Fisher & Sloan, 2003). Contrary to their expectations, however, women and men expressed similar fears of robbery. Such findings point to the important differences in men's and women's fear of crime levels as well as the importance of examining crime-specific fear by gender.

For example, women fear more for themselves than others, but men are more likely to express fear for people in their lives than for themselves (Warr & Ellison, 2000). Given all of these findings, researchers have developed theoretical ideas about the differential causes of fear among women and men. We first discuss the primary explanations for women's fear of crime, and then we turn to explanations for men's fear of crime.

Explaining Women's Fear of Crime

Scholars have focused much of their attention over the years attempting to explain women's greater fear of crime. Table 4.1 presents the theoretical ideas in concise form, and we discuss each in turn.

Table 4.1 Explanations of Women's Personal Fear of Crime

Explanation	Primary Argument
Demographic Characteristics	Women's race, social class, marital status, and parenting status determine their fear of crime levels.
Irrationality Perspective	Women's fear of crime levels are out of line with their actual risk of victimization.
Vulnerability	Women feel physically vulnerable to victimization or feel that their environment makes them socially vulnerable.
Socialization	Primary sources (parents, friends, and family) and secondary sources (media) teach women messages that induce fear.
Patriarchy and the Social Control of Women	Gender inequality oppresses women in society and victimization is a potential component of this oppression. Women are socially controlled to behave in certain ways that restrict their mobility and increase fear of crime.
Shadow of Sexual Assault	Women's fear of crime is really a fear of rape that "shadows" their fear of all crimes.
Hidden Victimization	Intimate crimes against women are underreported and undercounted in crime statistics. Considering these crimes, women's chances of victimization are actually much higher and likely correspond to high fear of crime levels.

Demographic Correlates That Affect Women's Fear of Crime

Although most theoretical attempts to understand women's heightened fear of crime focus on other issues, we first address some basic personal characteristics that research shows are related to fear of crime for women. These include race, social class, age, victimization status, marital status, and parenting status. While the impact of race, social class, and age on fear of crime generally are the focus of the next chapter, we note in this chapter that race, social class, and age affect men and women differently (Cobbina, Miller, & Brunson, 2008; Melde, 2009; Pantazis, 2000). For example, when researchers run different models for men and women, they often find that race, age, and income are not critical predictors of fear among women, although some of these variables predict fear of crime levels among men (May, Rader, & Goodrum, 2010; Rader & Cossman, 2011; Schafer et al., 2006). We discuss men's fear of crime after first focusing on women.

Social Class and Race

Studies show that the impact of social class varies by gender. For example, Pantazis (2000) examined how gender affects the relationship between age, poverty, and fear of crime levels among British residents. Her findings provide insight into these other important demographic correlates of fear of crime. Not surprisingly, Pantazis concluded that women were significantly more likely to fear crime than men. In fact, she determined that women were three times more likely than men to feel unsafe when alone on the streets at night. Probing further, she uncovered that both older and younger women were more likely to feel unsafe compared to middle-aged women and that women who had higher incomes were less afraid of crime than those with lower incomes. Pantazis also concluded that poor women were two-thirds more likely to fear crime than poor men, and wealthy women were twice as likely to feel unsafe than wealthy men. These results confirmed not only the consistent results that women are more afraid than men but also similar results that people of lower income are typically more afraid than those who have higher incomes (see also Warr, 1994). One of the most interesting findings from her study was that poor women were one and a half times more likely than wealthy women to feel unsafe. Yet, her study was one of the only published works to examine this issue and occurred in Britain, so it is unclear whether similar results hold for other countries, including the United States (Pantazis, 2000).

Supportive of results from several previous studies of fear of crime, Madriz's (1997) focus groups with women revealed that race was an important factor in predicting fear. As most studies have reported, she found that women were fearful of crime and took a variety of precautions to manage their fear of crime levels. Importantly, although the study was not specifically focused only on race, she found that both Black women and White women believed that White women were more likely to be the victim of criminal victimization and should fear crime more than other racial groups (Madriz, 1997). The beliefs expressed by these women were in direct contradiction to victimization statistics that show Black women have higher victimization rates than White women, including both non-sexual crime and sexual assault (Catalano et al., 2009). This contradiction may occur, because women may rely more on the knowledge they gain from secondary sources (e.g., news, media, or parents) than they do on their own victimization experiences, since victimization is actually relatively rare (Truman, 2011). For example, it is possible that both White and Black women may believe that what they see on television (for example, that most female victims are White), because they do not have much direct personal experience with victimization (Day, 2001; Hollander, 2001; Madriz, 1997; Rader, 2008).

Interestingly, as we discuss more in Chapter 6, Madriz (1997) also found race of others affected women's fear of crime. She noted that her respondents had stereotypes and perceptions of racial, cultural, and immigrant status differences that predicted their fear of crime, no matter the race of the woman. For example, she argued that women had "strongly racialized images of criminals, with Black and Latino men at the forefront of most women's fears" (Madriz, 1997, p. 98).

Marriage and Children

Another personal characteristic that may impact fear levels for women is their relationship status—whether they are married or in a relationship or have children. While there is not much focus on this topic to date, researchers have discovered that married women are less afraid of crime than non-married women (Rader, 2008) and that younger female parents are more afraid of crime for their children than older female parents for their children (Mesch, 2000).

Theoretical Explanations for Women's Fear of Crime

Because so many studies have shown that women are more afraid of crime than men are, much of the theoretical work focused on gender has been directed at explaining women's fear of crime. There are at least six specific theoretical ideas that have been developed to explain women's fear, and these include the irrationality perspective, the vulnerability perspective, the socialization perspective, the shadow of sexual assault perspective, the patriarchal or social control perspective, and the hidden victimization perspective. Although some of these distinct theoretical ideas are clearly connected, researchers developed them independently, and we discuss them separately.

Irrationality Perspective

One of the first ideas developed to explain women's heightened fear in the face of less victimization risk from street crime can be called the *irrationality perspective* (Lupton & Tulloch, 1999; Smith & Torstensson, 1997). As explained by Lupton & Tulloch (1999), this point of view assumes that because people do not know the true facts about their real victimization risk, they develop their own ideas and have an irrational response to them—or increased fear of crime. That is, researchers argued that women were more afraid than they should be because they were unreasonable, emotional, and/or not very rational (Hale, 1996; Lupton & Tulloch, 1999; Smith & Torstensson, 1997). Some researchers hypothesized that since women were considered more emotional than men, the best explanation for their behavior was that it was an emotional decision not based on facts. One criticism of this point of view is that it does not try to also explain men's irrationality (or, the fact that they have low fear but higher risk). In other words, scholars who promoted this argument did not explain why they thought women were irrational for fearing crime but men were not irrational for lacking fear of crime (Gilchrist, Bannister, Ditton, & Farrall, 1998). Possibly, because of these criticisms, this early theoretical idea has not received much attention in the literature in recent decades.

Vulnerability Perspective

Another early theory to explain women's heightened fear of crime despite their relatively low victimization risk from street crime focused on their physical and social vulnerability. Physical vulnerability involves the perceived physicality of individuals. Individuals may perceive themselves as physically weak or unable to protect themselves from a potential attack (Killias & Clerici, 2000). Social vulnerability occurs when a particularly disadvantaged group might be more vulnerable to criminal victimization. Many contextual indicators in the community might lead to social vulnerability, such as living in an impoverished area (Hale, 1996; LaGrange, Ferraro, & Supancic, 1992; Skogan & Maxfield, 1981).

Early on, researchers argued that because women were smaller and felt less able to fend off attackers, it made sense that they would be more afraid of crime. Specifically, they argued that women (and the elderly, too) were more afraid, because they did not believe they could protect themselves and because they worried about the consequences of victimization. That is, women realized that they might easily get hurt if they were victimized by crime. In turn, these scholars also argued that men feared crime at such low levels because they felt physically capable of protecting themselves from an attack (Ferraro, 1995; Hale, 1996; Killias, 1990; Skogan & Maxfield, 1981). For example, Skogan and Maxfield (1981) argued more than three decades ago that women were more afraid than men were because they braved more "openness to attack, powerlessness to resist attack, and exposure to physical (and probably emotional) consequences if attacked" (p. 69). Interestingly, in his review of the literature at the time, Ferraro (1995) discovered that older and younger women were more afraid than middle-aged women, which highlighted the possibility that perceived vulnerability varied with age. More recently, Franklin and Franklin (2009) investigated the relationship between perceived vulnerability, disorder, and social integration among women and men in the state of Washington. They found that as women got older, their fear of crime level decreased, and these authors argued that this decline in fear resulted from a decreased risk of sexual assault (Franklin & Franklin, 2009). This finding is interesting because it emphasizes how the vulnerability perspective and the sexual assault hypothesis (discussed in detail below) may work together to influence women's fear of crime.

The vulnerability perspective also later expanded beyond physical vulnerability to include social vulnerability, or neighborhood characteristics, that may make specific groups feel more vulnerable to victimization (Killias & Clerici, 2000; Scarborough et al., 2010). For example, a recent study by Rader, Porter, & Cossman (2012) examined both physical and social vulnerability. They concluded that physical vulnerability characteristics (defined as being female) were more likely to affect fear, independent of social vulnerability factors (defined as the percent of female-headed households in the county census tract). Although we discuss this more in Chapter 5, social vulnerability has also been an important theory used to explain the reason that minorities are often more afraid of crime than Whites (Chiricos, Hogan, & Gertz, 1997; Skogan & Maxfield, 1981).

Socialization

One of the theoretical ideas that continues as one of the key arguments explaining differences between women and men's fears about crime focuses on how they are socialized by primary sources, such as parents, family, and friends, and secondary sources, such as the media (Rader & Haynes, 2011). The argument, in essence, is that families and society at-large teach young girls that females are victimized in certain places (e.g., in public settings), at certain times of day (e.g., night), and by certain types of offenders (e.g., strangers) (Gardner, 1989; Hollander, 2001; Scott, 2003). However, the reality is that these socialization messages are not based on females' victimization statistics, which show that women are often victimized at home, during the day, and by known offenders (Stanko, 1995). These socialization messages influence girls and women to take a variety of precautionary measures (e.g., taking self-defense classes, avoiding certain public spaces, and carrying mace) to protect themselves from potential crime (Campbell, 2005; Cobbina et al., 2008; Keane, 1998). The argument then, is that gender socialization plays a major part in the construction of women's fear of crime (Madriz, 1997; Rader & Haynes, 2011).

The literature indicates that gender is a socially constructed concept (Connell, 2002). In other words, gender is not merely a biological (i.e., male/female) but also a social concept (i.e., masculine/feminine). Therefore, being female means that society expects one to act in certain ways (e.g., "ladylike" or passive) and being male means that one is expected to act in certain ways (e.g., "tough" or aggressive). The argument is that people teach children these expectations from a young age and expect them to act in ways appropriate for their gender (West & Zimmerman, 1987).

Males and females also receive messages about appropriate behavior related to safety and crime prevention. For example, some theorists argue that women are socialized to fear crime while men are taught that "real men" do not feel fear (Goodey, 1997). Women are taught that they should avoid situations where strangers are present, during the night, or when they are alone. Men are not socialized to avoid the same situations. Women learn that acting vulnerable, helpless, and dependent on men to protect them from crime is a natural part of being a woman (Gardner, 1989; Hollander, 2001; Stanko, 1995). These messages can come from a variety of socialization agents, including parents and the media.

Parents

Parents are an especially potent source of socialization for young people, and they also share safety messages with their children (Akers, 1973; Wallace & May, 2005). De Groof (2008), for example, recently argued that fear of crime may be intergenerationally transmitted. In other words, parents' fears can be passed on to their children through role modeling and/or children perceiving cues from parents on how to act in specific places or with specific persons. She found that parents who over-supervise their children were more likely to have both male and female children who expressed feelings of insecurity. Yet, she argued that some messages may vary by gender and may reflect a greater fear for daughters than for sons. As we discuss briefly later, fear for others has been called *altruistic fear* (Snedker, 2006; Warr & Ellison, 2000), and some scholars, such as De Groof, argue that parents may have greater fear for their girls compared to their boys. According to De Groof (2008), this can "induce long-term consequences for gender equity in adult life" (De Groof, 2008, p. 271).

May and colleagues (2002) and Wallace and May (2005) have also shown that parental interaction affects fear of crime. These scholars found that adolescent males that are more attached to their parents have lower levels of fear of crime than boys with fewer attachments to parents (May et al., 2002). Wallace and May's later study (2005) argued that having a strong attachment to parents served as an "insulator" against fear of crime for teenagers, but they found that this effect was stronger for boys. In essence, though, they found that when children are closer to their parents, they feel less afraid. Yet, May et al. (2002) also found that those boys who were *supervised* more by their parents were *more* afraid, which they argued might mean that parents that closely watched their children regularly shared messages with them about their need to be careful. These few studies indicate that parental socialization and parental attachment are important factors that may help explain variation in adolescents' fear of crime levels. Although there is not much data available to test the idea, some argue that parental messages may artificially inflate fear among girls and women if they are told to fear crime and to take responsibility for protecting themselves from victimization (e.g., by changing their dress or behaviors) (Lane, 2010).

Adding new ideas to these socialization arguments, Rader and Haynes (2011) recently argued for using guidance from Akers' Social Learning Theory (1973) as a base framework to examine the connections between the gendered nature of fear of crime and socialization. Rader & Haynes called their point of view a "social learning theory of gendered fear of crime," because it was modeled after Akers' ideas regarding associations, definitions, imitation, and reinforcement. Specifically, they argued that men and women get different fear of crime messages from others (associations), which leads to their defining fear of crime in gendered ways. These ideas (definitions) about what is scary are eventually confirmed by others (reinforced), which leads to both men and women modeling (imitating) others (associations) behaviors related to fear of crime. Rader and Haynes argued that men learn fear differently than women, but they also suggested that this learning is not consistent for each gender. Some women learn different things than other women, and the same is true for men. Rader and Haynes' (2011) ideas were examined with only a small group of people. Consequently, these ideas need much more testing through empirical work to determine their validity (e.g., their ability to predict fear of crime) and reliability (whether similar results will be found in other samples and places).

Media Impacts

Some scholars also believe that, accurate or not, the media provides important information to women and men about the gendered nature of victimization by repeatedly showing sensationalized stories (Eschholz, Chiricos, & Gertz, 2003). As researchers have suggested, the media are a particularly important source of information about crime, because most individuals do not directly experience criminal victimization (Eschholz et al., 2003). Most individuals learn about crime and victimization from the news, fictional crime dramas, reality television, etc. In addition, the media are more likely to showcase White females as victims of crime (even though they are the least likely race/ gender group to be the victim of violent crime) (Cavender, Bond-Maupin, & Jurik, 1999); Box 4.1 illustrates an example of how the media focuses on White female victims). Furthermore, the media tends to provide messages that blame female crime victims who do not follow the traditional rules of safety prevention (i.e., do not avoid going places alone, at night, or in public). Safety prevention "advice" like this that is implied by the media becomes a consistent source of messages for women about what is appropriate to fear and what the consequences will be for those who violate such rules (Chiricos, Padgett, & Gertz, 2000; Madriz, 1997; Scott, 2003). In Chapter 6, we focus more on the media and studies on how it affects fear of crime for both men and women.

Patriarchy (or Social Control)

Another primary theoretical model designed to explain women's greater fear of crime and resulting behavioral precautions in the face of lower actual victimization risk, focuses on the patriarchal (male-dominated) aspects of society. This theoretical approach is based on the premise that there are inherent power dynamics between men and women and that this societal circumstance oppresses women. Explaining and examining such power differentials are a primary focus for gender scholars generally (Belknap, 2001; Connell, 2002). Researchers who ascribe to this position often study the amount of equality between men and women in a variety of settings including education, employment, family, religion, politics, and even the criminal justice system (Kimmel, 2004). Research has found that gender inequality exists in a variety of capacities, including the division of labor (working outside of the home versus inside the home), educational attainment, occupational status, and wages earned. Even when experience, hard work, and other types of individual characteristics are accounted for, women are still unequal with men in these capacities (Belknap, 2001; Kimmel, 2004; Spade & Valentine, 2011).

Box 4.1 Case Focus
Natalee Holloway

On May 30, 2005, Natalee Holloway disappeared from a graduation trip to Aruba. Holloway was 18 years old. A Brookhaven, Alabama, native, Holloway graduated from high school with honors only one week before the trip. Natalee was a dance squad member, a national honor's society member, and was scheduled to attend the University of Alabama on a full scholarship (Liebler, 2010). While her remains were never found, she was pronounced dead on January 12, 2012.

While it is apparent that Natalee's death was a tragic loss of a young life, it was also clear that Natalee Holloway represented yet another example of a phenomenon coined "the missing white woman syndrome." The missing white woman syndrome occurs when women who fit the "damsel in distress" stereotype receive more media coverage and public concern than other types of crime victims such as male victims or female victims who are deemed as more responsible for their victimization. Typically, White, blond, young, pretty, female victims are believed to be more worthy and deserving of more public attention than victims with other demographic characteristics (Bing, 2009; Liebler, 2010).

Some argue that fear of crime is one by-product of the missing white woman syndrome. According to this view, the public views young, White, female victims as more worthy of "saving" than other types of victims. The media makes these victims relatable. This, in turn, causes increases in fear of crime among young, White, female victims or fear for other loved ones who are young, White, and female (Bing, 2009; Liebler, 2010).

Thought/Discussion Questions:
1. Does this argument make sense to you?
2. Can you think of another situation covered extensively in the media that fits this description?
3. Can you think of a situation involving someone who is not a White woman who received the same amount of coverage?
4. What do you think of when you picture a victim of crime? How would you describe the race, gender, or age of the person? What about the person's living situation, neighborhood, or career?
5. Can you name one female victim of crime? Can you name one famous White female victim of crime? Can you name one famous African American female victim of crime? Do you think the media contributes to your answers? Why or why not?
6. Should the media have a responsibility to present victims accurately? Why or why not?
7. Do you think the ways that the media presents crime victims influences fear of crime? Why or why not?

One key institution in which gender scholars have examined the dynamics between men and women is the criminal justice system. Scholars have noted that women are often invisible in the criminal justice system. This is in part because women are less likely to commit crime than men and less likely to be victims of crime (Daly & Chesney-Lind, 1988). In addition, gender scholars in criminology note that although women are not formally sanctioned by the criminal justice system as often as men, they often experience heightened social control in informal settings (e.g., family and school) that men do not experience (Belknap, 2001). With this backdrop, several scholars have focused specifically on explaining women's fear of crime levels and men's lack of fear of crime levels through understanding the societal circumstance of patriarchy (Cobbina et al., 2008; Day, 2001; Madriz, 1997; Stanko, 1995).

Several feminist researchers have argued that the reason women fear crime at much higher levels than men is because of the informal social control placed on women in the patriarchal society. Women learn to fear crime under circumstances in which they are unlikely to get hurt. For example, women are taught to fear stranger attacks in public places, even though these are rare. These lessons may teach girls that the only way to stay safe is to restrict mobility or depend on others, especially men, even though men are typically their victimizers (Day, 2001; Hollander, 2001; Keane, 1998).

Stanko (1995, 1996) argued that potential victimization at the hands of men is part of women's everyday lives—that the threat of victimization by men is an everyday occurrence for women. She was one of the first fear of crime scholars to argue that inducing fear of crime in women was one way that men controlled women. In addition, she made a compelling point that when policymakers, practitioners, and others tell women how to protect themselves from victimization (e.g., by controlling their dress, whereabouts, and behavior), they are putting the blame for men's behavior on women and consequently increasing their fears of crime. Law enforcement, then, reinforces traditional gender roles by teaching women to fear strangers and to remain at home during night time hours (Campbell, 2005; Stanko, 1996). Consequently, Stanko (1996, 1998) argued that to prevent violence against women, programming and informational messages should be directed at men, who commit the violence, not at women, who receive it. As we note below, Stanko (1995) was also one of the first to discuss the hidden victimization perspective (Lane, 2010).

More recently, Hollander (2001) examined the impact of perceived vulnerability and perceived dangerousness for women and men. She found that the majority of the participants in her study believed vulnerability was associated with being female (not with specific women or types of women). When men were identified as vulnerable, it was often based more on a particular individual's attributes (e.g., height) than on the fact that he was male. In contrast, men were identified as dangerous 95% of the time with only 3% of women identified as dangerous. She concluded that "the fact that these beliefs (i.e., women are vulnerable and men are violent) are maintained in the face of empirical evidence to the contrary speaks to the powerful role of discourse in constructing and reproducing gender" (Hollander, 2001, pp. 106–107).

Shadow of Sexual Assault

One theoretical perspective that has received a lot of attention and support in the literature is the *shadow of sexual assault* thesis (see Ferraro, 1995, 1996). According to Ferraro (1995, 1996), women are more afraid of crime generally because they are actually worried about the possibility of rape and the likely physical and emotional consequences (Ferraro, 1996; Fisher & Sloan, 2003; May, 2001; Wilcox et al., 2006). About a decade before Ferraro's seminal work on this topic, Warr (1984) examined both men and women's fears of specific crimes, and he argued that women were more likely to associate some offenses (e.g., begging and burglary) with other more serious crimes (e.g., rape and murder). He called these "perceptually contemporaneous offenses." Warr speculated that for many women "fear of crime *is* fear of rape" (Warr, 1984, p. 700). He then found that women feared rape more than any other offense (Warr, 1985). Ferraro (1995, 1996) later conducted empirical studies examining this particular argument, and asserted that fear of rape served as a "master offense" for women. For example, women may be fearful that a burglary, homicide, robbery, or physical assault might also involve sexual assault. He found fear of rape mattered more than perceived risk in predicting fear of personal crimes, and said that fear of rape was a key factor that could explain differences in fear of other offenses among men and women (Ferraro, 1996). Many studies following Ferraro's (1995, 1996) have found empirical support for this argument that fear of rape is a key factor in explaining women's fear of other crimes, but some also find that to a lesser extent it predicts men's fears of other crimes, too (Ferraro, 1996; Fisher & Sloan, 2003; Lane & Meeker, 2003; May, 2001; Warr, 1984; Wilcox, et al., 2006).

Fisher & Sloan (2003) specifically tested the shadow of sexual assault hypothesis among a sample of college students. It is particularly important to test this hypothesis with this young group because of the high reported rates of women who are sexually assaulted in college. They discovered that fear of sexual assault was most closely linked to fear of violent crime. Although fear of sexual assault was significant in conjunction with property crime, it was most significantly related to fear of other types of violent crime. This makes intuitive sense as one can see how a robbery or assault might produce a greater possibility of sexual assault, at least in theory.

As an extension of Fisher and Sloan's work, Barberet, Fisher, and Taylor (2004) and Wilcox et al. (2006) considered how the perceived relationship between a victim and a perpetrator affected the fear of sexual assault. This distinction is important because although women are often sexually assaulted by a known attacker, they have been taught to fear sexual assault by a stranger (Stanko, 1996). These studies suggested that college women feared sexual assault by a stranger more than fear of sexual assault by a known attacker, even though the majority of sexual assault victims had been victimized by a known person.

Lane & Meeker (2003) examined the impact of the shadow of sexual assault thesis on fear of gang crimes, and they were one of the first to find that fear of rape/sexual assault predicted fear of other crimes among men, too (see also May, 2001). Yet, one of their most important contributions from this work was their finding that fear of assault generally was a stronger predictor of other fears than fear of rape, even for women. Consequently, they argued that it may be the harm component of rape that is the scariest, even though fear of the sexual intrusion is not insignificant for either women or men. Later studies have also confirmed these results, as well as the results that perceived risk mattered more for men while fear of rape mattered more for women (e.g., Cook & Fox, 2012; Lane & Fox, 2013; Lane et al., 2009). Interestingly, May (2001), in finding that fear of rape predicted fear among both teen girls and boys, argued that some boys may feel what he called a "shadow of powerlessness" (p. 167), because they feel physically weaker and less powerful than other boys. We discuss this argument more later.

In sum, the shadow of sexual assault thesis has received a lot of support in the literature, but studies find that fear of rape sometimes predicts fear of other crimes among men, too. In addition, scholars have yet to determine for sure what it is about rape that is so scary—is it the threat of physical harm itself, the sexual intrusion, or the emotional consequences? Scholars will need to determine these answers through more empirical work.

Hidden Victimization Perspective

The last theoretical idea to explain greater fear among women that we discuss in detail is sometimes called the "hidden victimization" perspective, which was developed in direct response to the irrationality perspective. Gender scholars have argued that most victimization experienced by women is underreported because it often occurs behind closed doors, for example, at home (see Stanko, 1995; Young, 1992). Therefore, if official statistics could account for this hidden victimization, of which law enforcement is unaware, women's fear of crime levels would correspond better to crime data. In essence, the argument is that women's fear is not irrational but actually based on real experience with risk and victimization unknown to the police (Belknap, 2001; Stanko, 1995). In support of this argument, a recent Bureau of Justice Statistics report suggested that sexual assault is among the most underreported crimes, and estimated that about 65% of rape or sexual victimizations are not reported to the police (Langton, Berzofsky, Krebs, & Smiley-McDonald, 2012). Also recall the 2010 NCVS data discussed above, which indicated that, at least in that year, the rate of men's and women's victimization rates were converging (Truman, 2011). Because the NCVS asks people (in households) about their victimization experiences, this data source is better able to measure some of the victimizations that are not reported to the police (or what criminologists call "the dark figure of crime") than the Uniform Crime Reports (UCR), which publish only crimes known to the police and arrests (see www.fbi.gov).

In this section, we have discussed the many theoretical ideas developed by scholars to explain greater fear of crime among women in the face of lower victimization risk by street crime. Yet, some scholars have also tackled the problem of men's fear of crime, trying to explain the fact that men are unlikely to express fear of crime. In the next section, we discuss this research.

Men's Fear of Crime

As discussed above, men are less likely to report fear of crime than women are (Beaulieu et al., 2007). This has been perplexing to researchers for decades, because men are more likely to be victims of crime (Cooper & Smith, 2011). Although the "paradox of fear" mentioned above generally focuses on women, men are clearly part of this paradox. In fact, males are four times more likely to be the victim of homicide and more likely to be the victim of aggravated assault and robbery than females (Cooper & Smith, 2011; Truman & Rand, 2010). Statistics suggest that if fear were based on objective risk alone, men should be much more fearful of crime. Of course, as this book discusses throughout, there is much more to fear of crime than objective risk of coming face-to-face with a criminal offender.

Because of the overwhelming focus on explaining women's heightened fear of crime, there have been few studies or theoretical attempts specifically focused on explaining men's fear. As Beaulieu and colleagues (2007) state, "In the last few years, researchers have made progress to better understand men in general but only a few rare studies have been interested particularly in the fear of crime among men" (p. 337). The handful of researchers who study men's fear of crime (or lack thereof) primarily focus on the importance of socializa-

tion and definitions of masculine identity (Goodey, 1997). Studies that have
focused on men's fear argue that men underreport fear of crime levels for different reasons: (1) because of socialization practices that teach them to neutralize fear of crime, and (2) to only fear crime in specific situations (see Table
4.2 for a brief description of these points of view).

Table 4.2 Explanations of Men's Lack of Personal Fear of Crime

Name of Explanation	Description of Explanation
"Boys Don't Cry"	Men are also afraid of crime but are socialized to neutralize or not admit this fear of crime, because fear of crime is not a "manly" emotion.
Men's Fear Is Situational	Men are only afraid in specific locations, such as in large cities or when visiting a strange place.

"Boys Don't Cry"

Those studies that have examined men's fear of crime levels specifically have
determined that men either underreport fear of crime levels or they neutralize fear because of societal expectations concerning normative masculine gender roles (Brownlow, 2005). There are several reasons that men might
"neutralize" their fear of crime levels. Most of the leading explanations involve
the basic premise that men are not raised to fear crime. In fact, many men are
taught that being fearful is a sign of weakness (Goodey, 1997). According to
Goodey (1997), a researcher in Great Britain, "hegemonic masculinity" is a
primary reason that men do not feel comfortable admitting that they feel unsafe. Hegemonic masculinity refers to the societal circumstance in which young,
strong, heterosexual, White men are considered more important, while those
who are older, weaker, homosexual, and/or minority are considered less important. As Goodey (1997) so eloquently states "the popular understanding of
'maleness' is still constricted within the idea that 'boys don't cry'" (p. 402).
Men may fear crime but are unlikely to admit such fear to others (Gilchrist et
al., 1998; Sutton & Farrall, 2005). They may even feel social pressure to vocalize
an absence of fear (Sutton & Farrall, 2005). What this means for men is that
fear of crime is not expected, supported, or cultivated, and therefore, it is not
surprising that men neutralize fear of crime.

Interestingly, some researchers have suggested that only certain groups of males
are more likely to neutralize fear of crime. These often consist of men who are
employed, feel financially secure, and live up to images of the "hegemonic"

male (Connell, 2002; Rader, 2010). On the other hand, males who fall out-side of the scope of the hegemonic male are less likely to feel embarrassed by admitting fear of crime. Researchers have shown that non-White men, older men, and younger men are less likely be affected by the expectations inherent in hegemonic masculinity, and therefore are more willing to admit fear (Schafer et al., 2006). For example, Goodey (1997) argued that younger boys, not yet in their teens, may feel more comfortable expressing fear because they are ob-viously weaker due to age. As noted above, May (2001) might call this feeling "the shadow of powerlessness." In other words, men who feel powerlessness (due to physical size or other types of vulnerability) may feel afraid of crime, regardless of the type of crime. Such feelings of powerlessness were more ap-parent in his study among adolescents, where physical size of boys varied greatly. Smaller boys expressed this sense of powerlessness in a way that the larger boys did not. May argued that the shadow of powerlessness helped to understand variations in boys' and men's fear of crime levels.

Sutton & Farrall (2005) also provided guidance in interpreting such findings when they examined the possibility that men are more likely to respond to sur-vey questions in socially desirable ways when reporting their fear of crime. Using a lie scale score that was calculated for all respondents, they discovered that there was a significant relationship between fear of crime levels and lying among men. In other words, men who are most interested in appearing socially desir-able are least likely to report fear of crime. This study offers support for the "boys don't cry" (Goodey, 1997) or neutralization hypothesis. In addition, some work has specifically considered the role of fear for older men. Beaulieu and colleagues (2007) noted that little is known about the impact of both social and physical vulnerability on fear of crime in older men's lives. They found that being older (over 80 years), a previous victim, and having multiple illnesses contributed to men's fear of crime levels. In addition, they suggested that eld-erly men who lived alone or lacked social support were more likely to fear crime and engaged in a variety of precautionary measures (Beaulieu et al., 2007).

A recent study by Cops and Pleysier (2011) examined the impact of masculine identity on adolescents' fear of crime. These researchers discovered that both male and female juveniles who reported more masculine gender identities expressed lower fear of crime. This study would indicate that even masculine attitudes taken on by both boys and girls may have a neutralization effect on fear of crime.

Men's Fear Is Situational

As we discuss in detail in Chapter 6, a sizable body of literature focuses on the physical environment and fear of crime. Some of this work, especially the work done by geographers, focuses on fear producing or alleviating landscapes and environments. For example, areas with bushes, trees, lack of lighting, or problematic locations such as subways may all heighten fear levels. Several studies have also been conducted with "built environments" which may also contribute to avoidance of public space (Pain, 2000). In addition, other work has focused on how certain locations more generally are likely to provoke or reduce fear of crime levels (Day et al., 2003), and research shows fear-provoking areas exist for both men and women. For example, Fisher and Nasar (1992), examined fear of crime levels over three areas on a college campus for both men and women. They found that respondents felt most unsafe in areas where there was less likelihood of escape, in areas where offenders could lurk, and where there was limited visibility. While these studies are particularly relevant to women, they also show that there are some specific situations in which men are willing to admit fear. Specifically, men are more likely to express fear when they do not believe they are in control of the situation, and this is more likely in certain types of locations.

For example, studies have shown that men are more afraid when they are not familiar with an area, feel they would not be able to flee from an area, would not have back up from other men, or if they encounter others unlike them (Brownlow, 2005; Day et al., 2003; Schafer et al., 2006). Specifically, although Brownlow (2005) discovered that males were four times more likely than females to rate potentially fearful landscapes as "relatively safe," he found interesting results with the men he studied. Men often felt safer when in groups and when they had the ability to flee a dangerous situation. Regardless of the visual cues in the environment, men felt safer if they perceived they had control over the situation. Women, in contrast, reported surveying the environment constantly. Day and colleagues (2003) also found that perceived control was critical for men, and men were more likely to report more fear of crime in unfamiliar places. When men visited a strange city or location, they were more likely to say they had a heightened awareness of their surroundings due to a lack of familiarity with the people and community. This uncertainty in the environment led men to feel they would not be able to handle a conflict, should one arise, which increased their fear levels.

Yet, as we discuss more in Chapter 8, some scholars have argued that changing the way researchers ask men about their fears of crime may promote their ability to admit fear when they feel it. If it is true that most men are worried about appearing weak, as the socialization argument hypothesizes, then questions that allow them to admit fear while appearing strong may be an important methodological advancement. For example, Lane (2013) argued for asking men questions that "focus on how they portray strength, why they do so, and how often they feel it is necessary to do so" (p. 63). In addition, studies could ask men what they do to feel safer when they are in public, as a way of allowing them to express their experience of fear. For example, do they hang out in groups (or with a gang), carry a weapon, or carry themselves differently (e.g., stand taller or "puff up their chests")? Although fear researchers tend to consider these behavioral precautions rather than expressions of fear, asking men when they do these things and why may be one way that men can say they are afraid without using terms that indicate weakness. Brainstorming discussions among fear of crime researchers may promote even more ideas for increasing men's willingness to admit to fear of crime. For example, Lane and one of her graduate students recently presented work at a national conference in which they asked people how they would respond if placed in a position similar to the George Zimmerman-Trayvon Martin case. Options included things like scream, run away, pull a weapon other than a gun, pull a gun, etc. (Lane & Kuhn, 2013). Stephen Farrall, a male fear researcher, was in the audience and suggested that men would rarely say they would "scream," but they might say they would "holler" or "make noise," pointing to the importance of how we ask men about their fears and what they would do as a result (personal communication, November 20, 2013). Similar discussions might lead to better and more valid research on men's personal fear of crime. Yet, as fear is currently measured, studies do show that men are more willing to admit being afraid for other people in their lives. It is to this "altruistic" fear that we now turn our attention.

Altruistic Fear among Women and Men

One aspect of fear that has received much less attention in the literature is called "altruistic fear," and refers to fear for others, including spouses, children, other family members, and friends (Warr & Ellison, 2000). Results show that there are gender differences here, too. Several studies have noted that while men report less personal fear of crime than women, the same pattern is not evident when researchers ask about fear for others. In fact, several studies have pointed out that men may feel more social pressure to fear for other people, particularly women. This in part stems from society's notion and socialization messages that men are supposed to serve as protectors for women (Rader, 2010; Snedker, 2006). This sense of responsibility seems greatest among husbands. In fact, one of the first studies to examine fear for others (Warr & Ellison, 2000) discovered that 50% of married men reported that they feared their spouse might be victimized, while only 33% of married women worried about this possibility. Snedker (2006) also found that the men she interviewed felt an obligation to protect the women and children in their lives.

Rader's (2010) qualitative study provided interesting insight into how fear for others worked for men. Not only did male respondents acknowledge a fear for their partners, they noted that such fear heightened once they were married. Male respondents indicated that getting married made them realize that they were now responsible for their spouse's safety and they felt a heavy burden to keep their wives safe (Rader, 2010). Interestingly, Rader's married male respondents discussed masking their personal fear of crime to make their wife feel safer, confirming socialization arguments that men do not feel okay expressing personal fear of crime (Goodey, 1997).

Rader and Cossman (2011) later examined fear of crime for others among college students, a younger group than most studies of altruistic fear include. This study confirmed that college men were more likely to fear for others than college women were. Similar to studies focused on married men, college males that feared for others tended to fear for their female romantic partners. Possibly because they were childless, female respondents who expressed fear for others noted that they were most likely to fear for either a male or female friend or roommate. These results may indicate that when males are not available to serve as protectors, women rely on other women to help combat fear of crime.

Studies that include adult women, rather than college students, show that women tend to fear most for children, and some studies show that they are more likely to do so than men are (Rader, 2008; Snedker, 2006; Warr & Ellison, 2000). Interestingly, Snedker (2006) found that women also feared for children who were not their own, including those in the neighborhood. One study specifically focused on altruistic fear among Israeli mothers. Mesch (2000) argued that younger mothers were more likely to fear for their children than older mothers, perhaps because children seem more vulnerable at younger ages. In addition, Mesch (2000) discovered that women who were afraid of crime for their children were also more likely to have higher personal fear of crime levels. This connection between personal fear of crime and fear for others has rarely been addressed in this body of literature, and points to an important gap in the literature (but see Warr & Ellison, 2000).

Concluding Remarks

The body of scholarship that surrounds gender and fear of crime is now close to 40 years old. Findings in the 1970s showing that women were more afraid than men despite lower victimization risk led to many studies, beginning in the early 1980s, that focused on explaining women's greater fear of crime (Ferraro, 1996; Warr, 1984). Theorists have developed many theories to account for this discrepancy, including early ideas about women being driven by irrational emotion and feeling physically and environmentally vulnerable to later theories about women being socialized to be afraid, being controlled by men in a male-dominated society, being primarily afraid of rape, and responding to hidden victimization in private arenas that are not included in crime statistics. Because most studies have focused on women, there is less information about men. There is much to be learned about how much men fear crime, what they are afraid of, or why they are afraid. What scholars have learned is that men are less likely to report fear of crime than women and when they do report fear of crime, it is often only under specific circumstances (locations that are fear producing) or among certain groups of men (i.e., elderly men). More exploration into gender identity and the social construction of gender roles (i.e., masculinity and femininity) may help shed light on this conundrum, as will better approaches to measuring men's fear of crime. We know that men feel more comfortable expressing fear for others than for themselves, often fear for their partners. While women, in contrast, often fear more for their children as well as other people in their family and their friends. Future research will need to continue to tease out why men fear (or do not), how gender differences impact fear for others, the intersection between gender and other correlates and fear of crime, and to conduct longitudinal and mix-methods studies that can more adequately account for theoretical reasons that men and women fear crime. Box 4.2 includes some specific recommendations for future research specifically focused on the gender and fear of crime.

Our next chapter focuses more on the other personal characteristic that affect fear of crime, including age, income and race.

Box 4.2 Recommendations for Future Research on Gender and Fear

- Examine gender in combination with race, age, and class instead of separately (intersections).
- Conduct more studies on men's fear of crime, including what men fear and why.
- Study the gendered implications of fear for others, including men's and women's fear for others, and how their feelings differ or converge.
- Use methodologies that allow for longitudinal analysis of the gender socialization process so that researchers may gain better perspective on what is learned, from whom, and the impact of this learning process on men and women.

References

Akers, R.L. (1973). *Deviant behavior: A social learning approach*. Belmont, CA: Wadsworth.

Barberet, R., Fisher, B.S., & Taylor, H. (2004). *University student safety in the East Midlands*. United Kingdom: Home Office.

Beaulieu, M., Dube, M., Bergeron, C., & Cousineau, M. (2007). Are elderly men worried about crime? *Journal of Aging Studies, 21*(4), 336–346.

Belknap, J. (2001). *The invisible woman: Gender, crime, and justice* (2nd ed.). Belmont, CA: Wadsworth/Thomson Learning.

Bing, R. (2009). *Race, Crime, and the Media*. New York: McGraw Hill.

Brownlow, A. (2005). A geography of men's fear. *Geoforum, 36*(5), 581–592.

Campbell, A. (2005). Keeping the lady safe: The regulation of femininity through crime prevention literature. *Critical Criminology, 13*(2), 119–140.

Catalano, S. (2012). *Stalking victims in the United States—revised*. Washington, D.C.: Bureau of Justice Statistics.

Catalano, S., Smith, E., Synder, H., & Rand, M. (2009). *Female victims of violence*. U.S. Department of Justice Publications and Materials.

Cavender, G., Bond-Maupin, L., & Jurik, N.C. (1999). The construction of gender in reality crime tv. *Gender & Society, 13*(5), 643–663.

Chiricos, T., Hogan, M., & Gertz, M. (1997). Racial composition of neighborhood and fear of crime. *Criminology, 35*(1), 107–131.

Chiricos, T., Padgett, K., & Gertz, M. (2000). Fear, tv news, and the reality of crime. *Criminology, 46*, 755–785.

Cobbina, J.E., Miller, J., & Brunson, R.K. (2008). Gender, neighborhood danger, and risk-avoidance strategies among urban African-American youths. *Criminology, 46*(3), 673–709.

Connell, R.W. (2002). *Gender*. Cambridge: Polity Press.

Cook, C., & Fox, K. A. (2012). Testing the relative importance of contemporaneous offenses: The impacts of fear of sexual assault versus fear of physical harm among men and women. *Journal of Criminal Justice, 40*, 142–151.

Cooper, A., & Smith, E.L. (2011). Homicide trends in the United States, 1980–2008. In B. o. J. Statistics (Ed.), *Annual Rates for 2009–2010* (Vol. NCJ 236018, pp. 1–35): U.S. Department of Justice.

Cops, D., & Pleysier, S. (2011). 'Doing gender' in fear of crime: The impact of gender identity on reported levels of fear of crime in adolescents and young adults. *British Journal of Criminology, 51*, 58–74.

Daly, K., & Chesney-Lind, M. (1988). Feminism and Criminology. *Justice Quarterly, 5*(4), 497–538.

Day, K. (2001). Constructing masculinity and women's fear in public space in Irvine, California. *Gender, Place, & Culture, 8*(2), 109–127.

Day, K., Stump, C., & Carreon, D. (2003). Confrontation and loss of control: Masculinity and men's fear in public space. *Journal of Environmental Psychology, 23*(3), 311–322.

De Groof, S. (2008). And my mama said ... The (relative) parental influence on fear of crime among adolescent girls and boys. *Youth & Society, 39*(3), 267–293.

Eschholz, S., Chiricos, T., & Gertz, M. (2003). Television and fear of crime: Program types, audience traits, and the mediating effect of perceived neighborhood racial composition. *Social Problems, 50*(3), 395–415.

Ferraro, K.F. (1995). *Fear of crime: Interpreting victimization risk.* New York, NY: SUNY Press.

Ferraro, K.F. (1996). Women's fear of victimization: Shadow of sexual assault? *Social Forces, 75*(2), 667–690.

Fisher, B.S., & Nasar, J.L. (1992). Fear of crime in relation to three exterior site features. *Environment and Behavior, 24*(1), 35–65.

Fisher, B.S., & Sloan, J.J. (2003). Unraveling the fear of sexual victimization among college women: Is the "shadow of sexual assault" hypothesis supported? *Justice Quarterly, 20*(3), 633–659.

Franklin, C.A., & Franklin, T.W. (2009). Predicting fear of crime: Considering differences across gender. *Feminist Criminology, 4*(1), 83–106.

Gardner, C.B. (1989). Analyzing gender in public places: Rethinking Goffman's vision of everyday life. *The American Sociologist, Spring*, 42–56.

Gilchrist, E., Bannister, J., Ditton, J., & Farrall, S. (1998). Women and the fear of crime: Challenging the accepted stereotype. *British Journal of Criminology, 38*(2), 283–298.

Goodey, J. (1997). Boys don't cry: Masculinities, fear of crime, and fearlessness. *British Journal of Criminology, 37*(3), 401–418.

Hale, C. (1996). Fear of crime: A review of the literature. *International Review of Victimology, 4*, 79–150.

Harrell, E. (2012). *Violent victimization committed by strangers, 1993–2010.* Washington, D.C.: Bureau of Justice Statistics.

Hollander, J.A. (2001). Vulnerability and dangerousness: The construction of gender through conversation about violence. *Gender & Society, 15*(1), 83–109.

Karmen, A. (2010). *An introduction to victimology* (Vol. 7). Belmont, CA: Thomson/Wadsworth.

Keane, C. (1998). Evaluating the influence of fear of crime as an environmental mobility restrictor on women's routine activities. *Environment & Behavior, 30*(1), 60–81.

Killias, M. (1990). Vulnerability: Towards a better understanding of a key variable in the genesis of fear of crime. *Violence & Victims, 5*(2), 97–108.

Killias, M., & Clerici, C. (2000). Different measures of vulnerability in their relation to different dimensions of fear of crime. *British Journal of Criminology, 40*(3), 437–450.

Kimmel, M.S. (2004). *The gendered society* (Vol. 2). New York: NY: Oxford University Press.

LaGrange, R.L., Ferraro, K.F., & Supancic, M. (1992). Perceived risk and fear of crime: Role of social and physical incivilities. *Journal of Research in Crime and Delinquency, 29*(3), 311–334.

Lane, J. (2010). Stanko, Elizabeth A.: Gender, fear and risk. In F.T. Cullen & P. Wilcox (Eds.), *Encyclopedia of Criminological Theory* (pp. 878–880). Thousand Oaks, CA: Sage.

Lane, J. (2013). Theoretical explanations for gender differences in fear of crime: Research and prospects." pp. 57–67 In *Routledge International Handbook of Crime and Gender Studies*, edited by C. M. Renzetti, S. L. Miller, and A.R. Gover. New York: Routledge.

Lane, J., & Fox, K. A. (2012). Fear of crime among gang and non-gang offenders: Comparing the effects of perpetration, victimization, and neighborhood factors. *Justice Quarterly, 29*, 491–523.

Lane, J, & Fox, K.A. (2013). Fear of property, violent, and gang crime: Examining the shadow of sexual assault thesis among male and female offenders. *Criminal Justice and Behavior, 40*(5), 472–496.

Lane, J., Gover, A., & Dahod, S. (2009) Fear of violent crime among men and women on campus: The impact of perceived risk and fear of sexual assault. *Violence & Victims, 24*(2), 172–192.

Lane, J., & Kuhn, A.P. (2013, November). "In the Shoes of George Zimmerman: The Impact of Promotion of Mistrust, Subcultural Diversity, and Fear of Crime on Expected Personal Reactions." Paper presented at the American Society of Criminology Annual Meeting, Atlanta, GA.

Lane, J., & Meeker, J.W. (2003). Women's and men's fear of gang crimes: Sexual and nonsexual assault as perceptually contemporaneous offenses. *Justice Quarterly, 20*(2), 337–371.

Langton, L., Berzofsky, M., Krebs, C., & Smiley-McDonald, H. (2012). *Victimizations not reported to the police, 2006–2010*. Washington D.C.: Office of Justice Programs.

Lauritsen, J.L., & Rezey, M.L. (2013). *Measuring the prevalence of crime with the National Crime Victimization Survey*. Washington D.C.: Bureau of Justice Statistics.

Liebler, C.M. (2010). Me(di)a culpa?: The "missing white woman syndrome" and media self-critique. *Communication, Culture, & Critique, 3*(4), 549–565.

Lupton, D., & Tulloch, J. (1999). Theorizing fear of crime: Beyond the rational/irrational opposition. *British Journal of Sociology, 50*(3), 507–523.

Madriz, E.I. (1997). Images of criminals and victims: A study on women's fear and social control. *Gender & Society, 11*(3), 342–356.

May, D.C. (2001). The effect of fear of sexual victimization on adolescent fear of crime. *Sociological Spectrum, 21*(2), 141–174.

May, D.C., Rader, N.E., & Goodrum, S. (2010). A gendered assessment of the "threat of victimization": Examining gender differences in fear of crime, perceived risk, avoidance, and defensive behaviors. *Criminal Justice Review, 35*(2), 159–182.

May, D.C., Vartanian, L.R., & Virgo, K. (2002). The impact of parental attachment and supervision on fear of crime among adolescent males. *Adolescence, 37*(146), 267–287.

Melde, C. (2009). Lifestyle, rational choice, and adolescent fear: A test of a risk-assessment framework. *Criminology, 47*(3), 781–812.

Mesch, G. (2000). Women's fear of crime: The role of fear for the well-being of significant others. *Violence & Victims, 15*(3), 323–336.

Pain, R. (2000). Place, social relations, and the fear of crime: A review. *Progress in Human Geography, 24*(3), 365–387.

Pantazis, C. (2000). Fear of crime, vulnerability, and poverty. *British Journal of Criminology, 40*(3), 414–436.

Rader, N.E. (2008). Gendered fear strategies: Intersections of doing gender and fear management strategies in married and divorced women's lives. *Sociological Focus, 41*(1), 34–52.

Rader, N.E. (2010). Until death do us part? Husband perceptions and responses to fear of crime. *Deviant Behavior, 31*(1), 33–59.

Rader, N.E., & Cossman, J.S. (2011). Gender differences in U.S. college students' fear for others. *Sex Roles, 64*(7), 568–581.

Rader, N.E., Cossman, J.S., & Porter, J.R. (2012). Fear of crime and vulnerability: Using a national sample to examine two competing paradigms. *Journal of Criminal Justice, 40*(2), 134–141.

Rader, N.E., & Haynes, S.H. (2011). Gendered fear of crime socialization: An extension of Akers's social learning theory. *Feminist Criminology, 6*(4), 291–307.

Reid, L.W., & Konrad, M. (2004). The gender gap in fear: Assessing the interactive effects of gender and perceived risk on fear of crime. *Sociological Spectrum, 24*(4), 399–425.

Saad, L. (2010). Nearly 4 in 10 americans still fear walking alone at night. *GALLUP Poll Social Series: Crime.* Retrieved from http://www.gallup.com/poll/144272/Nearly-Americans-Fear-Walking-Alone-Night.aspx.

Scarborough, B.K., Like-Haislip, T.Z., Novak, K.J., Lucas, W.L., & Alarid, L.F. (2010). Assessing the relationship between individual characteristics, neighborhood context, and fear of crime. *Journal of Criminal Justice, 38*(4), 819–826.

Schafer, J.A., Huebner, B.M., & Bynum, T.S. (2006). Fear of crime and criminal victimization: Gender-based contrasts. *Journal of Criminal Justice, 34*(3), 285–301.

Scott, H. (2003). Stranger danger: Explaining women's fear of crime. *Western Criminology Review, 4*(3), 203–214.

Skogan, W.G., & Maxfield, M.G. (1981). *Coping with crime: Individual and neighborhood reactions.* Beverly Hills: CA: Sage.

Smith, W.R., & Torstensson, M. (1997). Gender differences in risk perception and neutralizing fear of crime. *British Journal of Criminology, 37*(4), 608–634.

Snedker, K.A. (2006). Altruistic and vicarious fear of crime: Fear for others and gendered social roles. *Sociological Forum, 21*(2), 163–195.

Spade, J.Z., & Valentine, C.G. (2011). *The kaleidoscope of gender: Prisms, patterns, and possibilities* (3rd ed.). Thousand Oaks: CA: Sage.

Stanko, E.A. (1995). Women, crime, and fear. *Annals of the American Academy of Political and Social Science, 539*(1), 46–59.

Stanko, E.A. (1996). Warnings to women: Police advice and women's safety in britain. *Violence Against Women, 2*(1), 5–24.

Stanko, E.A. (1998). Warnings to women: Police advice and women's safety in Britain. In S.L. Miller (Ed.), *Crime control and women: Feminist implications of criminal justice policy.* pp. 52–71. Thousand Oaks: Sage.

Sutton, R.M., & Farrall, S. (2005). Gender, socially desirable responding and the fear of crime: Are women really more anxious about crime? *British Journal of Criminology, 45*(2), 212–224.

Truman, J.L. (2011). *Criminal victimization, 2010.* Washington D.C.: Bureau of Justice Statistics.

Truman, J.L., & Rand, M.R. (2010). *Criminal victimization, 2009.* Washington, D.C.: Bureau of Justice Statistics.

Wallace, L.H., & May, D.C. (2005). The impact of parental attachment and feelings of isolation on adolescent fear of crime at school. *Adolescence, 40*(159), 458–474.

Warr, M. (1984). Fear of victimization: Why are women and the elderly more afraid? *Social Science Quarterly, 65*(3), 681–702.

Warr, M. (1985). Fear of rape among urban women. *Social Problems, 32*(3), 238–250.

Warr, M. (1994). Public perceptions and reactions to violent offending and victimization. In A. J. Reiss, Jr. & J. A. Roth, (Eds.). *Understanding and preventing violence: Consequences and control,* Vol 4. pp. 1–66. Washington D.C.: National Academy Press.

Warr, M., & Ellison, C.G. (2000). Rethinking social reactions to crime: Personal and altruistic fear in family households. *American Journal of Sociology, 106*(3), 551–578.

West, C., & Zimmerman, D. (1987). Doing gender. *Gender & Society, 1*(2), 125–151.

Wilcox, P., Jordan, C.E., & Pritchard, A.J. (2006). Fear of acquaintance versus stranger rape as a master status: Towards refinement of the shadow of sexual assault. *Violence & Victims, 21*(3), 355–370.

Young, V. (1992). Fear of victimization and victimization rates among women: A paradox? *Justice Quarterly, 9*(3), 419–441.

Chapter 5

How and Why Age, Race/ Ethnicity, and Socioeconomic Status Contribute to Fear of Crime

[T]he overwhelming evidence to date shows convincingly that age differences in fear of crime in adulthood are modest to trivial.... There really is no victimization/fear paradox by age as described in the literature.
Ferraro, 1995, p. 82

The increase in racial residential segregation, the expansion of popular fears to include economic insecurity, the movement of civil rights conflict to the courts and the workplace, and the media-driven images of a ubiquitous crime threat—these are just part of a changing historical context in which relationships among race, residence, and fear of crime are grounded.
Chiricos, Hogan, & Gertz, 1997, pp. 124–125

The last chapter focused on gender, the personal characteristic that is most consistently related to fear of crime. Yet, there are other personal factors that many studies also show are related to fear. Three of these are age, race/ethnicity, and social class. Researchers suggest that in certain situations, people in particular categories of these groups may feel more vulnerable to victimization. Sometimes people fit within more than one of these categories and so may feel even more vulnerable. This chapter discusses each of the factors in more detail, noting how personal characteristics might be correlated with perceived vulnerability and fear of crime. Specifically, we broadly discuss the primary theme connecting all of these personal factors—vulnerability—and then discuss each characteristic in turn. We first discuss age, which accounts for the bulk of this chapter, because it has received more attention in the literature. Equally important, we believe, are race and ethnicity and income, but these have received much less attention as the primary focus of studies to date. Consequently, the summaries of knowledge to date on these topics are leaner. As we note in Chapter 8, we believe the latter categories should receive much more attention by researchers in the future.

The Importance of Vulnerability

One key theoretical backdrop that helps explain differences in fear among different social groups focuses on vulnerability. Chapter 4 discussed vulnerability as one of the key arguments put forth to explain fear of crime among women. Recall that some scholars have argued that women feel more vulnerable to both victimization and harm should it occur, because they feel physically weaker than men. They do not necessarily believe they could fend off an attack if someone tried to hurt them (Hale, 1996; LaGrange, Ferraro, & Supancic, 1992; Skogan & Maxfield, 1981). The vulnerability perspective also includes the broader argument that some people, including some men, feel more vulnerable to victimization because of other factors in their lives. In addition to women (see Chapter 4), there are several other categories of people (e.g., minorities, lower income individuals, and the very young and very old) who may experience heightened fear of crime because of their physical or social vulnerability (see Skogan & Maxfield, 1981). Consequently, researchers have paid particular attention to explaining why such groups may feel vulnerable to victimization and what impact this vulnerability may have on fear of crime levels more generally (Hale, 1996; Katz, Webb, & Armstrong, 2003; Killias & Clerici, 2000).

This perceived vulnerability may be a result of facing real crime (e.g., witnessing it in the neighborhood or knowing people who commit crime, see Chapter 6), or it may be unrelated to a real risk of being victimized. For example, early research on fear showed that, like women, the elderly were more afraid than they should be based on their actual victimization risk, and some researchers set out to understand why this group might feel more vulnerable (Clemente & Kleiman, 1977; Lewis & Salem, 1986; Skogan & Maxfield, 1981; Yin, 1982). Yet, as measures of fear improved over the years, findings often showed that younger people, who are greater risk, are more afraid (Ferraro, 1995; Lane & Meeker, 2003a, 2003b, 2003c; Rountree, 1998; Rountree & Land, 1996). For some scholars, then, the early findings about the elderly being so afraid were problematic and because of poor measurement of fear rather than a large discrepancy in fear for this group (Ferraro & LaGrange, 1988; LaGrange & Ferraro, 1987; Yin, 1980, 1982). Yet, the vulnerability perspective (broadly considered) can serve as an important backdrop for understanding fear among many groups, including those elderly who really are afraid (Liu, Messner, Zhang, & Zhuo, 2009), but also people of color and people living in poverty.

Physical Vulnerability

As noted above and in Chapter 4, some people, including women, senior citizens, and young people may feel more crime-related fear because they feel physically unable to protect themselves from a potential attack. People might feel physically vulnerable because they are smaller than others (e.g., women and children), or because they are facing declining strength and/or health (e.g., senior citizens or those with a disability or physical injury) (Beaulieu, Dube, Bergeron, & Cousineau, 2007). The critical part of this argument is that people perceive of themselves as physically vulnerable to victimization, whether or not they could actually protect themselves if put in that situation (Stiles, Halim, & Kaplan, 2003) Some individuals may begin to feel fear because they have experiences where their physical weakness is obvious. For example, women might see in their everyday lives that men are often bigger, taller, and/or stronger than they are. Or, the elderly may realize that strength they once had to do everyday activities (e.g., lifting heavy objects), their eyesight (to see someone coming) and/or mental acuity (to think fast in scary situations) are no longer evident. Another reason they might feel more vulnerable is due to socialization from others. For example, people may be told by the media, family, or friends that crime happens to those who cannot defend themselves, at the hands of a stranger, and is typically violent, despite statistics to the contrary (Lauritsen & Rezey, 2013). Those who are already feeling weaker may be more affected by these messages than others, because they are already concerned about their health, size, etc. (Beaulieu et al., 2007; Killias & Clerici, 2000; Stanko, 1995).

Social Vulnerability

Social vulnerability refers to the fact that certain groups of people live in an environmental context where they are more vulnerable to many social ills, including crime. According to this argument, certain groups, such as the poor and minorities, may be more afraid because their lived experience in their neighborhoods and other frequented areas tell them they should be (Hale, 1996; LaGrange et al., 1992). That is, these groups are more socially vulnerable to crime. As we discuss in detail in Chapter 6, some environmental factors that can increase feelings of personal vulnerability include neighborhood racial and ethnic diversity, disorder (e.g., trash, rundown buildings, or graffiti), and decline (or the perception that the area is no longer as nice as it used to be) (Lane, 2002; Skogan, 1995).

For some scholars, this social vulnerability means more than just everyday experiences in communities and can be expanded to include a lack of social and political power. For example, Blacks may feel more unease generally and may feel more fear of crime because they have less social power than Whites (Chiricos, Hogan, & Gertz, 1997). In addition, poor people have less social power, including status and prestige, than middle and upper-income people. Because they feel less powerful generally, they may also feel less able to protect themselves from crime (Pantazis, 2000).

Age and Fear of Crime

As noted earlier, initial studies showed that age was an important predictor of fear of crime—that the elderly (also called senior citizens or older people in this chapter) were more afraid than younger people even though their risk of victimization was actually much lower (Baumer, 1978; Ferraro & La-Grange, 1987; Skogan & Maxfield, 1981; Warr, 1984). One of the key initial explanations was the vulnerability hypothesis—that senior citizens felt frail and defenseless, leading them to fear crime (McKee & Milner, 2000). For example, Skogan and Maxfield (1981, p. 71) noted that senior citizens are "not very agile, and may more easily fall victim to vigorous young males. In addition, they may suffer physical disabilities or a general reduction in acuity which makes it difficult for them to evade attack or fend off those who would harass them." Interestingly, Warr (1984) found that elderly females were more afraid than younger ones, but this difference was not apparent for males, showing that gender differences existed regardless of age.

Yet, early in the move to understand fear of crime among the elderly, Yin (1980, 1982) argued that they were not as afraid as people believed and criticized the measurement of fear (see Chapter 3). He also argued that social support might be a buffer that reduced fear of crime among senior citizens. But, he noted that there are more women who live into their upper years and elderly people tend to have lower incomes, which could be explanatory factors for higher fear levels sometimes found among the elderly (Yin, 1980). That is, as we discuss later, these personal factors work together to promote fear. Yin (1982) soon tested some of his arguments with survey data but with the general measures of fear rather than those that measured fear of specific offenses. However, he found that senior citizens rarely mentioned crime as a significant worry, supporting his belief that older people were not necessarily that afraid.

Ferraro & LaGrange (1987, 1988, 1989) soon wrote a series of articles in which they further questioned the assumption that older people were really afraid. They focused on key problems with questions used to measure fear of crime and suggested better ways to ask about fear of crime (e.g., mention crime and focus on specific offenses) (Ferraro & LaGrange, 1987, 1988; LaGrange & Ferraro, 1987). Then, they examined women and the elderly's fear of crime, using better measures. Specifically, they included perceived risk as a predictor and measured fear of specific offenses, comparing this approach to the typical NCS measure that did not specify fear of crime but measured fear of being alone in the neighborhood at night. While they found that women were more afraid than men no matter how fear was measured, they found that older people were no longer the most fearful when they were asked about specific offenses (LaGrange & Ferraro, 1989). As noted, later works that measure fear of specific offenses now regularly find that younger people are more fearful (see Ferraro, 1995; Ferraro & LaGrange, 1992; Warr, 2000). Some studies actually show that fear increases up to a certain age (e.g., for personal loss, age 45, and for personal harm, age 23) and then decreases as people get older (Moore & Shepherd, 2007). Interestingly, one study conducted by Franklin and Franklin found that women get less fearful as they age, but this was not true for men (2009). Still another found older people living in elderly-only housing towers were not very afraid of crime, but elderly living in mixed age public housing towers were more afraid than younger people there were. This study illustrated the importance of including context in understanding the impact of age on fear (DeLone, 2008).

Fear among the Elderly

Personal Characteristics

A few studies have focused specifically on understanding fear among older people, some have been quantitative and others qualitative. Studies of senior citizens generally find that women are more afraid than men are (e.g., Acierno, Rheingold, Resnick, & Kilpatrick, 2004; Akers, La Greca, Sellers, & Cochran, 1987; De Donder, Verte, & Messelis, 2005; LaGrange & Ferraro, 1989; Tulloch, 2000). We discussed reasons for women's greater fear and men's lesser fear in Chapter 4. Interestingly, Liska, Sanchiro, and Reed's (1988) work illustrated an intersection between age and gender. They discovered that women were more afraid of crime, regardless of age. However, men were more afraid of crime when they were younger and when they were older but not as much during the middle years. Schafer et al. (2006) found similar results, older men were more afraid of crime than younger men were while age had no effect on women's fear of crime levels. This may suggest that feelings of vulnerability vary more over time for men than for women.

Elderly people with lower incomes also tend to be more afraid (Akers et al., 1987). Rates of poverty tend to be higher among elderly people than among middle-aged adults, and so this might be a key factor relevant to fear among this group (Hale, 1996; Pantazis, 2000). In addition, Liska and colleagues (1988) concluded that the relationship between income and fear of crime levels was curvilinear (increased until individuals were in their middle ages and then decreased once individuals were older). Yet, as we show later in this chapter, lower incomes are often related to increased fear of crime.

Some studies also find that among the elderly, minorities (Acierno et al., 2004; Akers et al., 1987) and victims (e.g., Beaulieu et al., 2007; McCoy, Wooldredge, Cullen, Dubeck, & Browning, 1996; Yin, 1980) are more afraid. Likely because these results confirm those found in the general population, there is not much scholarly work attempting to explain these relationships among the elderly population in particular.

Why Some Senior Citizens Are Afraid

What might prompt elderly people who are afraid to worry about, or feel vulnerable to, crime? Despite now consistent findings that younger people are more afraid, some research does point to reasons that some senior citizens might fear crime. Although compared to gender, there are fewer theoretical efforts to explain fear among this group, some scholars have discussed possible causes for older people's fear.

One suggestion is that they often live alone, sometimes after having lived with someone else (e.g., a spouse) for many years. For example, Beaulieu and colleagues investigated fear of crime among elderly men, finding that those who lived alone were five times more likely to take protective measures in response to fear of crime (Beaulieu et al., 2007).

Another issue pertinent to older citizens in particular are health issues (Stiles et al., 2003). As we mentioned above, some elderly people may feel physically vulnerable and unable to ward off an attack and consequently are more afraid of crime (Cossman & Rader, 2011; McKee & Milner, 2000). In fact, Killias and Clerici (2000) found that age was no longer an important predictor of fear, once they controlled for physical vulnerability, meaning that physical issues were really important to understanding older people's fear. Beaulieu and colleagues (2007) also concluded that people who were sicker were more afraid of crime (see also Akers et al., 1987). Specifically, men, who had a chronic illness, were four times more likely to fear crime than those without chronic illnesses. However, it is the perception of health, more than actual health itself, that apparently matters most (Rader, Cossman, & Porter, 2012). For example, if someone is diagnosed with a debilitating illness but does not worry about it, the connection between poor health and fear of crime may not be as strong (Cossman & Rader, 2011).

Interestingly, some studies find that one important issue related to physical vulnerability, including perceptions of strength and health, is elderly people's belief in their ability to recuperate from a victimization experience (Greve, 1998; Yin, 1980). As Greve (1998) argued, even small injuries can have more serious implications for older people, especially if they think they would not be able to get better or adapt to the resulting physical limitations that came with an injury. They might worry about loss of independence if they were injured or worry about how they could face new problems created by the crime as they continue to struggle with ones they already have, such as illness (Greve, 1998).

One negative outcome for those older people who are afraid is to avoid places and restrict mobility which can have psychological impacts by increasing isolation and decreasing the number of social contacts they have (Chandola, 2001; Pain, 1997). One study found, for example, that people with more mental health issues (e.g., depression and anxiety) were also more likely to fear crime, as were those who had limited physical functioning (e.g., walking speed and lung functioning) (Stafford, Chandola, & Marmot, 2007). One problem is that this can become a cycle, where fear increases social isolation, depression, and other dissatisfaction with life, which can in turn increase fear. As noted, studies show that depression is related to fear (Acierno et al., 2004; Baldassare, 1986). Dissatisfaction with life, the local neighborhood, and housing is also related to fear among older people (McCoy et al., 1996).

Yet, as Yin (1982) argued, social support may serve as a buffer to reduce fear of crime. The aging literature generally shows that people who believe they will have social support if they need it tend to have better physical and mental health over time (Krause, 2001). Studies generally find that those who are married, and therefore probably have more social support and are less isolated, are less afraid (Ross, 1993; Ward, LaGory, & Sherman, 1986). In addition, people who have more neighborhood interaction tend to be less afraid (O'Bryant & Donnermeyer, 1991; Yin, 1980). Yet, some research finds that people generally vary in their tendency to be afraid. Some are frightened easily by many factors while others are rarely afraid (Ferraro & LaGrange, 1987; Gabriel & Greve, 2003). Despite the fact that the elderly are not as fearful as early studies showed, some of them are afraid, and some are very afraid.

There is still much to learn about this and many other aspects of senior citizens' fears about crime, including the intricacies of how, why, when and where they worry. For example, while studies show that elderly people in urban areas are more afraid than those in rural areas (Ward et al., 1986), the authors know of only a few published studies that specifically set out to vary the context in which they studied elderly fear. In the late 1980s, Akers et al. (1987) found that senior citizens living in retirement communities were less afraid than those living in more heterogeneous areas. Roncek (2002) studied older people living in public housing. Two residential towers were for the elderly only, while two others housed people of different ages. He found that people living in the buildings with a mixed-age population were much more afraid than those who lived around people of a similar age (see also DeLone, 2008). We now turn to fear of crime among the young, or those that more recent research shows tend to be more afraid.

Fear among the Young

Despite findings over the last two or more decades that younger people are more afraid of crime, there has not been much research focused on understanding the particular causes and consequences of their fear levels. More than a decade ago, May and Dunaway (2000) argued, "Despite the abundance of research examining fear of crime among adults, there has been scant attention paid to examining fear of crime among adolescents" (p. 152). Their point still rings true. Most fear of crime research uses adult samples. Only two articles have examined fear among youths generally without using school samples. Parker & Onyekwuluje (1992) found that most Black teens were not afraid in their neighborhoods. In contrast, in her qualitative study of Denver youths, Irwin (2004) found that most youths in her sample were afraid of fights and shootings, even though most of them did not have to face crime on a regular basis. Most studies on adolescent fear have focused on (1) fear at or on the way to and from school or (2) fear of crime among offenders. We will discuss studies in each of these areas first and then discuss some of the reasons that young people may or may not be afraid.

Fear of Crime among Youths at or to and from School

Because research on fear among young people is in its infancy, many of the first studies focused on how many high school students were actually afraid on their way to and from school. Findings indicated that fewer than half (between 14% and 47%) were afraid at or as they travelled to or home from school (Bailey, Flewelling, & Rosenbaum, 1997; Baker & Mednick, 1990; Bowen & Bowen, 1999; Everett & Price, 1995; Martin, Sadowski, Cotten, & McCarraher, 1996). Bowen and Bowen (1999) did find that about a third of students had experienced personally threatening situations in the area around where they lived during the previous month. In addition, a couple of studies found that a few kids missed school in the previous month, because they were afraid of victimization on their way to and from school (Lowrey et al., 1999; Malek, Change, & Davis, 1998). In their primarily Hispanic sample, Brown and Benedict (2004) found that almost ⅓ of students were afraid of being stabbed at school, and about ¼ worried about being shot there. Interestingly, Addington (2003) found that youths were not generally afraid at school, and only a few more (4%) were afraid across the country after the Columbine incident in 1999 where two students shot multiple students in Littleton, Colorado. Based on this study, then, even when school shootings happen, fear levels do not increase a lot in schools elsewhere. The school shooting in Newtown, Connecticut, in December 2012 where twenty elementary children were killed and six staff members were shot, however, is so recent that it's difficult to know the effects on school children nationally.

A few studies have analyzed the predictors of fear in middle and/or high school samples, and they found similar demographic predictors evident in research on adults. For example, girls are typically more afraid than boys (Alvarez & Bachman, 1997; Baker & Mednick, 1990; Brown & Benedict, 2004; May, 2001a; May & Dunaway, 2000). Youths of color are also more afraid than Whites (Alvarez & Bachman, 1997; Baker & Mednick, 1990) although May and colleagues (May, 2001a; May & Dunaway, 2000) found that was true only for males (Black teens were more afraid than White ones). As with other studies, age findings are inconsistent. Some studies have shown that younger teens are more afraid than older ones (Alvarez & Bachman, 1997; Brown & Benedict, 2004; May & Dunaway, 2000) while others show the age of the teen is not particularly relevant (e.g., Baker & Mednick, 1990). Also similar to studies on adults, the importance of prior victimization depends on the study. Some found it predicts fear (Alvarez & Bachman, 1997; Baker & Mednick, 1990) and other indicated it does not (May, 2001a; May & Dunaway, 2000). Interestingly, May and Dunaway (2000) found prior victimization only predicted fear among female teens, not males.

As Chapter 6 notes, context is an important factor in understanding fear of crime, and a few studies have examined the impact of neighborhood problems (e.g., disorder) on adolescent fear of crime. May and his colleagues (2001a; 2000) found that youths who lived in disorderly neighborhoods are more afraid, especially girls (May, 2001b).

Box 5.1 Case Focus
Phoebe Prince

A critical issue for young people, especially in school, is bullying, which recently has received a lot of media airtime. Part of the reason for the interest in bullying is that at least 25% of children experience bullying at school (Copeland, Wolke, Angold, & Costello, 2013). In addition, bullying is an important topic of study because it comes in many forms (e.g., emotional threats, cyber threats, threats of physical harm, psychological harm) and can have severe consequences for its victims (e.g., depression, anxiety, suicide) (Jeong & Lee, 2013). Another important consequence of bullying is fear (Copeland et al., 2013). Harm or the threat of harm by peers at school may cause victims to avoid going to school, change routine activities, or even carry weapons to school (Wilcox, May, & Roberts, 2006). For these reasons, bullying prevention policies are a key concern for criminal justice professionals, school administrators, and parents alike.

Many of these issues were brought to light by the national media in 2010 with the Phoebe Prince story. Phoebe Prince, a new girl who had recently moved from Ireland to Massachusetts, briefly dated a senior football player. When this relationship ended, she was repeatedly bullied by peers at South Hadley High School. On a daily basis, she was called names like "Irish slut," sent harassing text messages, and her property was damaged. On January 14, after months of experiencing bullying without reprieve and after just that day, a moving car threw a Red Bull can at her head, Phoebe Prince walked home and hung herself from her stair case. She was 15 years old. Even after her death, the bullying continued, with defaming comments and negative posts about her. Five students from South Hadley High School were charged and received either probation or community service for their role in Prince's death (Kennedy, 2010; Webley, 2011).

Thought/Discussion Questions:
1. What do you think should be done to prevent bullying in school?
2. Do school administrators (e.g., superintendents, principals, teachers) have a responsibility to prevent bullying? If so, what should their responsibility be?
3. What should the role of parents be in preventing bullying?
4. How can peers in school get involved in bullying prevention? Do you think they should be involved?
5. What do you think should be the punishment for bullies?
6. Many zero tolerance policies have been created to prevent bullying. Do you think this is a good idea? Why or why not?

Fear of Crime among Young Offenders

One of the newer trends in fear of crime research is to examine fear of crime among offenders, who face a greater objective risk of victimization due to their involvement in crime (Fagan, Piper, & Cheng, 1987; Sampson & Lauritsen, 1990). There are only a few studies focused specifically on offender fear of crime, and many of them focused on youthful populations. May (2001a) and his colleagues (May, Vartanian, & Virgo, 2002) were the first to publish studies focused on fear of crime among juvenile offenders. Their studies focused on more than 300 incarcerated youth in an Indiana facility for delinquent males. May (2001b) was primarily focused on testing his hypothesis that fear of crime would lead to defensive behaviors such as gun possession and gang membership, which could then contribute to violence, although the data did not support this conclusion. Yet, he also included models predicting fear of crime. He found that younger juvenile offenders, those who lived in neighborhoods with disorder, experienced blocked opportunities in life, and had more friends who were not in trouble were more afraid. Using the same sample, May et al. (2002) examined the effects of parental attachment and parental supervision on fear. Interestingly, youths who felt more attached to their parents expressed less fear, while those who were supervised more closely were more afraid but felt less at risk. May and colleagues reasoned that those parents who supervised their kids more closely may have been sharing their own concerns about crime with their children on a regular basis.

Lane (2009) also studied fear of crime among incarcerated youths. Most youths interviewed, both boys and girls, indicated they were not afraid of all crimes listed, except for being shot in the street and murdered. More boys said they were afraid of being shot in the street (54.9%) than not, and about half (49.6%) said they were afraid of being murdered. She found no significant differences between boys and girls in terms of their fear levels, but reasoned that this result may have been due to the small number of girls in the sample. She did find that boys were significantly more likely to say they were more likely to buy or secure a gun or carry a gun to avoid victimization, while girls were significantly more likely to say they arranged for a companion when they were going out.

Lane (2006) also studied fear among teenage offenders, but focused on juveniles on probation in the community. She again found that most youths were not afraid of the crimes measured (about 31–43%, depending on the crime), but the majority were afraid of serious crimes, including being shot in the street, drive-by shootings, and being murdered. Similar to her study of incarcerated youths, this study showed that juvenile offenders were more afraid of life-threatening crimes.

Explaining Fear Levels among Young People

Scholars have put forth several explanations for young people's fear levels, and these are primarily twists on the general theoretical ideas used to explain fear generally or in other groups—specifically physical vulnerability and socialization—are two of the primary explanations. In addition, because some of the few studies on youths focus specifically on kids who are in trouble, others have discussed the importance of a delinquent lifestyle.

Physical Vulnerability

One of the key explanations for fear among youths is physical vulnerability, because children are clearly physically smaller than adults. For example, Goodey (1994, 1997) argued that young boys are not yet one of those in the valued male category—that they are one of the groups at the bottom of the male social hierarchy, because they are smaller and weaker. She noted that they therefore feel more comfortable admitting fear while they are adolescents than they do when they grow into adults. May (2001b) also speculated younger children were more afraid because of their smaller physical size compared to adults. Building on the "shadow of sexual assault idea" developed to explain fear of crime among women, May (2001b, p. 167) argued that young boys may suffer from a "shadow of powerlessness," which prompted them to feel fear. More recently, Melde (2009) made a similar argument, indicating that younger teenagers feel more vulnerable to potential victimization.

Socialization

Socialization is another explanation provided by scholars to explain fear of crime levels among the young, this is in part because much of the socialization in life occurs during this developmental period. Younger people are continually influenced by both parents and peers. Therefore, it makes sense that fear of crime may be transmitted from these socialization agents to youth, which may in turn, increase their fear of crime levels. Goodey (1994) for example, argued that it is important for fear scholars to study gender socialization and fear of crime among children as a way to better understand the consistent gender differences in fear of crime among adults. In her later work, partly entitled "Boys Don't Cry," she argued that boys are taught to be fearless, which in reality means that they stifle their feelings and feel unable to express feelings of vulnerability as they grow older and work to fit into the valued categories in the hierarchy of men (Goodey, 1997). Girls, in contrast, are taught from a young age to be careful in how they dress, where they go, with whom they associate, etc. and that it is "feminine" to be passive and weak, meaning it is okay to express fear (Hollander, 2001).

A couple of studies have examined parental fear of crime as a way of understanding the socialization of children regarding when it is appropriate to feel fear. As noted above, May and colleagues (May et al., 2002) focused on parental attachment and supervision of children, finding that youth who were supervised more were more afraid but those who were more attached to their parents were less afraid. De Groof (2008) extended this work and argued that an intergenerational transmission of fear of crime may occur where parents pass fear of crime on to their children. De Groof specifically noted that "Parents explicitly teach their children to fear and avoid certain situations and things (strangers, spiders, heights, and desolate places, among others). As a consequence, children will often experience the fear of their parents" (p. 271). De Groof found that children with smothering or unattached parents had higher fear of crime levels. This was especially the case when over or under parental supervision stemmed from fathers.

Delinquent Lifestyle as a Possible Buffer to Fear

Recall that some studies have focused on fear among offending adolescents. If fear of crime were based on actual risk of victimization, one would expect offenders to have the highest fear of crime levels due to their real everyday experience with crime and/or troubled peers. Yet, as early studies found, objective risk of victimization (e.g., crime statistics) does not always correspond well with fear. The studies discussed above generally found that youths more immersed in the offending lifestyle (e.g., who were older or committed more serious crimes) were less afraid, except of serious crimes like being shot or murdered (Lane, 2006, 2009; Melde, 2009). A number of researchers have speculated on the reasons for this curious finding. Lane (2006) surmised that those who were more involved in crime might be able to distinguish between those crimes that they could survive and those that they could not. For example, she noted "It is possible that because of their life experiences and street knowledge, these youths felt more resilient and more able to handle whatever came at them, except when it involved a bullet," while those less involved in crime might feel less skilled in their own abilities to deal with a dangerous situation should it arise (Lane, 2006, p. 47). Lane (2009) later studied incarcerated youths, who expressed even less fear than those in her earlier study of youths in the community. She speculated that her subjects may have felt pressure to express toughness in the facility and therefore did not feel free to express fear, even when in a private area with a researcher. May (2001b) supposed that people more immersed in crime may be less willing to admit fear even if they feel it. His argument supported Anderson's (1999) point that those who commit crime must express "nerve," which includes showing no fear of personal harm (see also Miller, 2001). Melde, Taylor, and Esbensen compared school youths who were in gangs to those who were not, finding that those who were in gangs were less afraid over time. They argued that while many youths initially join gangs for protection, they may then feel safer—gaining "peace of mind"—because of the membership despite the fact that their actual risk of victimization increases (Melde, Taylor, & Esbensen, 2009, p. 588).

As this section illustrates, age has been a consistent predictor in the fear of crime literature, but depending on the research period in which the study occurred, results vary. For example, in the infancy period, when weaker measures of fear were included in studies, older people appeared more afraid. But, as fear of crime research developed and as scholars have moved into the maturation period of research (see Chapter 2), results have shown that younger people are more afraid. For each group, the old and the young, some researchers have made important strides in understanding what factors relate to increased or decreased fear of crime. We now turn to another important demographic factor that is related to fear of crime—specifically race and ethnicity.

Race/Ethnicity and Fear of Crime

Race and ethnicity are significant personal characteristics discussed among criminologists, but they receive the most attention in the literature focused on crime commission. Statistics and research show that Black people are more likely to be arrested for violent crimes and are also the most likely victim of most crimes (Kaufman, Rebellon, Thaxton, & Agnew, 2008). Therefore, researchers spend a considerable amount of time focusing on the role of race and ethnicity in the criminal justice system. Less time and research has been devoted to understanding race and ethnicity in relation to fear of crime levels, although researchers include race and/or ethnicity as predictors in most studies. Few researchers have made race and/or ethnicity and its relationship to fear of crime the central focus of their study (Chiricos et al., 1997; Eitle & Taylor, 2008). Before we discuss the theoretical ideas about fear of crime among racial and ethnic minorities, we first discuss research showing that these groups are typically more afraid of crime than Whites are.

Fear of Crime Experiences by Race/Ethnicity

Historically, studies generally find that non-Whites are more afraid of crime than Whites (Baumer, 1978; Ferraro, 1995, 1996; Ferraro & LaGrange, 1992; Parker, 1988; Skogan, 1995; Skogan & Maxfield, 1981; Warr, 1994). This is also true in studies that measure fear of specific perpetrators, such as gangs (Katz et al., 2003; Lane & Meeker, 2003b, 2011). Yet, once in a while, studies show that Whites are more afraid (Gainey, Alper, & Chappell, 2011). Other studies have found no significant differences when comparing Whites and non-Whites in terms of fear of crime levels (Ferguson & Mindel, 2007). Still, other studies have shown that the results depend on what type of fear the survey measures or what other predictor variables are in the model. For example, Lane & Fox (2012) found that among their adult offender sample, minorities were significantly more afraid of personal crime and gang crime, but not property crime (see also Lane & Fox, 2013). Lane & Meeker (2003c), in contrast, found that minorities were sometimes more afraid of gang crimes when fear of gang-related assault was included as a predictor, but not when fear of sexual assault was included instead. Still, studies overwhelmingly show that people of color are more afraid than Whites are, and this is true whether or not the minorities are African-American, Hispanic, or Asian (e.g., Vietnamese). In fact, studies that include Hispanics often find that they are more afraid than both Whites and Blacks (Chiricos, Padgett, & Gertz, 2000; Eitle & Taylor, 2008; Parker, McMorris, Smith, & Murty, 1993), and Vietnamese are often more afraid than even Hispanics (Lane & Meeker, 2004).

Explaining Fear among Racial and Ethnic Minorities

While the literature has not focused on explaining fear among racial and ethnic minorities as much as it has among women and among different age groups, there has been some discussion among scholars regarding the likely reasons for the increased fear of crime among non-Whites. The primary reason discussed in the literature is social vulnerability, but recent work has focused also on the likely importance of cultural and language barriers and socialization.

For a long time, researchers did not spend much effort trying to develop explanations for fear among racial and ethnic minorities, because their social vulnerability as a group was clear. Specifically, African Americans, who were the primary minority group in many research studies as a group are more likely to be victimized by crime, to live in areas where crime occurs, and to be offenders themselves than Whites are (Kaufman et al., 2008). Consequently, it is not a huge theoretical leap to say that as a group they should be more afraid than Whites are. A number of researchers have made this argument (Ferraro, 1995; Hale, 1996; Parker, 1988; Parker & Ray, 1990; Skogan & Maxfield, 1981). Interestingly, because this seems the obvious answer, not many researchers have considered other reasons for greater fear among minorities, despite the fact that research on gender and fear shows that actual risk is not necessarily "neatly" correlated with fear of crime.

Yet, a few studies have pointed to the possibility that for some minorities, especially immigrants, language and cultural barriers may also contribute to fear of crime. For example, Lee and Ulmer (2000) found that Koreans who did not speak English well were more afraid than those who did, as were those who were born outside the United States. This points to the importance of cultural and lifestyle differences among immigrant groups and people born and raised in the United States. In her qualitative work, Lane (2002) found that cultural differences were one of the primary reasons that long-term residents gave for being afraid of immigrants, and it may be that immigrants have the same concerns about those who they encounter in their newly adopted countries. As we discuss more in Chapter 6, when we discuss the importance of community context, the subcultural diversity argument points to the importance of racial, cultural, and language differences among residents as one of the key contributors to fear of crime (Merry, 1981). Yet, research that specifically focuses on minority fear has not necessarily incorporated this as a key argument.

In the last few years, some researchers have argued for the importance of studying socialization as a key factor predicting fear of crime among racial and ethnic minorities. Recently, Lane and Fox (2012, p. 516) argued "It may be that, like women, minorities in the USA are socialized generally to be more afraid as a way to protect children from harm and that this socialization carries throughout their lives (e.g., to be more aware of the possibility of crime around them than others might be)." Lane and Fox (2012) noted research from the psychological literature that focuses on "promotion of mistrust" in families of color where parents "emphasize the need for wariness and distrust in interracial interactions" (Hughes et al., 2006, p. 757), and argued for more research on whether these types of messages increase fear of crime in minority communities. The research in this area is just beginning, but Lane and Kuhn (2013) recently presented research examining whether promotion of mistrust messages received from parents affected the likelihood of choosing a violent response in a situation similar to the George Zimmerman-Trayvon Martin case, in which a Hispanic man followed an unarmed African-American teen in the neighborhood, eventually killing him (see Chapter 6 for more discussion of this case). They found that people who received promotion of mistrust messages were more likely to say they would shoot a gun in a similar situation, and they were more likely to shoot a gun if the person they were following was Black (Lane & Kuhn, 2013). There is much to be learned regarding socialization and the effects on fear among minority groups, and it is an important area to explore.

Some have argued that Whites also may be afraid of crime because they are socialized to be afraid especially of African-Americans (De Welde, 2003), despite the fact that crime tends to be intra-racial (or within one's own race) (Harrell, 2007; Skogan & Maxfield, 1981). According to Madriz (1997, p. 97),

The fear producing outlaw is exemplified in the image of the stranger, the dark-skinned man who haunts us from the shadows of alleys and public parks. This image is created and recreated in everyday conversations about criminals as men from other races, possibly immigrants, and certainly poor.

While Madriz (1997) found that women of many races typified criminals as minority, being socialized to be prejudiced may be especially relevant for Whites. For example, Skogan (1995) found that Whites who lived closer to Blacks were more afraid of crime as were prejudiced Whites. Chiricos, Hogan, and Gertz (1997) also found that Whites who perceived that they were a racial minority in the neighborhood were more afraid, but this was not true for Blacks. St. John and Heald-Moore (1996) also concluded that Whites were more afraid of African-American strangers than of White strangers, and that prejudiced Whites were even more afraid than were those who were not prejudiced.

This section has focused on racial differences in fear of crime and possible explanations for these differences, especially physical vulnerability and socialization. The next section focuses on income levels and their relationship to fear of crime.

Poverty, Vulnerability, and Fear of Crime

Research specifically on the relationship between poverty and fear of crime is sparse, although income is sometimes included in models predicting fear of crime. Income is not always included in the models, because some people are hesitant to share their incomes with researchers. When this is the case, the data set is often missing too much information on income to reliably understand the impact it has on fear of crime, and sometimes researchers include educational level as a proxy for social class.

Generally, the research that has been done on this relationship illustrates that lower income people are more afraid of crime than people who have more money (Hale, 1996; McKee & Milner, 2000; Pantazis, 2000; Rader et al., 2012). Yet this is not always true. For example, Franklin et al. (2008) recently found that those with lower incomes had higher levels of perceived risk but not fear of crime. Others have found that income matters only for some groups but not for others. For example, Schafer and colleagues (2006) found that lower income men were significantly more likely to fear crime than those of higher incomes, but this was not true for women. Another study found that lower income people were more afraid of crime generally, but not of gang crime

(Lane & Meeker, 2000). Yet, the bulk of the research supports the notion that those in poverty are more afraid of crime (Chiricos et al., 1997; McKee & Milner, 2000; Pantazis, 2000; Rader et al., 2012; Scarborough, Like-Haislip, Novak, Lucas, & Alarid, 2010).

While several studies cited above discuss income as a significant predictor of fear of crime, few studies focus primarily on the relationship between poverty and fear of crime. One of the few studies that did so was conducted by Christina Pantazis (2000). She determined that nearly half of the lower income individuals she studied felt unsafe from crime. Specifically, she found that lower income people were more afraid of rape, mugging, auto theft, theft, and burglary than those who were wealthier. In addition, she found that those who lived in diverse areas and neighborhoods with more incivilities were more afraid than poor people who lived in other areas (see Chapter 6 for a discussion of these issues). As in most other studies, women were much more afraid than men were, but lower income women were even more afraid. Based on these findings, she concluded: "To this effect, anxiety about crime and victimization can be seen as part of a long chain of insecurities, which may be experienced more acutely by people living in poverty" (p. 425).

Delone (2008) studied public housing residents from Nebraska, which some consider one of the poorest groups of residents. Two of the towers he studied included mixed age residents, while the other two housed elderly people only. He asked about fear of crime within their housing unit. Delone concluded that women, Whites, those who were unemployed, and those who perceived more incivilities in their units and those who were less integrated into the social environment were more afraid of crime than their counterparts.

In an earlier study, Will and McGrath (1995) examined the relationship between social class and fear of crime and they argued that lower income individuals would fear crime more than their counterparts because they lacked confidence in their business leaders and government. Their study found that the poor were significantly more afraid of crime than the non-poor. As Pantazis (2000) found, lower income women were more afraid than upper-income women were, but this difference was also apparent for men. Younger people who were poor were also more afraid than those who were not poor. In sum, the poor were more afraid, even after considering their age and gender, which the authors argued made sense due to their greater likelihood of victimization by crime.

In an interesting review of the literature, Vacha and McLaughlin (2000) explored the rare case of gun accidents, finding that they are more common among children in lower income homes. They found that adults in lower-income and urban areas are less likely to report owning a gun, but children in these areas have a lot of access to illegal guns. In addition, even legal guns kept in low-income homes are less likely to be stored safely (e.g., unloaded and locked) because they are kept for protection and make the people in the home feel safer. Yet, this study relied on data that was sparse, because such information is hard to come by. Specifically, it may be difficult to get poor people to talk to researchers, because they may be transient, without landline phones, or potentially less trusting of researchers than other groups, especially if they are engaged in illegal activity (such as illegally owning weapons).

Explaining Fear among Lower Income Groups

Although most research contributing to our understanding of the impact of income on fear is a result of studies that examine multiple factors, such as age, race, and incivilities, some scholars have discussed the reasons that poverty matters. Specifically, as for women, the elderly and, the young, much of the focus has been on the poor's perceived vulnerability to being victimized. In the case of lower income individuals, their actual risk of being victimized can be pretty high due to the higher crime in neighborhoods where they live, and so their perceived vulnerability may be closer to their objective reality (Chiricos et al., 1997; Scarborough et al., 2010; Skogan & Maxfield, 1981). In other words, place matters. In addition, those who live in poverty may not have the financial ability to access protective resources such as sturdy locks on doors and windows, security systems, or other target hardening measures (Vacha & McLaughlin, 2000). Yet, as this section has shown, there is much to be learned about the particular impact of poverty independent of other issues, such as neighborhood conditions. In truth, these problems are difficult to separate because they are highly correlated, but scholars could attempt to learn more about the specific perceived vulnerabilities related to poverty that are not particular to neighborhood conditions. For example, is fear of crime among the poor related to a larger "unease" about their place in society or their general higher level of stress due to the financial and other conditions that accompany their financial problems (e.g., family or job stress) (Pantazis, 2000)?

Concluding Remarks

This chapter focused on key personal characteristics other than gender that predict fear of crime—specifically, age, race and ethnicity, and poverty. We began with a discussion of the importance of physical and social vulnerability as the theoretical theme underlying most explanations of fear among the different subgroups we discuss—the old and the young, racial and ethnic minorities, and the poor.

We then discussed each subgroup, focusing on what we know about fear among the group as well as the theoretical ideas that researchers have developed to understand their greater fear levels. For example, while physical vulnerability (perceived and actual) is the primary reason that the elderly and the very young may fear crime, social vulnerability (perceived and actual) is the primary reason that racial/ethnic minorities as well as those who live in poverty fear crime. Yet, other ideas exist, too—for example, socialization may matter for both young people and for racial and ethnic minorities. And, for offenders, although it is counterintuitive, involvement in street crime may have a "buffering effect" to help youths and adults feel less afraid.

While little research has focused specifically on this issue, it should be clear from this chapter and Chapter 4 that these personal characteristics are often interconnected and work together to impact fear of crime. There are more examples but to highlight a few here, age is connected to gender in the sense that elderly men feel more vulnerable to victimization than younger men. Race and ethnicity are connected to social class in numerous ways, with minorities who are lower income fearing crime at higher levels than other groups. Age is connected to social class as well, with those young people living in poverty fearing crime at higher levels than their counterparts who live in different areas. The interconnection examples go on and on. What this means is that researchers must consider multiple factors that converge to induce fear of crime—e.g., people are not only a woman or only White or only lower class or only elderly (see Box 5.2 for recommendations for future research). Simply put, the causes of fear of crime are complex, and they go beyond the personal characteristics discussed in this chapter and Chapter 4, as the discussion of contextual factors in Chapter 6 illustrates.

Box 5.2 Recommendations for Future Research on Personal Characteristics Other than Gender

Age
- Continue to explore the impact of health on fear of crime, especially among the elderly
- Conduct more research to study the possible buffering effect of delinquent activity on fear of crime, despite increased actual and perceived risk of crime
- Focus on the impact of bullying and bullying prevention programs on fear of crime among elementary through high school students
- Study the effect of highly visible incidents, such as the Newtown, Connecticut school shootings, on fear among elementary through high school students
- Examine the causes and correlates of reduced fear of crime among the middle aged

Race and Ethnicity
- Conduct more studies that disaggregate samples by race and ethnicity
- Study all racial and ethnic groups, expanding beyond the traditional study of Whites and African-Americans
- Focus on immigrants, and include measures of language barriers and acculturation, which may impact fear
- Examine the differential importance of perceived risk for different racial and ethnic groups
- Compare the importance of race and ethnicity for fear of different offenses

Social Class/Income
- Continue to study the relative contributions of poverty combined with victimization experience, victimization risk, and other neighborhood conditions
- Examine the independent contributions of poverty, beyond neighborhood crime and living conditions, conducting quantitative and qualitative studies specifically focused on poverty as a critical predictor of fear
- Study the particular aspects of poverty that increase fear (e.g., financial stress, unemployment, and increased family disruption, fighting, or alcohol and drug abuse)

References

Acierno, R., Rheingold, A.A., Resnick, H.S., & Kilpatrick, D.G. (2004). Predictors of fear of crime in older adults. *Anxiety Disorders, 18,* 385–396.

Addington, L.A. (2003). Students' fear after Columbine: Findings from a randomized experiment. *Journal of Quantitative Criminology, 19,* 367–387.

Akers, R.L., La Greca, A.J., Sellers, C., & Cochran, J. (1987). Fear of crime and victimization among the elderly in different types of communities. *Criminology, 25,* 487–505.

Alvarez, A., & Bachman, R. (1997). Predicting the fear of assault at school and while going to and from school in an adolescent population. *Violence & Victims, 12*(1), 69–86.

Anderson, E. (1999). *Code of the street: Decency, violence, and the moral life of the inner city.* New York: W.W. Norton & Company.

Bailey, S.L., Flewelling, R.L., & Rosenbaum, D.P. (1997). Characteristics of students who bring weapons to school. *Journal of Adolescent Health, 20*(4), 261–270.

Baker, R.L., & Mednick, B.R. (1990). Protecting the high school environment as an island of safety: Correlates of student fear of in-school victimization. *Children's Environments Quarterly, 7*(3), 37–49.

Baldassare, M. (1986). The elderly and fear of crime. *Sociology and Social Research, 70*(3), 218–221.

Baumer, T.L. (1978). Research on fear of crime in the United States. *Victimology, 3,* 254–264.

Beaulieu, M., Dube, M., Bergeron, C., & Cousineau, M. (2007). Are elderly men worried about crime? *Journal of Aging Studies, 21*(4), 336–346.

Bowen, N.K., & Bowen, G.L. (1999). Effects of crime and violence in neighborhoods and schools on the school behavior and performance of adolescents. *Journal of Adolescent Research, 14*(3), 319–342.

Brown, B., & Benedict, W.R. (2004). Bullets, blades, and being afraid in hispanic high schools: An exploratory study of the presence of weapons and fear of weapon-associated victimization among high school students in a border town. *Crime & Delinquency, 50*(3), 372–394.

Chandola, T. (2001). The fear of crime and area differences in health. *Health & Place, 7*(2), 105–116.

Chiricos, T., Hogan, M., & Gertz, M. (1997). Racial composition of neighborhood and fear of crime. *Criminology, 35*(1), 107–131.

Chiricos, T., Padgett, K., & Gertz, M. (2000). Fear, tv news, and the reality of crime. *Criminology, 46*(3), 755–785.

Clemente, F., & Kleiman, M. (1977). Fear of crime in the United States: A multivariate analysis. *Social Forces, 56*(2), 519–531.

Copeland, W.E., Wolke, D., Angold, A., & Costello, E.J. (2013). Adult psychiatric outcomes of bullying and being bullied by peers in childhood and adolescence. *JAMA Psychiatry, 70*(4), 419–426.

Cossman, J.S., & Rader, N.E. (2011). Fear of crime and personal vulnerability: Examining self-reported health. *Sociological Spectrum, 31*(2), 141–162.

De Donder, L., Verte, D., & Messelis, E. (2005). Fear of crime and elderly people: Key factors that determine fear of crime among elderly people in West Flanders. *Ageing International, 30*(4), 363–376.

De Groof, S. (2008). And my mama said ... The (relative) parental influence on fear of crime among adolescent girls and boys. *Youth & Society, 39*(3), 267–293.

De Welde, K. (2003). White women beware!: Whiteness, fear of crime, and self-defense. *Race, Gender, & Class, 10*(4), 75–91.

DeLone, G.J. (2008). Public housing and the fear of crime. *Journal of Criminal Justice, 36*(2), 115–125.

Eitle, D., & Taylor, J. (2008). Are Hispanics the new threat? Minority group threat and fear of crime in Miami-Dade county. *Social Science Research, 37*(4), 1102–1115.

Everett, S.A., & Price, J.H. (1995). Student's perceptions of violence in public schools: The Metlife survey. *Journal of Adolescent Health, 17*(6), 345–352.

Fagan, J., Piper, E.S., & Cheng, Y. (1987). Contributions of victimization to delinquency in inner cities. *Journal of Criminal Law and Criminology, 78*(3), 586–613.

Ferguson, K.M., & Mindel, C.H. (2007). Modeling fear of crime in Dallas neighborhoods: A test of social capital theory. *Crime & Delinquency, 53*(2), 322–349.

Ferraro, K.F. (1995). *Fear of crime: Interpreting victimization risk.* New York, NY: SUNY Press.

Ferraro, K.F. (1996). Women's fear of victimization: Shadow of sexual assault? *Social Forces, 75*(2), 667–690.

Ferraro, K.F., & LaGrange, R.L. (1987). The measurement of fear of crime. *Sociological Inquiry, 57*(1), 70–101.

Ferraro, K.F., & LaGrange, R.L. (1988). Are older people afraid of crime? *Journal of Aging Studies, 2*(3), 277–287.

Ferraro, K.F., & LaGrange, R.L. (1992). Are older people most afraid of crime? Reconsidering age differences in fear of victimization. *The Journal of Gerontology, 47*(5), S233–S244.

Franklin, C.A., & Franklin, T.W. (2009). Predicting fear of crime: Considering differences across gender. *Feminist Criminology, 4*(1), 83–106.

Franklin, T.W., Franklin, C.A., & Fearn, N.E. (2008). A multilevel analysis of the vulnerability, disorder, and social integration models of fear of crime. *Social Justice Research, 21*(2), 204–227.

Gabriel, U., & Greve, W. (2003). The psychology of fear of crime: Conceptual and methodological perspectives. *British Journal of Criminology, 43*(3), 600–614.

Gainey, R., Alper, M., & Chappell, A.T. (2011). Fear of crime revisited: Examining the direct and indirect effects of disorder, risk perception, and social capital. *American Journal of Criminal Justice, 36*(2), 120–137.

Goodey, J. (1994). Fear of crime: What can children tell us? *International Review of Victimology, 3*(3), 195–210.

Goodey, J. (1997). Boys don't cry: Masculinities, fear of crime, and fearlessness. *British Journal of Criminology, 37*(3), 401–418.

Greve, W. (1998). Fear of crime among the elderly: Foresight, not fright. *International Review of Victimology, 5*(5), 277–309.

Hale, C. (1996). Fear of crime: A review of the literature. *International Review of Victimology, 4*(2), 79–150.

Harrell, E. (2007). *Black victims of violent crime.* Washington D.C.: Bureau of Justice Statistics.

Hollander, J.A. (2001). Vulnerability and dangerousness: The construction of gender through conversation about violence. *Gender & Society, 15*(1), 83–109.

Hughes, D., Rodriguez, J., Smith, E.P., Johnson, D.J., Stevenson, H.C., & Spicer, P. (2006). Parents' ethnic-racial socialization practices: A review of research and directions for future study. *Developmental Psychology, 42*(5), 747–770.

Irwin, K. (2004). The violence of adolescent life: Experiencing and managing everyday threats. *Youth & Society, 35*(4), 452–479.

Jeong, S. & Lee, B.H. (2013). A multilevel examination of peer victimization and bullying prevention in schools. *Journal of Criminology, 2013,* 1–10. Article ID 735397.

Katz, C.M., Webb, V.J., & Armstrong, T.A. (2003). Fear of gangs: A test of alternative theoretical models. *Justice Quarterly, 20*(1), 95–130.

Kaufman, J.M., Rebellon, C.J., Thaxton, S., & Agnew, R. (2008). A general strain theory of racial differences in criminal offending. *The Australian and New Zealand Journal of Criminology, 4*(3), 421–437.

Kennedy, H. (2010). Pheobe Prince, South Hadley High School's 'new girl' driven to suicide by teenage cyber bullies. *New York Daily News,* March 29. Retrieved from http://www.nydailynews.com/news/national/phoebe-prince-south-hadley-high-school-new-girl-driven-suicide-teenage-cyber-bullies-article-1.165911.

Killias, M., & Clerici, C. (2000). Different measures of vulnerability in their relation to different dimensions of fear of crime. *British Journal of Criminology, 40*(3), 437–450.

Krause, N. (Ed.). (2001). *Social support* (5th ed.). San Diego, CA: San Diego Academic Press.

LaGrange, R.L., & Ferraro, K.F. (1987). The elderly's fear of crime: A critical examination of the research. *Research on Aging, 9*(3), 372–391.

LaGrange, R.L., & Ferraro, K.F. (1989). Assessing age and gender differences in perceived risk and fear of crime. *Criminology, 27*(4), 697–719.

LaGrange, R.L., Ferraro, K.F., & Supancic, M. (1992). Perceived risk and fear of crime: Role of social and physical incivilities. *Journal of Research in Crime and Delinquency, 29*(3), 311–334.

Lane, J. (2002). Fear of gang crime: A qualitative examination of the four perspectives. *Journal of Research in Crime and Delinquency, 39*(4), 437–471.

Lane, J. (2006). Exploring fear of general and gang crimes among juveniles on probation: The impacts of delinquent behaviors. *Youth Violence and Juvenile Justice, 4*(1), 34–54.

Lane, J. (2009). Perceptions of neighborhood problems, fear of crime, and resulting behavioral precautions: Comparing institutionalized girls and boys in Florida. *Journal of Contemporary Criminal Justice, 25*(3), 264–281.

Lane, J., & Fox, K. (2012). Fear of crime among gang and non-gang offenders: Comparing the effects of perpetration, victimization, and neighborhood factors. *Justice Quarterly, 29*(4), 491–523.

Lane, J., & Fox, K. (2013). Fear of property, violent, and gang crime: Examining the shadow of sexual assault thesis among male and female offenders. *Criminal Justice and Behavior, 40*(5), 472–496.

Lane, J., & Kuhn, A.P. (2013). *In the shoes of George Zimmerman: The impact of promotion of mistrust, subcultral diversity and fear of crime on expected personal reactions.* Paper presented at the American Society of Criminology, Atlanta, GA.

Lane, J., & Meeker, J.W. (2000). Subcultural diversity and the fear of crime and gangs. *Crime & Delinquency, 46*(4), 497–521.

Lane, J., & Meeker, J.W. (2003a). Ethnicity, information sources, and fear of crime. *Deviant Behavior, 24*(1), 1–26.

Lane, J., & Meeker, J.W. (2003b). Fear of gang crime: A look at three theoretical models. *Law & Society Review, 37*(2), 425–456.

Lane, J., & Meeker, J.W. (2003c). Women's and men's fear of gang crimes: Sexual and nonsexual assault as perceptually contemporaneous offenses. *Justice Quarterly, 20*(2), 337–371.

Lane, J., & Meeker, J.W. (2004). Social disorganization perceptions, fear of gang crime, and behavioral precautions among Whites, Latinos, and Vietnamese. *Journal of Criminal Justice, 32*(1), 49–62.

Lane, J., & Meeker, J.W. (2011). Combining theoretical models of perceived risk and fear of gang crime among Whites and Latinos. *Victims and Offenders, 6*(1), 64–92.

Lauritsen, J.L., & Rezey, M.L. (2013). *Measuring the prevalence of crime with the National Crime Victimization Survey.* Washington D.C.: Bureau of Justice Statistics.

Lee, M.S., & Ulmer, J.T. (2000). Fear of crime among Korean Americans in Chicago communities. *Criminology, 38*(4), 1173–1206.

Lewis, D.A., & Salem, G. (1986). *Fear of crime: Incivility and the production of a social problem.* New Brunswick, NJ: Transaction Books.

Liska, A.E., Sanchirico, A., & Reed, M.D. (1988). Fear of crime and constrained behavior: Specifying and estimating a reciprocal effects model. *Social Forces, 66*(3), 827–837.

Liu, J., Messner, S.F., Zhang, L., & Zhuo, Y. (2009). Socio-demographic correlates of fear of crime and the social context of contemporary urban China. *American Journal of Community Psychology, 44*(1–2), 93–108.

Lowrey, R., Cohen, L.R., Modzeleski, W., Kann, L., Collins, J.L., & Kolbe, L.J. (1999). School violence, substance use, and availability of illegal drugs on school property among U.S. high school students. *Journal of School Health, 69*(9), 347–355.

Madriz, E.I. (1997). Images of criminals and victims: A study on women's fear and social control. *Gender & Society, 11*(3), 342–356.

Malek, M.K., Change, B.H., & Davis, T.C. (1998). Fighting and weapon-carrying among seventh-grade students in Massachusetts and Louisiana. *Journal of Adolescent Health, 23*(2), 94–102.

Martin, S.L., Sadowski, L.S., Cotten, N.U., & McCarraher, D.R. (1996). Response of African-American adolescents in North Carolina to gun carrying by schoolmates. *Journal of School Health, 66*(1), 23–26.

May, D.C. (2001a). *Adolescent fear of crime, perceptions of risk, and defensive behaviors: An alternative explanation of violent delinquency.* Lewiston, NY: Edwin Mellen.

May, D.C. (2001b). The effect of fear of sexual victimization on adolescent fear of crime. *Sociological Spectrum, 21*(2), 141–174.

May, D.C., & Dunaway, R.G. (2000). Predictors of fear of criminal victimization at school among adolescence. *Sociological Spectrum, 20*(2), 149–168.

May, D.C., Vartanian, L.R., & Virgo, K. (2002). The impact of parental attachment and supervision on fear of crime among adolescent males. *Adolescence, 37*(146), 267–287.

McCoy, H.V., Wooldredge, J.D., Cullen, F.T., Dubeck, P., & Browning, S.L. (1996). Lifestyles of the old and not so fearful: Life situation and older persons' fear of crime. *Journal of Criminal Justice, 24*(3), 191–205.

McKee, K.J., & Milner, C. (2000). Health, fear of crime and psychosocial functioning in older people. *Journal of Health Psychology, 5*(4), 473–486.

Melde, C. (2009). Lifestyle, rational choice, and adolescent fear: A test of a risk-assessment framework. *Criminology, 47*(3), 781–812.

Melde, C., Taylor, T.J., & Esbensen, F. (2009). 'I got your back': An examination of the protective function of gang membership in adolescence. *Criminology, 47*(2), 565–594.

Merry, S.E. (1981). *Urban danger: Life in a neighborhood of strangers.* Philadelphia, PA: Temple University Press.

Miller, J. (2001). *One of the guys: Girls, gangs, and gender.* New York: NY: Oxford University Press.

Moore, S., & Shepherd, J. (2007). The elements and prevalence of fear. *British Journal of Criminology, 47*(1), 154–162.

O'Bryant, S.L., & Donnermeyer, J.F. (1991). Fear of crime and perceived risk among older widowed women. *Journal of Community Psychology, 19*(2), 166–177.

Pain, R. (1997). Old age and ageism in urban research: The case of fear of crime. *International Journal of Urban and Regional Research, 21*(1), 117–128.

Pantazis, C. (2000). Fear of crime, vulnerability, and poverty. *British Journal of Criminology, 40*(3), 414–436.

Parker, K.D. (1988). Black-white differences in perceptions of fear of crime. *Journal of Social Psychology, 128*(4), 487–498.

Parker, K.D., McMorris, B.J., Smith, E., & Murty, K.S. (1993). Fear of crime and the likelihood of victimization: A bi-ethnic comparison. *Journal of Social Psychology, 133*(5), 723–732.

Parker, K.D., & Onyekwuluje, A.B. (1992). The influence of demographic and economic factors on fear of crime among African Americans. *The Western Journal of Black Studies, 16*(3), 132–140.

Parker, K.D., & Ray, M.C. (1990). Fear of crime: An assessment of related factors. *Sociological Spectrum, 10*(1), 29–40.

Rader, N.E., Cossman, J.S., & Porter, J.R. (2012). Fear of crime and vulnerability: Using a national sample to examine two competing paradigms. *Journal of Criminal Justice, 40*(2), 134–141.

Roncek, D.W. (2002). A comparative analysis of victimization, fear of crime, and social-order problems in elderly-only and mixed-population public housing. Washington D.C.: National Institute of Justice.

Ross, C.E. (1993). Fear of victimization and health. *Journal of Quantitative Criminology, 9*(2), 159–175.

Rountree, P.W. (1998). A reexamination of the crime-fear linkage. *Journal of Research in Crime and Delinquency, 35*(3), 341–372.

Rountree, P.W., & Land, K.C. (1996). Perceived risk versus fear of crime: Empirical evidence of conceptually distinct reactions in survey data. *Social Forces, 74*(4), 1353–1376.

Sampson, R.J., & Lauritsen, J.L. (1990). Deviant lifestyles, proximity to crime, and the offender-victim link in personal violence. *Journal of Research in Crime and Delinquency, 27*(2), 110–139.

Scarborough, B.K., Like-Haislip, T.Z., Novak, K.J., Lucas, W.L., & Alarid, L.F. (2010). Assessing the relationship between individual characteristics, neighborhood context, and fear of crime. *Journal of Criminal Justice, 38*(4), 819–826.

Schafer, J.A., Huebner, B.M., & Bynum, T.S. (2006). Fear of crime and criminal victimization: Gender-based contrasts. *Journal of Criminal Justice, 34*(3), 285–301.

Skogan, W.G. (1995). Crime and the racial fears of white Americans. *The Annals of the American Academy of Political and Social Science, 539*(1), 59–71.

Skogan, W.G., & Maxfield, M.G. (1981). *Coping with crime: Individual and neighborhood reactions.* Beverly Hills: CA: Sage.

Stafford, M., Chandola, T., & Marmot, M. (2007). Association between fear of crime and mental health and physical functioning. *American Journal of Public Health, 97*(11), 2076–2081.

Stanko, E.A. (1995). Women, crime, and fear. *Annals of the American Academy of Political and Social Science, 539*(1), 46–59.

Stiles, B.L., Halim, S., & Kaplan, H.B. (2003). Fear of crime among individuals with physical limitations. *Criminal Justice Review, 28*(2), 232–253.

St. John, C. & Heald-Moore, T. (1996). Racial prejudice and fear of criminal victimization by strangers in public settings. *Sociological Inquiry, 66,* 267–284.

Tulloch, M. (2000). The meaning of age differences in the fear of crime. *British Journal of Criminology, 40*(3), 451–467.

Vacha, E.F., & McLaughlin, T.F. (2000). The impact of poverty, fear of crime, and crime victimization on keeping firearms for protection and unsafe gun-storage practices: A review and analysis with policy recommendations. *Urban Education, 35*(4), 496–510.

Ward, R.A., LaGory, M., & Sherman, S.R. (1986). Fear of crime as person/environment interaction. *The Sociological Quarterly, 27*(3), 327–341.

Warr, M. (1984). Fear of victimization: Why are women and the elderly more afraid? *Social Science Quarterly, 65*(3), 681–702.

Warr, M. (1994). Public perceptions and reactions to violent offending and victimization. In A.J. Reiss, Jr. & J.A. Roth, (Eds.). *Understanding and preventing violence: Consequences and control,* Vol 4. pp. 1–66. Washington D.C.: National Academy Press.

Warr, M. (2000). Fear of crime in the United States: Avenues for research and policy. In D. Duffee (Ed.), *Measurement and Analysis of Crime and Jus-*

tice: Crime Justice (Vol. 4, pp. 451–490). Washington, D.C.: Department of Justice.

Webley, K. (2011). Teens who admitted to bullying Phoebe Prince sentenced. *Time.com* (May 5). Retrieved from http://newsfeed.time.com/2011/05/05/teens-who-admitted-to-bullying-phoebe-prince-sentenced/

Will, J.A., & McGrath, J.H. (1995). Crime, neighborhood perceptions, and the underclass: The relationship between fear of crime and class position. *Journal of Criminal Justice, 23*(2), 163–176.

Yin, P. (1980). Fear of crime among the elderly: Some issues and suggestions. *Social Problems, 27*(4), 492–504.

Yin, P. (1982). Fear of crime as a problem for the elderly. *Social Problems, 30*(2), 240–245.

Chapter 6

The Influence of Contextual Predictors on Fear of Crime: Personal Experience, Indirect Victimization, and Community

[A]ttitudes of citizens regarding crime ... derive [from] mass media reports about crime, "what people say," and the highly visible signs of what they regard as disorderly or disreputable behavior in their community—insobriety, untidiness, boisterousness.
Biderman, Johnson, McIntyre, & Weir, 1967, p. 160

[T]he danger of the city is at the heart the fear of strangers ... of unfamiliar cultural groups, of people who are not committed to the established urbanite's life style or social order, who express their antagonisms in part through crime.
Merry, 1981, p. 219

Think about the times when you have been afraid that something would happen to you—that someone might hurt you or steal your stuff. Why did you think that? Was it based on prior experiences in a particular area (for example, seeing police cars or an altercation on that block) or with particular people (such as troublemakers in your neighborhood or at school) or based on something you had heard about on television or from your friends (for example, news stories or rumors about crime)? Was it something around you—a visual indication (such as darkness or bars on house windows) or auditory cue (such as a loud noise or footsteps approaching)? Research shows that fear of crime is affected by one's life context, including personal experiences with crime, indirect victimization through friends, family and the media, neighborhood characteristics, and immediate situational cues that provoke a sense of danger. This chapter focuses on what we know about how these factors affect fear (See Box 6.1).

Box 6.1 Contextual Factors Related to Fear of Crime

Direct personal experience
  • Personal victimization
  • Witnessing victimization of others
  • Participating in crime
Indirect victimization (or experience)
  • Media influences—newspapers, television, radio, and the Internet
  • Personal influences—friends, family, and community police officers
Community-level cues
  • Subcultural diversity/racial heterogeneity
  • Disorder/incivilities
  • Community concern/decline
Immediate situational cues about possible danger

Before fear of crime research began in earnest in the late 1960s and 1970s, it seemed obvious to assume that people who were most at risk of (or most likely to face) criminal victimization (such as young males and people living in high crime areas) or people who were actually victimized would be most afraid of crime. Yet, research in the 1970s quickly showed that this assumption was erroneous and that explaining and predicting people's fear of crime was more complicated (see Garofalo, 1979). Early research foreshadowed the now consistent finding that women are more afraid, even though they face little comparative risk of being victimized by street crime compared to males (see Chapter 4). Early studies also found that the elderly (i.e., people over 60) were more afraid of crime than their victimization risk (or real likelihood of being victimized) would predict (Baumer, 1978). More recent findings with more valid measures of fear of crime, however, often show that younger people are more afraid (see Chapter 5; Ferraro, 1995, 1996; Keane, 1995; Lane & Meeker, 2003b; Warr, 1994). These early findings regarding gender and age, termed the "paradox of fear," led many researchers to focus more on life or community context rather than demographic factors alone to understand why people were afraid of crime (Warr, 1994, p. 12). Some of the factors that researchers have focused on include personal experiences with crime, indirect experiences with crime, and contextual factors and situational cues in the community or in the immediate surroundings.

Personal Experiences with Crime— Victimization, Observation, and Criminal Behavior

There are three types of direct personal experiences with crime that are relevant to understanding fear—personally experiencing a crime, witnessing another person being victimized, or participating in crime and therefore putting oneself at greater objective risk of victimization by others. Importantly, the likelihood of these types of experiences (or one's risk) varies by one's personal life situation and living context (e.g., what their family is like and the socioeconomic characteristics of the neighborhood they live or work in).

Personal Victimization

One factor that varies by one's environmental context is personal experience with criminal victimization. That is, people living in certain families and places are more likely to be victimized than others (Sampson & Groves, 1989; Pinchevsky & Wright, 2012). Personal victimization is relatively rare in the general population (Truman, 2011), but many studies of fear over the years have included a measure of personal victimization as a predictor of fear because it might increase or decrease fear depending on one's psychological or behavioral reactions to the experience. If the experience was very stressful or painful, it might increase fear if it leads to feelings of powerlessness or to worry about the psychological, life, or health consequences should it happen again. Someone might worry, for example, if he/she could live through a similar experience the next time. However, if victimization prompts someone to take behavioral precautions to protect him/herself (such as buying more locks for doors or avoiding certain areas), it may actually lead to less fear if he/she consequently feels more able to protect against the victimization happening again.

Empirical results have been mixed with regard to the importance of victimization in predicting fear. Some studies have found that being victimized, particularly by personal crime and especially rape, increases fear (e.g., Bachman, Randolph, & Brown, 2011; Ferguson & Mindel, 2007; Garofalo, 1979; Kanan & Pruitt, 2002; Katz, Webb, & Armstrong, 2003; Keane, 1995; Skogan, 1987; Skogan & Maxfield, 1981; Smith & Hill, 1991; Tyler, 1980; Wilcox, 1998), and others have found that it was not a significant predictor of fear (e.g., Ferraro, 1995). Even when victimization is a predictor, however, it is often not as strong a statistical predictor as other variables included in the model (see Agnew,

1985; DuBow et al., 1979; Tyler, 1980). Still other studies have indicated that although personal victimization does not directly predict fear, it has an indirect effect on fear because it increases one's perceived risk of victimization, which increases fear (Lane & Meeker, 2003a; Ferraro, 1995).

These mixed results over time with regard to the impact of personal victimization on fear of crime have led to different interpretations of their meaning. Some have argued that measurement issues mask results (such as measuring only recent victimization, only measuring presence of victimization but not the number of times, or using cross-sectional data that cannot take into account the temporal sequencing of events). Others argue that results would be different depending on whether the victimization was against property, which may not be so serious, or against a person, especially involving injury, which would induce more fear (DuBow, McCabe, & Kaplan, 1979; Skogan & Maxfield, 1981). Yet, Reiss (1982, p. 564) controversially argued that victimization did not affect fear of crime much because victims, even of serious crimes, often are not hurt and therefore consider the experience "inconsequential" (see Skogan, 1987). In contrast, Agnew (1985, p. 224) argued that victims may "neutralize" the impact of victimization, or convince themselves that the victimization was not hurtful, so that they can continue to live a normal life. He argued that victims sometimes compare themselves to others or to what might have happened or convince themselves that they have power to control future victimization experiences, that they are not to blame for the experience, that the offender will get caught and punished, or that they were victimized in pursuit of something important (like saving someone else).

Skogan and Maxfield (1981) asserted that controlling confounding factors (such as gender and age) allowed for the impact of victimization to be more apparent. Further, Skogan (1987) noted that the effects of victimization on fear may be immediate and may lessen over time. He found that people who had been more recently victimized were more likely to express crime worry and that they were more likely to take precautions to protect themselves from crime. Skogan also noted that people who were fearful before the victimization may become even more afraid after victimization occurs, or that some people are more primed to be psychologically impacted by victimization. Warr (1984) made a similar argument after he found that some people are more sensitive to their perceived risk (e.g., women and senior citizens), or that perceived risk creates more fear in some than others. Recently, researchers have not focused much of their efforts on specifically understanding and explaining the impact of personal victimization, because many of the studies have tried to determine other factors that might increase fear in people who have not been exposed to crime.

Witnessing Victimization of Others

One context that varies greatly across people is their environmental experience with crime—whether or not they have witnessed someone else be victimized in their family or neighborhoods (Salzinger, Feldman, Stockhammer, & Hood, 2002). It is easy to imagine instances in which an individual might view someone else being hurt and such a personal experience might affect the person's own fear of crime. For example, living in a neighborhood where people are regularly hurt through criminal behavior and/or gang activity or in a family where abuse on others (e.g., parents or siblings) occurs might increase fear of crime. Research shows that children living in disadvantaged neighborhoods see and hear more violence than those living in other areas (Gibson, Morris, & Beaver, 2009). As Jenkins and Bell (1997) noted, "many children, particularly those in urban areas, are exposed to considerable amounts of life-threatening violence in their homes and communities," and they often are close to the people they see victimized (p. 9; see also Martinez & Richters, 1993; Osofsky, 1999). In fact, Dubrow and Garbarino (1989) found in their study of public housing projects in Chicago that almost all of the children there had seen a shooting by the time they were five years old (see also Garbarino & Kostelny, 1997). Richters and Martinez (1993) found that 97% of older elementary school youths (5th and 6th grade) and 61% of younger ones (1st and 2nd grade) had reported seeing violence inflicted on others. Interestingly, Salzinger et al. (2002) reported that children in homes where interpersonal violence between family members occurred were also more likely to witness violence in their communities.

There has not been much research by fear of crime scholars focused specifically on this particular aspect of indirect victimization. In the late 1970s, DuBow et al. (1979, p. 20) observed "Anecdotal information is available that would indicate that under some circumstances witnessing a crime can be a powerful experience" but noted that the data and findings were not yet available to test this idea empirically. Over thirty years later, there are still no published studies that focus specifically on the impact of witnessing crime on others, either in the home or in the neighborhood, and its subsequent effects on fear of personal victimization. Yet, there are studies that speak to the impact of witnessing crime generally. Specifically, there is some psychological research focused on children who witness violence either in the home or on the streets, terming this "co-victimization" (e.g., Shakoor & Chalmers, 1991; Warner & Weist, 1996). Most studies focus on the effects of witnessing violence on psychological (e.g., post-traumatic stress disorder, depression, anxiety) and behavioral outcomes (e.g., aggressive behavior, sleep problems, poor academic performance) other than fear. A few studies mention that fear of being victimized is one result (see Jenkins & Bell, 1997; Margolin & Gordis, 2000; Osofsky, 1999; Warner & Weist, 1996, for a review). For example, Shakoor & Chalmers (1991) found that three-quarters of the teenage boys and about 10% of girls in their school and educational workshop sample had seen someone else shot, stabbed, robbed or killed. They argued that these experiences had multiple negative effects on the youths, including causing "persistent fear, anxiety, [and] lack of trust" (Shakoor & Chalmers, 1991, p. 236). A more recent large scale study of detained youth in Cook County (Chicago), Illinois found that witnessing violence was the most common trauma experienced by youth held there, with almost ¾ reporting that they had witnessed or heard someone get hurt badly or killed (Abram et al, 2013).

In their review, Warner & Weist (1996) found that depending on the study, a few to a majority of children report seeing domestic violence in the home. They also reported that a number of studies have shown that youth often report witnessing violence committed toward others in the community. Some of these studies present findings that lead to the conclusion that these experiences increase fear and consequently point to the importance of studying this topic. Specifically, Pynoos & Nader (1988) who reported on ten children who had seen their mothers sexually assaulted by strangers, noted that after the event most of the children wanted to stay physically close to their parents and were afraid to leave their homes. They indicated that the children "were hyper vigilant about personal safety and all became conscious about the security of their homes; checking the locks became a nightly ritual" (Pynoos & Nader, 1988, p. 570). A couple of the youths they studied kept weapons by their beds, many were afraid to be alone, and some thought they might be attacked at any time. Pynoos & Nader (1990) later reported that children who have witnessed violence, including suicides and murders, experienced fears of specific places, things or behaviors that reminded them of what happened and also expressed more general fear at times when they were alone.

Other researchers reported similar results. For example, Martinez & Richters (1993) found that kids who had seen guns and drugs in their home were more afraid both at school and at home. Another study published the same year reported that youths who had witnessed violence experienced more symptoms of stress, including fear for their own safety (Osofsky, Wewers, Hann, and Fick, 1993). Farrell and Bruce (1997), however, found that seeing community violence was unrelated to emotional issues for boys or girls, but they did not specifically measure effects on fear of crime. Still, Margolin and Gordis (2000) noted that many studies show that exposure to violence among children leads to a number of psychological issues, including anxiety (see also Jenkins & Bell, 1997). While the studies they reviewed did not focus specifically on the impact on fear of crime itself and none included adults, the consistent finding that witnessing violence leads to anxiety begs the question of whether or not this includes anxiety about one's safety from crime. It would seem logical that witnessing violence would increase fear of crime, and it provides an important avenue of fear research yet to be fully explored by criminologists and victimologists who specialize specifically in understanding crime-related fear.

Criminological studies sometimes discuss the effects of witnessing violence on fear but generally not as the primary focus of the study. For example, in her St. Louis study of young African-American men and women who were in trouble or at risk of being in trouble, Miller (2008) found that almost all of her respondents had seen people being hit or assaulted, and most had seen someone shot. About half had seen someone stabbed. Many had seen someone killed. She noted that many of her respondents thought their neighborhoods were not safe for anyone living there. Interestingly, she found that for girls the perceived danger was often sexual (supporting the shadow of sexual assault hypothesis, see Chapter 4), while for men the danger was related to gang and drug-related violence. Contrary to the arguments of feminist scholars that women's fear can be based on "hidden" victimization in the home (e.g., Stanko, 1985; Young, 1992), many of Miller's (2008) subjects reported seeing violence against women in public, rather than privately behind closed doors. Miller argued that the visibility of this danger to women especially heightened the girls' sense of awareness and vulnerability, while some felt they were not at risk because they defined some of the victims whom they witnessed as worthy of the negative treatment. Still many reported staying inside buildings or at home to avoid victimization. More recently, Nellis (2012) reported that juveniles sentenced to life in prison ("lifers") experienced an overwhelming amount of violence in their lives prior to going to prison. Over 70% reported seeing violence in their communities and about half said they saw it at least once a week. The majority indicated that they thought they were unsafe in their neighborhoods. The fear of crime literature, however, has basically ignored the direct effects of witnessing crime, especially violence, on perceived risk and personal fear of crime. There is much to learn about both the short-term and long-term effects of witnessing violence on fear of crime among both children and adults. For example, an interesting question that remains is whether or not the effect of witnessing crime on fear is only immediate, continues to increase over time or if children or adults in these circumstances get so used to it that they become less fearful over time.

Participating in Crime

Another way that one might experience crime is to be an offender and therefore know about what happens first hand, which could increase or decrease one's fear of crime. As with fear, one's likelihood of committing crime partly depends upon environmental context. For example, research indicates that people who live in neighborhoods with a lot of poverty, crime, and gangs are more likely to be involved in serious crime themselves, and in the United States, these people are more likely to be African-American or Hispanic (National Research Council and Institute of Medicine, 2001). It is also true that people who live in urban areas tend to be more afraid of crime than those living in more rural ones (Hindelang, Gottfredson, & Garofalo, 1978). Yet, there is not much research on fear of crime among offenders in high crime, urban areas. Studies of juvenile offenders have found that they were not very afraid of crime, except for serious crimes like being shot or murdered (Lane, 2006, 2009; see also May, 2001a), but Melde, Taylor, and Esbensen (2009) found that juvenile gang members were less afraid over time than non-gang youths were. Lane and Fox (2012) found that adult gang members felt more at risk of property, personal, and gang victimization than non-gang members but expressed less fear than those not in a gang. They also found that the number of crimes committed was unrelated to fear of crime.

The results so far seem counterintuitive because it is natural to expect that people who are involved in offending would be more afraid of crime. After all, their daily context includes increased risk of being victimized due to their participation in criminal behavior (e.g., Chen, 2009; Lauritsen, Sampson, & Laub, 1991; Sampson & Lauritsen, 1990). They likely know firsthand the risks that they face and know the real consequences of victimization, either at their own hands or at the hands of others. In addition, gang research often shows that one of the reasons people join gangs is for protection, which would indicate that they felt fear at least initially (e.g., Decker, 1996, Decker & Van Winkle, 1996; Klein, 1995; Melde et al., 2009; Padilla, 1992; Peterson et al., 2004), although some research shows that they do not necessarily express fear once they are in the gang (e.g., Lane & Fox, 2012; Melde et al., 2009). Still, Jankowski (1991) found that fear of victimization by rival gangs can prompt gang members to launch proactive attacks (see also Vigil, 1998), implying that gang members sometimes do express fear.

This offending and fear of crime relationship is complex and scholars do not yet have enough studies to make strong conclusions about the intricacies of fear for people who commit crime. Specifically, the research is very limited regarding whether or not offenders are afraid of crime, but most indicates that they do not fear crime as much as they theoretically should based on their high violent victimization risk. Yet, qualitative studies often show that people who commit crime express some fear or need for protection. Melde et al. (2009) argued that gang-involved youths may feel protected by their membership in the group. In other words, it may be that offenders generally feel more protected by their criminal knowledge and experience, their weapons, and their friends (see Cobbina et al., 2008; Lane & Fox, 2012), even though they may actually experience more objective risk of victimization due to their behavior and participation in these groups. In contrast, the public may express fear specifically because they have abstract images of people who might hurt them as culturally, racially and/or ethnically different from themselves but no first-hand victimization experience to counteract their mental images (Madriz, 1997; Merry, 1981). Still others argue that researchers might ask about fear in different ways, so that people who are embarrassed to admit fear might be more willing to share their concerns. For example, their preference to hang out with other gang members rather than alone or a belief that one needs to have a weapon all the time might really be an expression of fear, even if someone does not admit it (see Lane, 2013). The bottom line is that the scholarly and policy communities need much more research on the relationship between participation in crime and the effects on fear as contextualized by other factors such as personal and neighborhood characteristics.

Indirect Experiences with Crime — Media, Friends, Family, and Community Policing Officers

Because early studies on context were attempting to explain the results often showing that people with objective risk of victimization were more afraid (such as women and the elderly), there has been much more research on the effects of what has been termed "indirect victimization" than on actual personal experiences with crime. There are basically two ways one might be indirectly victimized by crime, other than witnessing it firsthand. First, one might hear about victimization of others through media sources, such as television, newspapers, radio, or the Internet. According to Warr (2000), the most common source of crime news for the public is the mass media, although it is clear that media reports contain much more violence than the "real" world (Fishman, 1978; Graber, 1980; Heath & Gilbert, 1996) and often sensationalize crime without discussing its context (Glassner, 1999). Second, one might hear about

crime from people he/she knows, such as family, friends, acquaintances, coworkers, or community policing officers. Tyler (1980, 1984) argued that this type
of communication was more fear inducing than crime stories by the media.
Debates continue about which matters more for inducing fear of crime, but more
studies have focused on the impact of media.

Newspapers and Television

Some studies have focused specifically on the impact of crime-related newspaper stories on fear, and these studies sometimes find that reading about crime
increases one's fear level. Heath (1984, p. 263) found that people who read newspapers that printed a lot of crime news were more likely to express fear if the reported crimes were "sensational" or "random," but they were less afraid if these
crime stories occurred far away geographically rather than near them. Liska and
Baccaglini (1990) likewise found that local crime stories increased fear of crime
but nonlocal stories decreased it. They noted that stories about murder were
more fear inducing than others, especially if they were in the first few pages of
the paper. Williams and Dickinson (1993) also found that people who read
newspapers that contained more salient crime reports expressed more fear of
crime. In contrast, Perkins and Taylor (1996) noted that stories about disorder
crimes increased fear but stories about serious crimes did not. Still, Koomen, Visser,
and Stapel (2000) found that the effect of a crime story on fear was dependent
upon the credibility of the newspaper. Yet other results showed that reading
newspapers was unrelated to fear of crime (Chiricos, Eschholz, and Gertz, 1997).[1]

Still other studies have reported that watching television news increases fear
of crime, but reading newspapers decreases it (O'Keefe & Reid-Nash, 1987)
or that television viewing matters while newspaper readership does not. For example, Lane & Meeker (2003a) showed that for Whites, relying on newspaper
for crime news had a negative indirect impact on fear of crime through perceived risk (meaning it decreased their fear), while relying on television as the
primary source had no impact on fear for Whites. In contrast, among Latinos, relying on newspapers for crime news had no effects on their fear levels,
but using television as a primary source of crime news had both a positive direct and indirect effect on fear of crime through perceived risk (meaning it in-

---

1. Grabe and Drew (2007) purported to measure the impact of different media sources
on fear of crime, but actually measured perceived likelihood of property and violent victimization, which fear researchers call "perceived risk." They found that frequency of reading newspapers had a stronger impact on perceived risk than television viewing did (cf.
Lane & Meeker, 2003a).

creased their fear). Weitzer and Kubrin (2004) later reported that people who listed the local news as their most important source of crime information were more afraid, and they were significantly more afraid than those who listed the national news or newspaper as their most important source. When they examined the effects for different racial groups, they found that focusing on local news was a significant predictor for African-Americans but not for Whites. In addition, they noted that people who lived in high crime areas and who focused on local news were more afraid of crime than others.

Some studies have focused specifically on the impact of television on fear of crime. The results show that the effect on fear depends on audience characteristics and type of programming (Chiricos, Padgett, & Gertz, 2000; Heath & Gilbert, 1996). One line of research in the 1970s assumed that watching a lot of television caused people to be afraid of crime, regardless of their personal characteristics, and this was called the "cultivation hypothesis" (Gerbner & Gross, 1976; Gerbner et al., 1977, 1978). Researchers soon set out to test these arguments under the assumption that personal characteristics should have an impact on how television viewing affects fear of crime. Many studies found that after controlling for personal characteristics, such as an individual's age, race, and sex, television viewing did not impact their fear of crime (e.g., Doob & Macdonald, 1979; Hirsch, 1981; Hughes, 1980; Potter, 1986; Reith, 1999; Sacco, 1982; Tyler, 1984; Wober, 1978). In response to these findings, Gerbner, Gross, Morgan, & Signorielli (1980) offered the resonance hypothesis, or the idea media impacts fear of crime more when the content fits well with the viewer's own experiences and circumstances. Consequently, they argued, those individuals at highest risk of victimization by crime (e.g., residents of high-crime neighborhoods, non-Whites, and individuals of lower socioeconomic status) will become even more fearful when viewing crime-related media. The counterargument to the resonance hypothesis is the substitution hypothesis (Adoni & Mane, 1984), or the idea that the media impact is stronger for people with lower rates of crime victimization (e.g., elderly, wealthy, and Whites).

Some studies did find that television viewing was correlated with fear, but only for certain people or certain areas (e.g., Chiricos et al., 1997, 2000; Gerbner et al., 1980; O'Keefe & Reid-Nash, 1987; Schlesinger, Tumber, & Murdock, 1991). For example, one study found that people who lived in high crime, urban areas and watched more television were more afraid (Doob & Macdonald, 1979). Another found that watching crime-related programming was related to crime fear when people did not learn about crime through other sources such as friends, family or personal experience (Weaver & Wakshlag, 1986). Chiricos et al. (1997) found that watching television news was correlated with fear of crime for White women and people who had been victimized.

Chiricos and his colleagues (2000) later reported that the frequency of watching local and national news was related to fear even after controlling for personal characteristics and perceived risk. When they examined fear based on ethnic group, they found that frequency of watching the local television news was related to fear for Whites and African-Americans (especially in high crime areas), but not Hispanics (unless they lived in low crime areas).

Eschholz, Chiricos, & Gertz (2003) also found that audience characteristics were very important in determining how different types of television viewing affected fear. For example, they found that for their whole sample, people who watched local news more often during the week and who watched crime drama and crime reality shows more often in a month were more afraid. But, when they did separate analyses for different demographic groups, they found the details of who was more afraid depended on which program they were watching more often. For example, younger people were more afraid if they watched more tabloid, reality or crime dramas, but this was not true for older people. Women who watched more tabloid shows, and men who watched more violent reality shows and crime dramas were more afraid. Those with higher incomes were more afraid if they watched more crime dramas. In contrast, those with lower incomes were more afraid for all types of shows measured *except* crime dramas. Also, Blacks and Whites who lived in areas with more Blacks were more afraid if they watched more crime-related television. Heath and Petraitis (1987) found that watching more television was related to fear of victimization in cities that were far away but not of one's own living environment. Interestingly, Eschholz (2002) showed that for Blacks, more time watching television was related to higher fear of crime levels; yet, for Whites the frequency of Black offenders in television programs mattered more than the amount of television they viewed.

In sum, the findings on the importance of media—television and newspapers—are inconsistent, but more recent research shows that the personal characteristics of the reader or watcher are relevant to how these sources impact fear of crime. Yet, there is not enough research on the causal order of media use and fear. It is possible that people watch more news because they are fearful. Although the Internet has been widely available to the public since the mid-1990s, there are not yet published studies on how use of the Internet to obtain crime news and stories specifically affects fear of crime. There is much to learn in this arena as more people in more households come into daily contact with the internet through personal, work and school computers. According to the Census Bureau, over three quarters of people have access to the Internet, so it is likely a major source of information about local, national, and international crime news yet its impact on fear of crime is virtually unknown (U.S. Census Bureau, 2009).

Friends, Family, and Community Police Officers

The other primary source of indirect victimization is learning about crime through family, friends, neighbors, coworkers, community police officers, and others. According to Skogan (1986, p. 211), "[p]eople make extensive use of information gathered secondhand through social networks" and people regularly talk to their neighbors about crime. Tyler also argued in the 1980s that social communication with others is the critical factor that increases fear of crime rather than media reports (Tyler, 1980, 1984). The idea is that more local social ties (e.g., knowing one's neighbors) or social integration may increase fear of crime through discussions of crime going on in the area as well as people sharing their personal experiences with crime (Skogan & Maxfield, 1981).

There has been some empirical support for this argument, although there is less research on this specifically. Skogan and Maxfield (1981) found, for example, that when people feel there is serious crime in their neighborhood, they are more likely to talk to their neighbors about crime, especially when they have strong social ties in their communities. Taylor and Hale (1986) examined the effect of social networks on fear, and found that they were not a significant predictor of fear per se but did influence worry about crime. Covington and Taylor (1991) later found that in neighborhoods where people heard about more neighborhood burglaries, fear was higher and that people who heard about them were more afraid. Lane (2002) also found that people were afraid of gangs, in part, because they heard about crime in the area through friends, neighbors and community police officers. Her respondents said they heard through "word of mouth" or "neighborhood news," and people in the middle- and upper-income neighborhoods said that reports by community police officers were critical sources for them to understand crime in their neighborhoods (Lane, 2002, p. 459). In line with this idea, recent research has found that perceived neighborhood collective efficacy (or close enough cohesion among people living in the area that they are also willing to step in to make a difference if necessary) is associated with more fear of crime, not less (Lane & Fox, 2012; Roman & Chalfin, 2008; Sampson, Raudenbush, & Earls, 1997; Thomas, 2007). Yet, some research indicates that social integration does not matter (Kanan & Pruitt, 2002), meaning there is more that scholars and policymakers need to know on this topic to unpack this relationship.

A few studies have noted that more broadly shared but unsubstantiated rumors about crime may prompt fear. For example, Best and Hutchinson (1996) discussed the spreading of urban legends regarding gangs driving around in motor vehicles without their headlights on and then shooting the person who warned them, or the "lights out" urban legend (see Donovan, 2004). Other urban legends that might affect fear of crime include children being stolen from malls and body parts being sold on the black market (Donovan, 2004) and the old rumor that at Halloween, some people put razor blades in apples and other contaminants in candy when they hand these goodies out to children (see Best & Horiuchi, 1985). Urban legends like these might be spread by the media or by friends through emails or social media. Yet, fear of crime researchers have yet to specifically examine how many of these urban legends people hear or read about (or whether they ignore them), how much they believe them, or how much these rumors affect fear or resulting behavioral precautions. For example, do people check all their children's Halloween loot before allowing them to eat or do they not flash headlights at people who are driving with them off because they are afraid of victimization?

The research on the specific impact of community policing on fear of crime has also been inconsistent. Some studies have found that community policing and related strategies (e.g., foot patrol) reduce fear of crime (e.g., Dammert & Malone, 2006; Kelling et al., 1981; Moore, 1992; Pate et al., 1986; Roh & Oliver, 2005; Xu, Fiedler, & Flaming, 2005; Weisburd & Eck, 2004; Zhao et al., 2002), and others have found that they increase it (e.g., Hinkle & Weisburd, 2008; Lane, 2002) or do not affect fear (e.g., Roh, Kwak, & Kim, 2013; Scheider, Rowell, & Bezdikian, 2003). Unfortunately, the studies do not lead scholars to a definitive conclusion about the ways that police officers who have close interaction with the communities affect residents (e.g., studies have yet to consider what information is shared or how crime information affects neighborhood fear). These studies also do not provide strong indications of how community policing might affect fear depending on an individual's age, race and ethnicity, gender, type of community they reside in, etc. That is, there are many unanswered questions, and scholars have a lot to learn.

Community-Level Cues That Crime May Be Near — Subcultural Diversity, Disorder, and Community Decline

Research has generally shown throughout time that people who are poor and who live in urban areas are more afraid than others, and they are also generally at greater risk of being victimized by crime (Hindelang, Gottfredson, & Garofalo, 1978; Keane, 1987; Like, 2011; Skogan, 1987). Yet, as noted above, the research on personal characteristics in the 1970s indicated that women and the elderly were more afraid, despite their lower victimization risk compared to males and younger residents. Findings such as these led to calls for better fear of crime measures (e.g., Ferraro & LaGrange, 1988; LaGrange & Ferraro, 1987, 1989; see Chapter 3) and parallel attempts to theorize about why victimization risk did not neatly match up with fear. There are three micro-level theoretical models focused on environmental characteristics that might prompt people to be more afraid than they should be based on actual crime rates and victimization risk: subcultural diversity (also called racial heterogeneity), disorder (also called incivilities) and community concern (also called decline).

Social Disorganization Framework

The social disorganization framework has been the key theoretical perspective used to develop micro-level ideas designed to understand how neighborhood characteristics and environmental living conditions can affect individuals' fear of crime. Early social disorganization theorists (e.g., Shaw & McKay, 1972 [1942]) found that low-income neighborhoods also experienced frequent residential turnover and racial diversity which decreased their ability to maintain social control and stop crime, which in turn contributed to increasing crime rates compared to other areas (Bursik, 1988). Fear of crime researchers have focused on the symbols of social disorganization in the community that lead people to fear that crime is a problem in their communities, even when they may not directly observe criminal behavior (Taylor & Covington, 1993). Although concerns about diversity, disorder, and decline can all happen at once, most of the studies have treated them as distinct concepts and so each will be discussed here individually and in terms of the theoretical and empirical connections among them.

Subcultural Diversity/Racial Heterogeneity

The idea behind the subcultural diversity model is that people who live in areas without close friendship networks will be more afraid of strangers who are racially, ethnically, and/or culturally different from themselves (Merry, 1981; see also Bursik & Grasmick, 1993; Covington & Taylor, 1991: Skogan, 1995). Merry (1981) found in her ethnographic study of a housing project that residents were unable to interpret the mannerisms and behaviors of people who looked and acted differently than they did and had trouble believing that people who were different shared their own values and concern about the community. So, for example, if people do not act and dress the same way, meaning they do not accept "our" way of life, they appear to be dangerous (Lewis & Salem, 1986). For example, Madriz (1997) found that people often hold stereotypes of immigrants and minorities as dangerous, which led to fear among both White and minority women. Quantitative studies have supported these ideas, finding that the racial composition of the area matters (Liska, Lawrence, & Sanchirico, 1982), especially for Whites (Chiricos, Hogan, & Gertz, 1997). In addition, living in a predominately Black neighborhood or perceiving one's self as racially different than the bulk of the neighborhood leads to more fear (Covington & Taylor, 1991). Studies have shown that concern about diversity predicts fear of crime generally and fear of specific perpetrators, e.g., gangs. Diversity concerns can directly affect fear or can affect other concerns about the neighborhood like worries about disorder or community decline which then induce fear (Katz, Webb, & Armstrong, 2003; Lane, 2002; Lane & Meeker, 2000, 2003b, 2005, 2011).

Disorder/Incivilities

The second of the theoretical models focusing on perceptions of environmental context concentrates on people's vision of the community as disordered or characterized by social or physical incivilities. Social incivilities include the perceived presence of homeless people, prostitutes, drug users, gangs, and kids hanging out in the neighborhood. Physical incivilities include the perceived presence of problems like bars on windows, graffiti, trash, rundown or abandoned buildings, disheveled yards, etc. (Skogan, 1990). The model posits that people who see these characteristics in their neighborhoods believe that they signal deeper, fundamental issues in the area, thereby making them feel more vulnerable and more afraid of crime (Lewis & Salem, 1986; Skogan, 1990; Taylor, 2001). Interestingly, much of the research shows that it is not the actual presence of these issues but the perceptions that they exist that matters most in predicting fear of crime generally (e.g., Brunton-Smith & Sturgis, 2011; Ferguson & Mindel, 2007; LaGrange et al., 1992; Lewis & Maxfield, 1980; Robinson et al., 2003; Scarborough et al., 2010; Skogan & Maxfield, 1981; Taylor, 2001; cf. Perkins & Taylor, 1996; Wyant, 2008) and fear of gangs (Katz et al., 2003; Lane & Meeker, 2003b, 2005, 2011). One study found not only that perceptions of disorder increased fear, but people who thought incivilities were getting worse became more afraid (Robinson et al., 2003). Yet, Carvalho and Lewis (2003, p. 791) found that most people in poor neighborhoods reacted to disorder and crime in the reverse way, by feeling safe because they "contextualized" them and they were "ordinary" or easy to attach to certain places or people. These authors argued that "[l]ocal problems become part of the neighborhood routine and of one's life, losing, at the same time, their potential to scare" (Carvalho & Lewis, 2003, p. 792). Still, those that did feel fear indicated that disorder mattered a lot. Wyant (2008) found that people who saw more disorder were more afraid, but he also found that people in some neighborhoods felt more at risk and people in those neighborhoods were more afraid (see Box 6.2 for a real world case in which contextual factors were relevant).

Box 6.2 Case Focus
George Zimmerman and Trayvon Martin Case,
Sanford, Florida, February 2012

On February 26, 2012, George Zimmerman, a 28-year-old Hispanic neighborhood watch member, shot and killed unarmed Trayvon Martin, a 17-year-old African-American teen who was walking to a family friend's home in the rain with his sweatshirt hood over his head after going to a 7-Eleven to buy a drink and candy. Zimmerman called police, saying to the dispatcher that he was "suspicious" and "up to no good." The dispatcher told Zimmerman not to follow Martin because police were on the way, but he did. There was a scuffle, Martin was shot in the chest, and Zimmerman claimed self-defense when the police arrived (Botelho, 2012). After this incident, there was much debate in the media, among commentators, and among the public about what really happened, whether Zimmerman really was defending himself, and whether he was racially profiling Martin as a criminal because he was Black (Kuhn and Lane, 2013). The discussion about this case continued with renewed vigor and protests erupted across the country after Zimmerman was acquitted of second-degree murder in July 2013 (Fallout over Zimmerman Verdict Continues, 2013).

The Trayvon Martin case is a real-world example of the how contextual factors can converge to cause fear of crime and affect subsequent behavioral reactions. The neighborhood itself was diverse—about 50% White, 20% Black, and 20% Hispanic—home values had been decreasing significantly, and more renters had moved to the area. There had been eight home burglaries over the previous year in Zimmerman's neighborhood, and people believed the burglars were Black. Interviewed residents indicated that there had been many other reports of attempted break-ins, and fear in the neighborhood had increased (Francescani, 2012). Recall that the subcultural diversity/racial heterogeneity model argues that in areas where people do not have close friendships, people will be afraid of others who are racially and ethnically different than themselves. Zimmerman was Hispanic and Martin was black, and Zimmerman immediately categorized Martin as "suspicious." The diversity model also argues that when people dress differently (Martin was wearing a "hoody" sweatshirt) and have different mannerisms (Martin was described by Zimmerman as "on drugs or something" and "just walking around") (Botelho, 2012), community residents have difficulty understanding them and worry that the others do not share their own values and concern about the community. Zimmerman told the dispatcher that "they always get away" (The Washington Post, 2012). His use of "they" implies that he considered Martin one of these "others" who were different from himself, and in the context of recent burglaries with black suspects, it may help explain why he was suspicious of Martin and why he followed him. This case also apparently happened in the context of heightened indirect victimization by neighborhood residents sharing stories of people casing the area and attempting other burglaries, which theory indicates increases fear among residents (Francescani, 2012). Moreover, this situation happened in Florida, where a broad Stand Your Ground law allows people to shoot others when they feel threatened with serious harm, without requiring them to try get away if they can (i.e., retreat) (Fla. Stat. §776.013).

Thought/Discussion Questions:
1. In this context, how do you think you would have reacted if in Zimmerman's shoes?
2. Would you have been afraid?
3. Would you have been suspicious of Martin?
4. Would you have followed him?
5. If you had, and a confrontation had ensued, would you have considered pulling and/or shooting a gun?
6. Do you think Zimmerman was justified in his behavior?
7. Do you think he should have been convicted of second-degree murder?
8. If you had been in Martin's shoes, how might you have reacted when Zimmerman started treating you as suspicious or when he started following you?

Community Concern/Decline

The community concern/decline model was first articulated in the 1970s, when scholars discussed the possibility that fear of crime was specifically an expression of concern over community decay (Conklin, 1975; Garofalo & Laub, 1978) or what some have more recently called "community decline" (Lane, 2002; Lane & Meeker, 2005). As with the subcultural diversity model, the belief is that concern about community decline heightens when people are not connected with others in their communities (see Hunter & Baumer, 1982). There are few studies that examine the community concern model alone, because many see it as a feeling resulting from concerns about disorder (e.g., Garofalo & Laub, 1978; Skogan, 1990; Skogan & Maxfield, 1981; Taylor & Hale, 1986). However, findings indicate that in areas where people believe the neighbors would call the police if they saw problematic activity, fear of crime is lower (Covington & Taylor, 1991). And, studies have found that community concern was a direct predictor of fear of gangs (Lane & Meeker, 2003b, 2005, 2011).

The Connections between the Environmental Context Models

Although each of the models posit a different focus and discuss distinct constructs related to perceptions of the environmental context, scholars have examined the connections among them as a way to better understand the thought process that leads people to fear crime. For example, researchers have long believed that community concern often results from concern about disorder (e.g., Garofalo & Laub, 1978; Skogan, 1990; Skogan & Maxfield, 1981).

That is, when people see disorder in their neighborhoods, they believe their community is declining, which leads them to fear crime more. Taylor and Hale (1986) tested the disorder only model and then compared it to the disorder plus decline model. They found that when community concern was in the model predicting fear, the significant impact of disorder was only indirect through community concern, although its direct impact on worry remained. Lane and Meeker (2003b) later tested the disorder model and community concern model separately and then the disorder plus decline model on fear of gang crime, finding that the multi-model analysis was more predictive of fear. What these results showed was that the connections between the theoretical concepts were important to predicting fear of crime. They later found that disorder led to concerns about decline among Whites, but for Latinos this relationship did not hold, possibly because the Latinos had not lived in the same neighborhoods long enough to see it decline (Lane & Meeker, 2005). Lane (2002) found in her qualitative research that concerns about ethnic and cultural differences (especially undocumented immigrants) led people to worry about increasing disorder in their neighborhoods leading them to believe the neighborhood was declining, and increasing their fear of gang crime. Indirect victimization through conversations with neighbors and community policing officers fueled these beliefs, as did direct observation over time. Lane and Meeker (2011) later tested these theoretical connections in a larger data set, finding that concerns about diversity predicted concerns about disorder and then decline which predicted perceived risk and then fear of gang crime for both Whites and Latinos. Disorder also had a direct, positive effect on perceived risk for both groups, meaning that it had an impact on fear by affecting people's perceived risk.

Wilson and Kelling (1982) in an early famous article argued that disorder issues that are not corrected increase the likelihood of more problems related to disorder because people see it as a sign that the community does not care. From this point of view, as disorder increases, more fear and isolation occur among residents, which eventually leads to more crime because people stay inside and offenders come to believe that they can do what they want. That is, fear of crime not only affects the quality of life of the person who is afraid, but it also can reduce the neighborhood's ability to overcome its problems.

Immediate Situational Cues That Crime May Occur

Another approach to thinking about how environmental context can affect fear is to consider the effect of immediate situational cues. Over thirty years ago, Garofalo (1981, p. 841) noted that "actual fear of crime is triggered by some cue," while "anticipated fear" is something that people *think* would happen in specific types of situations. Specific contexts that provoke fear include being in a new or dark area (in areas with little lighting or out at night), where there are areas for potential offenders to hide (e.g., behind buildings, in alleys, or in foliage), and when they feel they could not easily escape if they were threatened (Fisher & Nasar, 1992a, 1992b; Warr, 1990). Being alone heightens fear in these situations (Day, 1999; Fisher & Nasar, 1992; Nasar & Jones, 1997). For example, in one study, women noted that they avoided alleys, tunnels, some stairways, narrow walkways, and parking lots (Day, 1999). These types of areas have been called "fear spots" (see Fisher & Nasar, 1995). Studies have found that although these effects happen for both men and women, women often express more fear in these situations (e.g., Fisher, Sloan, & Wilkins, 1995), confirming most research that finds that women are more afraid than men (see Chapter 4).

Concluding Remarks

This chapter has provided a summary of the research to date on how context affects fear of crime. It has discussed (1) personal experience with crime, including personal victimization, witnessing victimization of others and participating in criminal behavior; (2) indirect experience with crime, including impacts of media, friends and family, and community policing officers; (3) community-level cues that signal crime might near, including factors related to social disorganization (subcultural diversity/racial heterogeneity, disorder/incivilities, and community concern/decline); and the immediate situational cues that might provoke fear, including things like darkness, places for offenders to hide, being alone, and feeling that there are few escape options. There has been much learned from the research conducted over the last three or more decades, but there are many issues related to context that still need to be explored. Box 6.3 provides directions for future research.

**Box 6.3 Recommendations for Future Research:
Some Key Unanswered Questions on Context**

1. **Effects of Witnessing Crime.**
   - On different groups of people
     - e.g., older adults versus young adults versus children, women versus men, whites versus other racial and ethnic groups, people in urban versus rural areas
   - Of witnessing different types of violence
     - e.g., a fight versus murder versus domestic abuse
   - Of witnessing one violent event versus sustained exposure over time
     - e.g., in a violent neighborhood or home
   - Of witnessing crimes other than violence
     - e.g., drug dealing, weapon carrying, or property crime

2. **Effects of Witnessing Crime Events on Television (or via Internet feed).**
   - Of watching a real crime event (sometimes played over and over)
     - e.g., the 9/11 planes flying into the World Trade Center in September 2001 or the Boston Marathon bombing in April 2013
   - Of just hearing about a story on the television news versus seeing the actual events on television (or Internet replay)
   - Of seeing events that happen far away versus near, in the context of continual replay

3. **The Impact of the Internet on Fear of Crime.**
   - Of the wide availability (Pew, 2012) and use of the Internet for crime news
   - Of access to papers and other news sources that one might not normally see

4. **Effects of Context on Fear of Specific Perpetrators.**
   - Are people more afraid of strangers, gangs or terrorism when they are in particular places (like certain neighborhoods or large urban areas or on airplanes)
   - Are people more afraid of people they know when they are in specific contexts (e.g., when the other has been drinking or when they are in private rather than public?

References

Abram, K.M., Teplin, L.A., King, D.C., Longworth, S.L., Emanuel, K.M., Romero, E.G., McClelland, G.M., Dulcan, M.K., Washburn, J.J., Welty, L.J., & Olson, N.D. (2013). *PTSD, Trauma, and Comorbid Psychiatric Disorders in Detained Youth*. Washington D.C.: Office of Juvenile Justice and Delinquency Prevention.

Adoni, H., & Mane, S. (1984). Media and the social construction of reality: Toward an integration of theory and research. *Communication Research, 11* (3), 323–340.

Agnew, R.S. (1985). Neutralizing the impact of crime. *Criminal Justice and Behavior, 12*(2), 221–239.

Bachman, R., Randolph, A., & Brown, B.L. (2011). Predicting perceptions of fear at school and going to and from school for African American and White students: The effects of school security measures. *Youth & Society, 43*(2), 705–726.

Baumer, T.L. (1978). Research on fear of crime in the United States. *Victimology: An International Journal, 3,* 254–264.

Best, J., & Horiuchi, G.T. (1985). The razor blade in the apple: The social construction of urban legends. *Social Problems, 32*(5), 488–499.

Best, J., & Hutchinson, M.M. (1996). The gang initiation rite as a motif of contemporary crime discourse. *Justice Quarterly, 13*(3), 383–404.

Biderman, A.D., Johnson, L.A., McIntyre, J., & Weir, A.W. (1967). *Report on a Pilot Study in the District of Columbia on Victimization and Attitudes toward Law Enforcement.* Retrieved from https://www.ncjrs.gov/pdf-files1/Digitization/737NCJRS.pdf.

Black, D. (1983). Crime as social control. *American Sociological Review, 48*(1), 34–45.

Boggs, S.L. (1971). Formal and informal crime control: An exploratory study of urban, suburban, and rural orientations. *Sociological Quarterly, 12*(3), 319–327.

Botelho, G. (2012). What happened the night Trayvon Martin died. (May 23). Accessed August 7, 2013. http://www.cnn.com/2012/05/18/justice/florida-teen-shooting-details.

Brunton-Smith, I., & Sturgis, P. (2011). Do neighborhoods generate fear of crime? An empirical test using the British crime survey. *Criminology, 49*(2), 331–369.

Bursik, R.J., Jr. (1988). Social disorganization and theories of crime and delinquency: Problems and prospects. *Criminology, 26*(4), 519–551.

Bursik, R.J., Jr., & Grasmick, H.G. (1993). *Neighborhoods and Crime: The Dimensions of Effective Community Control.* New York: Lexington Books.

Carvalho, I., & Lewis, D.A. (2003). Beyond community: Reactions to crime and disorder among inner-city residents. *Criminology, 41*(3), 779–812.

Chen, X. (2009). The link between juvenile offending and victimization: The influence of risky lifestyles, social bonding, and individual characteristics. *Youth Violence and Juvenile Justice, 7*(2), 119–135.

Chiricos, T., Eschholz, S., & Gertz, M. (1997). Crime, news, and fear of crime: Toward an identification of audience effects. *Social Problems, 44*(3), 342–357.

Chiricos, T., Hogan, M., & Gertz, M. (1997). Racial composition of neighborhood and fear of crime. *Criminology, 35*(1), 107–131.

Chiricos, T., Padgett, K., & Gertz, M. (2000). Fear, TV news, and the reality of crime. *Criminology, 38*(3), 755–785.

CNN. (2013). Fallout over Zimmerman Verdict Continues. Accessed August 7, 2013. Available at: http://earlystart.blogs.cnn.com/2013/07/18/fallout-over-zimmerman-verdict-continues/?iref=allsearch.

Cobbina, J.E., Miller, J., & Brunson, R.K. (2008). Gender, neighborhood danger, and risk-avoidance strategies among urban African-American youths. *Criminology, 46*(3), 673–709.

Conklin, J. (1975). *The impact of crime.* New York: Macmillan.

Covington, J., & Taylor, R.B. (1991). Fear of crime in urban residential neighborhoods: Implications of between- and within-neighborhood sources for current models. *The Sociological Quarterly, 32*(3), 231–249.

Dammert, L., & Malone, M.F.T. (2006). Does it take a village? Policing strategies and fear of crime in Latin America. *Latin American Politics and Society, 48*(4), 27–51.

Day, K. (1999). Strangers in the night: Women's fear of sexual assault on urban college campuses. *Journal of Architectural and Planning Research, 16(4),* 289–312.

Decker, S.H. (1996). Collective and normative features of gang violence. *Justice Quarterly, 13*(2), 243–264.

Decker, S.H., & Van Winkle, B. (1996). *Life in the gang: Family, friends and violence.* New York: Cambridge University Press.

Doob, A.N., & Macdonald, G.E. (1979). Television viewing and fear of victimization: Is the relationship causal? *Journal of Personality and Social Psychology, 37*(2), 170–179.

Donovan, P. (2004). *No way of knowing: Crime, urban legends, and the internet.* New York: Routledge.

DuBow, F., McCabe, E., and Kaplan, G. (1979). *Reactions to crime: A critical review of the literature.* Washington D.C.: Law Enforcement Assistance Administration.

DuBrow, N.F., & Garbarino, J. (1980). Living in the war zone: Mothers and young children in a public housing development. *Child Welfare, 68*(1), 3–20.

Eschholz, S. (2002). Racial composition of television offenders and viewers' fear of crime. *Critical Criminology, 11*(1), 41–60.

Eschholz, S., Chiricos, T., & Gertz, M. (2003). Television and fear of crime: Program types, audience traits, and the mediating effect of perceived neighborhood racial composition. *Social Problems, 50*(3), 395–415.

Farrell, A.D., & Bruce, S.K. (1997). Impact of exposure to community violence on violent behavior and emotional distress among urban adolescents. *Journal of Clinical Child Psychology, 26*(1), 2–14.

Ferguson, K.M., & Mindel, C.H. (2007). Modeling fear of crime in Dallas neighborhoods: A test of social capital theory. *Crime & Delinquency, 53*(2), 322–349.

Ferraro, K.F. (1995). *Fear of crime: Interpreting victimization risk.* New York: State University of New York Press.

Ferraro, K.F. (1996). Women's fear of victimization: Shadow of sexual assault? *Social Forces, 75,* 667-690.

Ferraro, K.F., & LaGrange, R.L. (1988). Are older people afraid of crime? *Journal of Aging Studies, 2*(3), 277–287.

Ferraro, K.F., & LaGrange, R.L. (1987). The measurement of fear of crime. *Sociological Inquiry, 57*(1), 70–101.

Fisher, B., & Nasar, J.L. (1992a). Fear of crime in relation to three exterior site features: Prospect, refuge and escape. *Environment & Behavior, 24*(1), 35–65.

_____. (1992b). Students' fear of crime and its relation to physical features of the campus. *Journal of Security Administration, 15*(2), 65–75.

_____. (1995). Fear spots in relation to microlevel physical cues: Exploring the overlooked. *Journal of Research in Crime and Delinquency, 32*(2), 214–239.

Fisher, B.S., Sloan, J.J., & Wilkins, D.L. (1995). Fear of crime and perceived risk of victimization on an urban university campus: A test of multiple models. pp. 179–209 in B.S. Fisher & J.J. Sloan (Eds.). *Campus Crime: Legal, Social and Policy Perspectives.* Springfield, IL: Charles C. Thomas.

Fishman, M. (1978). Crime waves as ideology. *Social Problems, 25*(5), 531–543.

Fla. Stat. §776.013 (2012).

Francescani, C. (2012). George Zimmerman: Prelude to a shooting. *Reuters* (April 25). Accessed August 7, 2013. Available at: http://www.reuters.com/article/2012/04/25/us-usa-florida-shooting-zimmerman-idUSBRE83O18H20120425.

Garbarino, J. & Kostelny, K. (1997). What children can tell us about living in a war zone. In J.D. Osofsky (Ed.), *Children in a Violent Society,* pp. 32–41. New York: The Guilford Press.

Garofalo, J. (1979). Victimization and the fear of crime. *Journal of Research in Crime and Delinquency, 16*(1), 80–97.

Garofalo, J. (1981). The fear of crime: Causes and consequences. *The Journal of Criminal Law and Criminology, 72*(2), 839–857.

Garofalo, J., & Laub, J. (1978). The fear of crime: Broadening our perspective. *Victimology, 3*(3–4), 242–253.

Gerbner, G., & Gross, L. (1976). Living with television: The violence profile. *Journal of Communication, 26*(2), 172–194.

Gerbner, G., Gross, L., Elcey, M.F., Jackson-Beeck, M., Jeffries-Fox, S., & Signorielli, N. (1977). TV violence profile no. 8: The highlights. *Journal of Communication, 27*(2), 171–180.

Gerbner, G., Gross, L., Jackson-Beeck, M., Jeffries-Fox, S., & Signorielli, N. (1978). Cultural indicators: Violence profile no. 9. *Journal of Communication, 28*(3), 176–207.

Gerbner, G., Gross, L., Morgan, M., & Signorielli, N. (1980). The "mainstreaming" of America: Violence profile no. 11. *Journal of Communication, 30*(3), 10–29.

Gibson, C.L., Morris, S.Z., & Beaver, K.M. (2009). Secondary exposure to violence during childhood and adolescence: Does neighborhood context matter? *Justice Quarterly, 26*(1), 30–57.

Glassner, B. (1999). *The culture of fear: Why Americans are afraid of the wrong things.* New York: Basic Books.

Grabe, M.E. & Drew, D.G. (2007). Crime cultivation: Comparisons across media genres and channels. *Journal of Broadcasting & Electronic Media, 51*(1), 147–171.

Graber, D.A. (1980). *Crime news and the public.* New York: Praeger.

Heath, L. (1984). Impact of newspaper crime reports on fear of crime: Multimethodological investigation. *Journal of Personality and Social Psychology, 47*(2), 263–276.

Heath, L., & Gilbert, K. (1996). Mass media and fear of crime. *American Behavioral Scientist, 39*(4), 379–386.

Heath, L., & Petraitis, J. (1987). Television viewing and fear of crime: Where is the mean world? *Basic and Applied Social Psychology, 8*(1–2), 97–123.

Hindelang, M.J., Gottfredson, M.R., & Garofalo, J. (1978). *Victims of personal crime: An empirical foundation for a theory of personal victimization.* Cambridge, MA: Ballinger.

Hinkle, J.C., & Weisburd, D. (2008). The irony of broken windows policing: A micro-place study of the relationship between disorder, focused police crackdowns, and fear of crime. *Journal of Criminal Justice, 36*(6), 503–512.

Hirsch, P.M. (1981). On not learning from one's own mistakes: A reanalysis of Gerbner et al.'s findings on cultivation analysis, part II. *Communication Research, 8*(1), 3–37.

Hughes, M. (1980). The fruits of cultivation analysis: A reexamination of some effects of television viewing. *Public Opinion Quarterly, 44*(3), 287–302.

Hunter, A., & Baumer, T.L. (1982). Street traffic, social integration, and fear of crime. *Sociological Inquiry, 52*(2), 122–131.

Jankowski, M.S. (1991). *Islands in the street: Gangs and American urban society.* Berkeley: University of California Press.

Jenkins, E.J., & Bell, C.C. (1997). Exposure and response to community violence among children and adolescents. In J.D. Osofsky (Ed.), *Children in a Violent Society,* pp. 9–31. New York: The Guilford Press.

Kanan, J.W., & Pruitt, M.V. (2002). Modeling fear of crime and perceived victimization risk: The (in)significance of neighborhood integration. *Sociological Inquiry, 72*(4), 527–548.

Katz, C.M., Webb, V.J., & Armstrong, T.A. (2003). Fear of gangs: A test of alternative theoretical models. *Justice Quarterly, 20*(1), 95–130.

Keane, C. (1995). Victimization and fear: Assessing the role of offender and offence. *Canadian Journal of Criminology, 37*(3), 431–455.

Kelling, G.L., Pate, A., Ferrara, A., Utne, M., & Brown, C.E. (1981). *The Newark foot patrol experiment.* Washington D.C.:The Police Foundation.

Klein, M.W. (1995). *The American street gang: Its nature, prevalence, and control.* New York: Oxford University Press.

Koomen, W., Visser, M., & Stapel, D.A. (2000). The credibility of newspapers and fear of crime. *Journal of Applied Social Psychology, 30*(5), 921–934.

Kuhn, A. & Lane, J. (2013). Racial socialization, fear, and expected reactions to a suspicious person. Paper presented at the 10th Annual Spring Lecture and Panel Discussions, At Close Range: The Curious Case of Trayvon Martin. UF Levin College of Law, March 20. http://scholarship.law.ufl.edu/cgi/viewcontent.cgi?article=1003&context=csrrr_events.

LaGrange, R.L., & Ferraro, K.F. (1987). The elderly's fear of crime: A critical examination of the research. *Research on Aging, 9*(3), 372–391.

LaGrange, R.L., & Ferraro, K.F. (1989). Assessing age and gender differences in perceived risk and fear of crime. *Criminology, 27*(4), 697–719.

LaGrange, R.L., Ferraro, K.F., & Supancic, M. (1992). Perceived risk and fear of crime: Role of social and physical incivilities. *Journal of Research in Crime and Delinquency, 29*, 311–334.

Lane, J. (2002). Fear of gang crime: A qualitative examination of the four perspectives. *Journal of Research in Crime and Delinquency, 39*(4), 437–471.

Lane, J. (2006). Exploring fear of general and gang crimes among juveniles on probation: The impacts of delinquent behaviors. *Youth Violence and Juvenile Justice, 4*(1), 34–54.

Lane, J. (2009). Perceptions of neighborhood problems, fear of crime and resulting behavioral precautions: Comparing institutionalized girls and boys in Florida. *Journal of Contemporary Criminal Justice, 25*(3), 264–281.

Lane, J., & Fox, K.A. (2012). Fear of crime among gang and non-gang offenders: Comparing the effects of perpetration, victimization, and neighborhood factors. *Justice Quarterly, 29*(4), 491–523.

Lane, J., & Meeker, J.W. (2000). Subcultural diversity and the fear of crime and gangs. *Crime & Delinquency, 46*(4), 497–521.

Lane, J. & Meeker, J.W. (2003a). Ethnicity, information sources, and fear of crime. *Deviant Behavior, 24*(1), 1–26.

Lane, J. & Meeker, J.W. (2003b). Fear of gang crime: A look at three theoretical models. *Law & Society Review, 37*(2), 425–456.

Lane, J., & Meeker, J.W. (2004). Social disorganization perceptions, fear of gang crime, and behavioral precautions among Whites, Latinos, and Vietnamese. *Journal of Criminal Justice, 32*(1), 49–62.

Lane, J. & Meeker, J.W. (2005). Theories and fear of gang crime among Whites and Latinos: A replication and extension of prior research. *Journal of Criminal Justice, 33*(6), 627–641.

Lane, J. & Meeker, J.W. (2011). Combining theoretical models of perceived risk and fear of gang crime among Whites and Latinos. *Victims and Offenders, 6*(1), 64–92.

Lauritsen, J.L., Sampson, R.J., & Laub, J.H. (1991). The link between offending and victimization among adolescents. *Criminology, 29*(2), 265–292.

Lewis, D.A., & Maxfield, M.G. (1980). Fear in the neighborhoods: An investigation of the impact of crime. *Journal of Research in Crime and Delinquency, 17*(2), 160–189.

Lewis, D.A., & Salem, G. (1986). *Fear of crime: Incivility and the production of a social problem.* New Brunswick, N.J.: Transaction Books.

Like, T.Z. (2011). Urban inequality and racial differences in risk for violent victimization. *Crime & Delinquency, 57*(3), 432–457.

Liska, A.E., & Baccaglini, W. (1990). Feeling safe by comparison: Crime in the newspapers. *Social Problems, 37*(3), 360–374.

Liska, A.E., Lawrence, J.J., & Sanchirico, A. (1982). Fear of crime as a social fact. *Social Forces, 60*(3), 760–770.

Madriz, E. (1997). *Nothing bad happens to good girls: Fear of crime in women's lives.* Berkeley: University of California Press.

Margolin, G. & Gordis, E.B. (2000). The effects of family and community violence on children. *Annual Review of Psychology, 51*(1), 445–479.

Martinez, P. &. Richters, J.E. (1993). The NIMH community violence project: II. Children's distress symptoms associated with violence exposure. *Psychiatry, 56*(1), 22–35.

May, D.C. (2001a). *Adolescent fear of crime, perceptions of risk, and defensive behaviors: An alternative explanation of violent delinquency.* Lewiston, NY: Edwin Mellen Press.

McGarrell, E.F., Giacomazzi, A.L., & Thurman, Q.C. (1997). Neighborhood disorder, integration, and the fear of crime. *Justice Quarterly, 14*(3), 479–500.

Melde, C., Taylor, T.J., & Esbensen, F.A. (2009). I got your back: An examination of the protective function of gang membership in adolescence. *Criminology, 47*(2), 565–594.

Merry, S.E. (1981). *Urban danger: Life in a neighborhood of strangers.* Philadelphia: Temple University Press.

Miller, J. (2008). *Getting played: African American girls, urban inequality, and gendered violence.* New York: New York University Press.

Moore, M.H. (1992). Problem-solving and community policing. *Crime and Justice, 15,* 99–158.

National Research Council and Institute of Medicine. (2001). *Juvenile crime, juvenile justice.* Panel on Juvenile Crime: Prevention, Treatment and Control. Joan McCord, Cathy Spatz Widom, and Nancy A. Corwell (eds.). Committee on Law and Justice and Board on Children, Youth, and Families. Washington D.C.: National Academy Press.

Nellis, A.M. (2009). Fear of terrorism. In K. Borgeson & R. Valeri (eds.), *Terrorism in America* (pp. 117–144). Boston: Jones and Bartlett Press.

Nellis, A. (2012). *The lives of juvenile lifers: Findings from a national survey.* Washington D.C.: The Sentencing Project. Accessed July 16, 2013. Available at: http://sentencingproject.org/doc/publications/publications/jj_The_Lives_of_Juvenile_Lifers.pdf.

Nellis, A.M., & Savage, J. (2012). Does watching the news affect fear of terrorism? The importance of media exposure on terrorism fear. *Crime & Delinquency, 58*(5), 748–768.

O'Keefe, G.J., & Reid-Nash, K. (1987). Crime news and real-world blues: The effects of the media on social reality. *Communication Research, 14*(2), 147–163.

Osofsky, J.D. (1999). The impact of violence on children. *The Future of Children: Domestic Violence and Children, 9,* 33–49. http://www.futureofchildren.org/futureofchildren/publications/docs/09_03_2.pdf.

Osofsky, J.D., Wewers, S., Hann, D.M., & Fick, A.C. (1993). Chronic community violence: What is happening to our children? *Psychiatry, 56*(1), 36–45.

Padilla, F.M. (1992). *The gang as an American enterprise.* New Brunswick, NJ: Rutgers University Press.

Pate, A.M., Wycoff, M.A., Skogan, W.G., & Sherman, L.W. (1986). Reducing fear of crime in Houston and Newark. Washington D.C.: Police Foundation.

Perkins, D.D., Florin, P., Rich, R.C., Wandersman, A., & Chavis, D.M. (1990). Participation and the social and physical environment of residential blocks: Crime and community context. *American Journal of Community Psychology, 18*(1), 83–115.

Perkins, D.D., Meeks, J.W., & Taylor, R.B. (1992). The physical environment of street blocks and resident perceptions of crime and disorder: Implications for theory and measurement. *Journal of Environmental Psychology, 12*(1), 21–34.

Perkins, D.D., & Taylor, R.B. (1996). Ecological assessments of community disorder: Their relationship to fear of crime and theoretical implications. *American Journal of Community Psychology, 24*(1), 63–107.

Peterson, D., Taylor, T.J., & Esbensen, F.A. (2004). Gang membership and violent victimization. *Justice Quarterly, 21*(4), 793–815.

Pew Research Center for the People and the Press. (2012). *Trends in news consumption: 1991–2012; In changing news landscape, even television is vulnerable.* Washington D.C. Pew Research Center.

Pinchevsky, G.M., & Wright, E.M. (2012). The impact of neighborhoods on intimate partner violence and victimization. *Trauma, Violence & Abuse, 13*(2), 112–132.

Potter, W.J. (1986). Perceived reality and the cultivation hypothesis. *Journal of Broadcasting and Electronic Media, 30*(2), 159–174.

Pynoos, R.S. & Nader, K. (1988). Children who witness the sexual assaults of their mothers. *Journal of the American Academy of Child and Adolescent Psychiatry, 27*(5), 567–572.

Pynoos, R.S., & Nader, K. (1990). Children's exposure to violence and traumatic death. *Psychiatric Annals, 20*(6), 334–344.

Reiss, A.J., Jr. (1982). How serious is serious crime? *Vanderbilt Law Review, 35*(3), 541–585.

Reith, M. (1999). Viewing crime drama and authoritarian aggression: An investigation of the relationship between crime viewing, fear, and aggression. *Journal of Broadcasting and Electronic Media, 43*(2), 211–221.

Richters, J.E., & Martinez, P. (1993). The NIMH Community Violence Project: I. Children as victims of and witnesses to violence. *Psychiatry, 56*(1), 7–21.

Robinson, J.B., Lawton, B.A., Taylor, R.B., & Perkins, D.D. (2003). Multilevel longitudinal impacts of incivilities: Fear of crime, expected safety, and block satisfaction. *Journal of Quantitative Criminology, 19*(3), 237–274.

Roh, S., Kwak, D., & Kim, E. (2013). Community policing and fear of crime in Seoul: A test of competing models. *Policing: An International Journal of Police Strategies and Management, 36*(1), 199–222.

Roh, S. & Oliver, W.M. (2005). Effects of community policing upon fear of crime: Understanding the causal linkage. *Policing: An International Journal of Police Strategies & Management, 28*(4), 670–683.

Roman, C.G., & Chalfin, A. (2008). Fear of walking outdoors: A multilevel ecologic analysis of crime and disorder. *American Journal of Preventive Medicine, 34*(4), 306–312.

Ross, C.E., & Jang, S.J. (2000). Neighborhood disorder, fear and mistrust: The buffering role of social ties with neighbors. *American Journal of Community Psychology, 28*(4), 401–420.

Rountree, P.W., & Land, K.C. (1996). Perceived risk versus fear of crime: Empirical evidence of conceptually distinct reactions in survey data. *Social Forces, 74*(4), 1353–1376.

Sacco, V.F. (1982). The effects of mass media on perceptions of crime: A reanalysis of the issues. *The Pacific Sociological Review, 25*(4), 475–493.

Salzinger, S., Feldman, R.S., Stockhammer, T., & Hood, J. (2002). An ecological framework for understanding risk for exposure to community violence and the effects of exposure on children. *Aggression and Violent Behavior, 7*(5), 423–451.

Sampson, R.J., & Groves, W.B. (1989). Community structure and crime: Testing social-disorganization theory. *The American Journal of Sociology, 94*(4), 774–802.

Sampson, R.J., & Lauritsen, J.L. (1990). Deviant lifestyles, proximity to crime, and the offender-victim link in personal violence. *Journal of Research in Crime and Delinquency, 27*(2), 110–139.

Sampson, R.J., Raudenbush, S.W., & Earls, F. (1997). Neighborhoods and violent crime: A multilevel study of collective efficacy. *Science, 277*(5328), 918–924.

Scarborough, B.K., Like-Haislip, T.Z., Novak, K.J., Lucas, W.L., & Alarid, L.F. (2010). Assessing the relationship between individual characteristics, neighborhood context, and fear of crime. *Journal of Criminal Justice, 38*(4), 819–826.

Scheider, M.C., Rowell, T., & Bezdikian, V. (2003). The impact of citizen perceptions of community policing on fear of crime: Findings from twelve cities. *Police Quarterly, 6*(4), 363–386.

Schlesinger, P., Tumber, H., & Murdock, G. (1991). The media politics of crime and criminal justice. *British Journal of Sociology, 42*(3), 397–420.

Shakoor, B.H., & Chalmers, D. (1991). Co-victimization of African-American children who witness violence: Effects on cognitive, emotional and behavioral development. *Journal of the National Medical Association, 83*(3), 233–238.

Shaw, C.R., & McKay, H.D. (1972 [1942]). *Juvenile delinquency and urban areas.* Chicago: University of Chicago Press.

Skogan, W. (1986). Fear of crime and neighborhood change. In Albert J. Reiss & Michael Tonry (Eds.), *Communities and Crime*, pp. 203–229. Chicago: University of Chicago Press.

Skogan, W.G. (1987). The impact of victimization on fear. *Crime & Delinquency, 33*(1), 135–154.

Skogan, W.G. (1990). *Disorder and decline: Crime and the spiral of decay in American neighborhoods.* New York: The Free Press.

Skogan, W.G. (1995). Crime and the racial fears of White Americans. *The annals of the American Academy of Political and Social Science, 539*(1), 59–71.

Skogan, W.G. & Maxfield, M.G. (1981). *Coping with Crime: Individual and Neighborhood Reactions.* Beverly Hills: Sage.

Smith, L.N. & Hill, G.D. (1991). Victimization and fear of crime. *Criminal Justice and Behavior, 18*(2), 217–239.

Stafford, M.C., & Galle, O.R. (1984). Victimization rates, exposure to risk, and fear of crime. *Criminology, 22*(2), 173–185.

Stanko, E.A. (1985). *Intimate intrusions: Women's experience of male violence.* London: Routledge & Kegan Paul.

Swartz, K., Reyns, B.W., Henson, B., & Wilcox, P. (2011). Fear of in-school victimization: Contextual, gendered, and developmental considerations. *Youth Violence & Juvenile Justice, 9*(1), 59–78.

Taylor, R.B. (1996). Neighborhood responses to disorder and local attachments: The systemic model of attachment, social disorganization, and neighborhood use value. *Sociological Forum, 11*(1), 41–74.

Taylor, R.B. (2001). *Breaking away from broken windows: Baltimore neighborhoods and the nationwide fight against crime, grime, fear and decline.* Boulder, CO: Westview Press.

Taylor, R.B., & Covington, J. (1993). Community structural change and fear of crime. *Social Problems, 40*(3), 374–397.

Taylor, R.B., & Hale, M. (1986). Testing alternative models of fear of crime. *The Journal of Criminal Law & Criminology, 77*(1), 151–189.

Taylor, R.B., Shumaker, S.A. & Gottfredson, S.D. (1985). Neighborhood-level links between physical features and local sentiments: Deterioration, fear of crime, and confidence. *Journal of Architectural & Planning Research, 2,* 261–275.

Thomas, S.A. (2007). Lies, damn lies, and rumors: An analysis of collective efficacy, rumors, and fear in the wake of Katrina. *Sociological Spectrum, 27*(6), 679–703.

Truman, J.L. (2011). *Criminal victimization, 2010.* Washington D.C.: Bureau of Justice Statistics.

Tyler, T.R. (1980). Impact of directly and indirectly experienced events: The origin of crime-related judgments and behaviors. *Journal of Personality and Social Psychology, 39*(1), 13–28.

Tyler, T.R. (1984). Assessing the risk of crime victimization: The integration of personal victimization experience and socially transmitted information. *Journal of Social Issues, 40*(1), 27–38.

U.S. Census Bureau. (2009). *Internet use in the United States: October 2009.* http://www.census.gov/hhes/computer/publications/2009.html (accessed January 20, 2012).

Vigil, J.D. (1988). *Barrio gangs: Street life and identity in Southern California.* Austin: University of Texas Press.

Warner, B.S., & Weist, M.D. (1996). Urban youth as witnesses to violence: Beginning assessment and treatment efforts. *Journal of Youth and Adolescence, 25*(3), 361–377.

Warr, M. (1984). Fear of victimization: Why are women and the elderly more afraid? *Social Science Quarterly, 65*(3), 681–702.

Warr, M. (1990). Dangerous situations: Social context and fear of victimization. *Social Forces, 68*(3), 891–907.

Warr, M. (1994). Public perceptions and reactions to violent offending and victimization. In A.J. Reiss & J.A. Roth (Eds.), *Understanding and preventing violence: Consequences and Control* (Vol. 4), pp. 1–66. Washington D.C.: National Academy Press.

Warr, M. (2000). Fear of crime in the United States: Avenues for research and policy. In D. Duffee (Ed.), *Crime and Justice 2000: Vol. 4*, pp. 451–489. *Measurement and Analysis of Criminal Justice.* Washington D.C.: National Institute of Justice.

The Washington Post. (2012). Audio: Calls from Zimmerman, neighbor capture last minutes of Martin's life (May 20). Accessed August 5, 2013. Available at: http://www.washingtonpost.com/wp-srv/special/nation/last-minutes-trayvon-martin-911-calls/index.html.

Weaver, J., & Wakshlag, J. (1986). Perceived vulnerability to crime, criminal victimization experience, and television viewing. *Journal of Broadcasting & Electronic Media, 30*(2), 141–158.

Weisburd, D., & Eck, J.E. (2004). What can police do to reduce crime, disorder, and fear? *ANNALS, 593*(1), 42–65.

Weitzer, R. & Kubrin, C.E. (2004). Breaking news: How local TV news and real-world conditions affect fear of crime. *Justice Quarterly, 21*(3), 497–520.

Wilcox, P., Ozer, M.M., Gunbeyi, M., & Gundogdu, T. (2009). Gender and fear of terrorism in Turkey. *Journal of Contemporary Criminal Justice, 25*(3), 341–357.

Wilcox Rountree, P. (1998). A reexamination of the crime-fear linkage. *Journal of Research in Crime and Delinquency, 35*(3), 341–372.

Williams, P., & Dickinson, J. (1993). Fear of crime: Read all about it?: The relationship between newspaper crime reporting and fear of crime. *British Journal of Criminology, 33*(1), 33–56.

Wilson, J.Q., & Kelling, G.L. (1982). Broken windows: The police and neighborhood safety. *Atlantic Monthly* (March): 29–38.

Wober, J.M. (1978). Televised violence and paranoid perception: The view from Great Britain. *Public Opinion Quarterly, 42*(3), 315–321.

Wyant, B.R. (2008). Multilevel impacts of perceived incivilities and perceptions of crime risk on fear of crime: Isolating endogenous impacts. *Journal of Research in Crime and Delinquency, 45*(1), 39–64.

Xu, Y., Fiedler, M.L., & Flaming, K.H. (2005). Discovering the impact of community policing: The broken windows thesis, collective efficacy, and citizens' judgment. *Journal of Research in Crime and Delinquency, 42*(2), 147–186.

Young, V. (1992). Fear of victimization and victimization rates among women: A paradox? *Justice Quarterly, 9*(3), 419–441.

Zhao, J.S., Scheider, M., and Thurman, Q.C. (2002). The effect of police presence on public fear reduction and satisfaction: A review of the literature. *The Justice Professional, 15*(3), 273–299.

Chapter 7

Consequences of Fear of Crime: Physical, Psychological, Behavioral, and Social Effects

People often react to their fear of crime by reducing contact with others and by avoiding situations that might lead to their victimization. They also take various security measures, such as purchasing firearms or installing burglar alarms. These changes harm the community at the same time that they may protect specific individuals. They erect barriers between neighbors and they generate distrust.

Conklin, 1975, p. 105

The guns really helped me 'cause I needed to have protection. I could have just ran from those guys, I didn't think like that.

excerpt from an interview with Edmundo, an incarcerated juvenile, in May & Jarjoura, 2006, p. 76

Fear affects humans in a multitude of ways. Fear may induce physiological, psychological, and behavioral changes. Thus, fear has physiological, psychological, and social consequences for people. We begin this chapter with a broad discussion of the consequences of fear then turn to a focused discussion on the behavioral consequences of fear of crime. We divide these behavioral consequences into avoidance, defensive, and weapons behaviors, discuss the impact of fear of crime on each of these types of behavior, then close the chapter with recommendations for future research in the area of behavioral consequences of fear of crime (see Box 7.1 for a summary).

Box 7.1 Consequences of Fear of Crime

1. Physical consequences
   - Increased heart rate
   - Rapid breathing
   - Increased epinephrine

2. Social/Behavioral consequences
   - Avoidance behaviors
     - Avoiding particular areas at particular times
     - Avoiding particular activities
     - Creation of defensible spaces
     - Crime Prevention through Environmental Design (CPTED)
   - Defensive behaviors
     - Home security systems
     - Watchdog
     - Installation of additional locks
     - Installation of additional lighting
     - Installation of burglar alarms
     - Enrollment in self-defense classes
   - Weapons behaviors
     - Purchase firearms
     - Carry firearms in pubic
     - Carry mace or other weapons in public

Physical Consequences of Fear

The presence of fear in an individual produces a number of physical changes. Fear causes an increased heart rate and perspiration and changes the electrical conductance of the skin (Darwin, 1910). Fear may also cause paleness of the skin, hair standing on end, pupil dilation, increased tension and blood flow in the muscles, trembling, dryness and tightness of the mouth, constriction of the chest and rapid breathing, nausea, bladder and rectum contractions which create an urge to pass urine or feces, tingling in the hands and feet, and a sensation of faintness or falling (Marks, 1978). The experience of fear also is often accompanied by a reduction in body temperature (Rime & Giovannini, 1986).

Kemper (1978) cites several studies that suggest that fear produces increased levels of epinephrine. Epinephrine is a hormone that produces a rise in blood pressure by accelerating the pumping of the heart. Fear also can bring about a tightening of muscles. When the individual is terrified, fear normally brings about one of two reactions. Fear may cause the individual to become motionless and mute; or, fear may cause the individual to become startled, scream, and run away (Izard, 1977; Marks, 1978). Fear rarely lasts longer than an hour, and usually lasts less than five minutes. Intense fear is an emergency response, and is thus a short-lived reaction (Ricci-Bitti & Scherer, 1986).

Psychological Consequences

In addition to physiological consequences, fear also produces a number of psychological consequences. Fear can cause mental activity to be slow, narrow in scope, and rigid in form and may have a very marked effect on the individual's perception, thought, and action. The emotions associated with fear can range from apprehension to terror. The fearful person often senses uncertainty, insecurity, and imminent danger and feels a high degree of tension and a moderate degree of impulsiveness. In extreme situations, fear may cause "tunnel vision," where the victim becomes functionally blind to a large proportion of potential behavioral alternatives. Strong fear supports only one type of behavior—escape (Izard, 1977). Fears can embed themselves within an individual's psyche and can spread to all aspects of an individual's life, distorting and dominating it (Cole, 1964).

Social Consequences of Fear

Along with physical and psychological consequences, fear also has social consequences. In other words, fear affects an individual's ability to interact with others in a social context. At the extreme, phobias may restrict people's movement so much that they cannot be employed, attend school, or even participate in leisure activities like shopping or exercising. Fears may also be situational and yet may occur even when an individual has not personally experienced the fear-inducing situation. Humans are conditioned to react to a wide variety of stimuli, many of which they may never have encountered (Scruton, 1986). For example, many people who fear snakes have had no contact with snakes (Gray, 1971). Because of this fear of snakes, whether realistic or unrealistic, some individuals choose not to engage in activities such as hiking in the woods where they might encounter these reptiles.

Behavioral Consequences

That is, fear can greatly reduce behavioral alternatives. When people fear an event or situation, they often limit their behaviors so they can avoid it. This fear may even have drastic consequences for their everyday lives. For example, an individual fearful of eating in public may refuse to eat in a restaurant, choosing to dine only at home.

The behavioral consequences of fear of crime mirror those of fear in general. Just as a person fearful of eating in public will rarely eat in a restaurant, people fearful of what they perceive to be rampant crime in the metropolitan area and/or near their home may refuse to participate in the activities that city offers at night (e.g., plays, movies, or festivals) or in their neighborhoods, and thus are deprived of what could be a tremendously enjoyable experience. Furthermore, just as people often experience fear of some everyday objects or situations that they may never have encountered (snakes, flying in a plane, etc.), they may also fear crime even if they have had no personal experience with victimization and never have witnessed any crime. People adjust their fears to the world in which they reside, and thus, in a society with so much exposure to crime, many people fear criminal victimization even though it may not ever happen to them (Warr, 2000).

While a variety of disciplines discuss behavioral responses to certain types of fear (e.g., fear of snakes, crowds, or small spaces), research around behavioral consequences of fear of crime has largely been restricted to criminology (May & Dunaway, 2000; Warr, 2000). Fear of crime researchers have determined there are numerous behavioral responses to fear of crime and have labeled these behaviors "constrained behaviors" (Ferraro, 1995; Giblin, Burrus, Corsaro, & Schafer, 2012; Rader & Haynes, 2012). Constrained behaviors can be defined as the behaviors individuals take to protect themselves from criminal victimization (Rader & Cossman, 2011). These behaviors are commonly found to be associated with both fear of crime and perceptions of risk, although there is debate about whether they are the *result* of fear and risk (Giblin et al., 2012) or *precursors* to fear and risk (Rader & Haynes, 2012).

Defining Constrained Behaviors

Most fear of crime researchers divide constrained behaviors into one of two types: avoidance behaviors or protective behaviors. Although scholars often consider weapons behaviors to be defensive protective behaviors, we argue that weapons behaviors have both distinctive predictors (e.g., gender and socioeconomic status) and consequences. Recent research by Rader and Haynes (2012) found that weapons for protection are used differently by men and women. Wilcox, May, & Roberts (2006) argued that weapon possession for protection has a "triggering" effect that does not only prevent crime, it often escalates situations into criminal events. Thus, we treat weapons behaviors as a third, distinct category and discuss constrained behaviors as avoidance behaviors, protective behaviors, and weapons behaviors.

For the purposes of this chapter, avoidance behaviors are defined as behaviors taken by individuals that are passive, that is, that restrict where individuals go and what they do (May, Rader, & Goodrum, 2010). Protective behaviors are those behaviors in which individuals engage that require them to take some form or action (Rader & Haynes, 2012). Some of these behaviors designed to reduce fear of personal victimization include enrolling in self-defense classes; behaviors designed to reduce fear of property crime include installation of locks on doors and windows, engraving identification numbers on personal property, installing additional lighting and/or burglar alarms and security systems, and keeping a guard dog in the home.

The final category involves weapons behaviors. These behaviors also require action, in that an individual must obtain or purchase a weapon for protection, but researchers have found that owning a weapon as a protective behavior has distinctly different consequences than buying locks or taking a self-defense class. Therefore, we deem weapons behaviors as a separate type of constrained behavior for this discussion (Rader & Haynes, 2012).

Research on Constrained Behaviors

Polls that ask adults in the United States how often they participate in constrained behaviors reveal that a substantial minority of Americans engage in these behaviors. As part of their annual crime poll in 2007, Gallup researchers asked their sample of adult respondents how often they engaged in seven different types of constrained behaviors. In Table 7.1, we present their findings. Of the behaviors they examined, the most frequent behavior in which respondents engaged was avoiding certain neighborhoods or areas they might otherwise go to because of concerns about crime (48%). Approximately one in three respondents said they kept a dog for protection (31%) or had installed a burglar alarm in their homes (31%), while approximately one in four respondents (23%) had purchased a gun to protect themselves and their homes. Smaller proportions had personally carried mace or pepper spray (14%), a knife (12%), or a gun for defense (12%) (Carroll, 2007).

Rader and Haynes (2012) examined avoidance, protective, and weapons behaviors using data collected via telephone in 2009 from the National Survey of Attitudes toward Juvenile Justice to examine the relationship between gender, concern about crime, and perceived risk on these behaviors. Avoidance behaviors included whether the respondent had "avoided specific areas during the day," "avoided specific areas during the night," and "limited or changed

Table 7.1 Constrained Behaviors among Adults in the United States

Next, I'm going to read some things people do because of their concern over crime. Please tell me which, if any, of these things you, yourself, have done.	Yes %	No %
Avoid going to certain places or neighborhoods you might otherwise want to go to?	48	52
Keep a dog for protection?	31	68
Had a burglar alarm installed in your home?	31	69
Bought a gun for protection of yourself and your home?	23	76
Carry mace or pepper spray?	14	86
Carry a knife for defense?	12	87
Carry a gun for defense?	12	88

Adapted from results from Gallup's Annual Crime Poll (conducted October 4–7, 2007) presented at http://www.gallup.com/poll/102418/How-Americans-Protect-Themselves-From-Crime.aspx.

their daily activities." Protective behaviors included "carried mace or pepper spray," "taken a self-defense class," "added outside lighting or purchased dead-bolt locks for your residence," and "owned a watchdog." Weapons behaviors included whether or not the respondent had "carried a knife" and "carried a firearm" (Rader & Haynes, 2012, p. 8).

Rader and Haynes (2012) did not present estimates of each of these behaviors individually; rather, they collapsed the behaviors into the aforementioned categories (avoidance, protective, and weapons) and presented estimates of how often individuals engaged in each category of behavior. Respondents were most likely to engage in protective behaviors (73%), followed by avoidance behaviors (45%), and weapons behaviors (16%).

Nellis (2009) also examined responses to fear of terrorism among 527 adults that lived in New York and Washington D.C. in 2006. She asked respondents about eight behaviors in which they engaged " ... when they hear the terror alert has been raised." She found that both male and female respondents were most likely to (1) use more caution in their daily routines (37% for males and 50% for females), (2) avoid certain cities that had been victims of terrorist attacks (25% vs. 49%), (3) and avoid public transportation (23% vs. 41%). Both males and females were least likely to buy protective gear (12% vs. 13%, respectively) when the terror alert was raised. Thus, no matter what type of fear is considered, a substantial amount of adults alter their behaviors because of fear.

Avoidance Behaviors

One of the most common responses to fear of crime is to avoid a fear producing situation all together. Fear of crime researchers have examined (1) avoidance behaviors of individuals (e.g., examining why specific individuals avoid places and people due to fear of crime) and (2) the avoidance producing nature of environments (e.g., examining why certain places and spaces are fear producing). Early research indicated that individuals were likely to avoid certain places at night, in the dark, and when walking alone (Ferraro and LaGrange, 1987; Keane, 1998; Liska, Sanchirico, and Reed, 1988; Gordon and Riger, 1989; Skogan & Maxfield, 1981). The fictional case study presented in Box 7.2 provides a scenario based on a university campus where students might make those choices.

More recent research (Nellis, 2009) suggests that individuals may even avoid specific places (e.g., tall buildings and public transportation or certain areas on college campuses) and activities in specific time frames (e.g., avoiding going out at night for entertainment or walking in parks at night) because of their fear of crime (Fisher & Nasar, 1995; Fisher & Nasar, 1992; Keane, 1998). Fisher

---

Box 7.2 Fictional Case Study at Blissful University

Blissful University (BU) has recently heard complaints from their student affairs office that the number of students attending campus events at night had declined dramatically. This decline has been particularly noticeable among female students. In the past two months, the BU police have also noticed a dramatic increase in the number of weapons they have seen on-campus; in every case where they confiscated a weapon, a male student was either carrying the weapon or it was found in his dormitory room. Two months ago, in the space of a week, three students reported violent assaults against them while walking alone on campus. Since those assaults, fewer students go out at night and many students admit they are fearful of more assaults occurring.

Thought/Discussion Questions:
1. In this context, how do you think you would have reacted if you attended BU?
2. Would you have been afraid?
3. Would you have changed your behavior, either at night or during the day, while on-campus?
4. Would you consider carrying a weapon, even though the university regulations prohibit weapons on campus? Why or why not?
5. Why are females less likely to attend campus events and males more likely to have weapons on campus?
6. What should university officials do to reduce the fear of crime in this situation?
7. What other avoidance, defensive, and weapons behaviors might students consider as a result of their fear of crime?

and Nasar (1995) suggested that people are more likely to fear places that offer potential offenders the most refuge and offer potential victims the lowest prospect (open views of the area) and escape; they also argued that fear will be highest in these places.

Another notable study in this area was conducted by Liska, Sanchirico, and Reed (1988). They examined both avoidance and protective behaviors using data from the National Crime Survey with 2,000 respondents who were 16 years or older. The authors discovered that individuals were likely to constrain their behaviors and, in fact, they found that constrained behaviors might actually increase individuals' fear of crime. Further, in regards to avoidance behavior, they concluded that:

> People who fear crime tend to constrain their behavior to safe areas during safe times, avoiding unsafe areas of cities and the restaurants, shops, jobs, and residences located in them. People who are unable to constrain their behavior to safe areas, because of age or income, frequently become prisoners in their own homes, afraid to walk the streets in their own neighborhoods (p. 828).

Finally, they found age differences in these behaviors, discovering that older individuals were more likely to engage in avoidance behaviors than younger individuals.

Another influential study on constrained behaviors was conducted by Keane (1998). Keane used data from the Violence against Women Survey in Canada to assess fear of crime and the use of precautionary behaviors among women 18 years or older. Specifically, he examined if women would use traditional fear producing spaces (i.e., walking alone in their neighborhood and using parking garages when alone) if they felt more safe. He concluded that:

> What appears to be happening, then, is that some women because of fear are unable (or at least unwilling) to take full advantage of their immediate environments. Hence, many women may be currently restricting their daily activities to avoid the settings described here, and likely many other settings, because of worries about their personal safety (p. 70).

In addition, he discovered that other demographic characteristics were important, determining that women living in urban areas, younger individuals, and single people claimed that they would use these spaces if they felt safer.

As Keane (1998) shows, demographic characteristics are important in determining use of avoidance behaviors. Researchers have examined what types of individuals are likely to engage in avoidance behaviors and have focused on personal characteristics. This research has found that women, White people, and the elderly were more likely to engage in avoidance behaviors than their counterparts (Beaulieu, Dubé, Bergeron, & Cousineau, 2007; De Welde, 2003a; Madriz, 1997).

Gender, or being female, is an important predictor of fear of crime (see Chapter 4 for this discussion), and studies show that women are more likely to engage in avoidance behaviors as well (Lane, 2009; May et al., 2010; Nellis, 2009). Researchers have found that women are likely to be taught that they should be afraid of public spaces because of stranger danger, a myth particularly scary for women (Madriz, 1997; Scott, 2003; Stanko, 1997; see Chapter 4). A fear of public spaces may lead women to avoid going out late at night, going to certain places, and going alone (Hollander, 2001; Rader & Haynes, 2012; Stanko, 1997).

One example of a recent study that provided insight into the relationship between gender and avoidance behaviors comes from a study conducted by Lane (2009). In Lane's study of incarcerated adolescent girls and boys, about half of the girls (compared to only one third of the boys) stated they avoided areas of the city because of fear of crime when they were in the community. These results suggest that while avoidance behaviors affect both males and females, women are more likely to use avoidance behaviors (Madriz, 1997; Rader, Cossman, & Allison, 2009; San-Juan, Vozmediano, & Vergara, 2012; Stanko, 1997).

To a lesser extent, research also has examined the relationship between avoidance behaviors and other correlates including race and age. Madriz (1997), for example, found that White women were more likely than women of color to avoid places at night or when alone due to their fear of crime. She also found the avoidance of spaces because of fear stemmed from the belief that women (particularly White women) were more likely to be the victim of crime and violent stranger-induced crime.

A number of scholars also have determined that older individuals are more likely to engage in avoidance behaviors than their younger counterparts. Beaulieu and colleagues (2007) discussed the types of avoidance behaviors taken by elderly individuals (over the age of 65). Their research found that when individuals reach the age of 65, they are more likely to avoid activities in which they used to engage, especially at night. This was particularly relevant for elderly men who lived alone; these men were five times more likely to engage in avoidance behaviors than those who did not live alone. Therefore, the role of age and living status is particularly important for avoidance behaviors. The primary reason that elderly individuals engaged in avoidance behaviors is an increased sense of vulnerability. As their bodies age, they lose muscle mass, agility, and strength, all of which may make elderly people feel more vulnerable to victimization and cause them to avoid situations they deem as potentially dangerous (Chandola, 2001; Cossman & Rader, 2011; McKee & Milner, 2000; Pain, 1997).

Environmental Design and Fear of Crime

Beyond individual avoidance reactions to fear of criminal victimization are more macro-approaches, or policy and practitioner approaches to reducing problems that create fear. Specifically, architects and planners now focus on designing public spaces to reduce fear of crime in the spaces in which individuals reside, recreate, and work. These designs allow people to avoid criminogenic individuals or situations by reducing the likelihood that they will interact with these individuals or high-risk situations. The idea that spaces could be designed to reduce fear of crime has often been attributed to Oscar Newman's defensible space theory. Thus, we begin the discussion of environmental design and fear of crime with his work.

Newman (1972) created the idea of defensible space, primarily as a concept in deterring crime. In this perspective, defensible space involves a residential setting where the designed physical layout and other architectural characteristics of that setting allow the inhabitants to engage in their own active crime prevention. Among other ideas, Newman suggested that areas are safer (and residents of those areas feel safer) when these areas are defensible spaces. Thus, crime and fear of crime can be reduced by environmental design.

Newman (1972) argued that well-designed and well-maintained spaces could reduce both crime and fear of crime by (1) creating natural surveillance (designing spaces so that residents have the greatest visibility of those spaces), (2) reducing opportunity for crime by making spaces more visible and thus more easy to defend, and (3) increasing the likelihood that residents would (or could) use and/or protect their space.

Newman (1972) suggested that four factors are necessary for a space to be defensible. These factors include territoriality, natural surveillance, image, and milieu. Territoriality is the ability of the legitimate users of an area to "own," or lay claim to that area. When residents identify the area as their own, they are much more likely to do their part in protecting it from crime. Natural surveillance is the idea that an area can be designed so that it maximizes the ability of residents in that area to observe daily activities of both the neighborhood residents and strangers entering and leaving the area. The idea of image supports the notion that areas can be designed in such a way that they appear invulnerable to penetration by would-be criminals. Finally, milieu suggests that the surroundings in which a neighborhood is located impact the criminality of the designed area; areas located in low crime, high surveillance zones will thus have less crime and fear of crime than areas located in other zones.

Since 1972 when Newman originated the idea of defensible space, a number of studies have examined whether designing communities with defensible space principles reduces crime in those communities. In general, these studies have indicated that defensible spaces do have less crime than areas not using those principles. This only occurs when the residents in those areas commit to fulfilling the roles required by them to make defensible space work by engaging in actions such as active surveillance and enforcement of territorial boundaries (Newman, 1996).

At about the same time as Newman's principles of defensible space were articulated, C. Ray Jeffrey published *Crime Prevention through Environmental Design*. In this work, he articulated a crime control model that advocated social control through management of environmental characteristics. Jeffrey argued that the amount of crime in an area hinges on the features of the physical environment of that area, and these features can be manipulated to reduce crime (Jeffrey, 1971). Thus, the goal of crime prevention through environmental design (CPTED) is to identify social and physical conditions of an environment that increase the likelihood of crime then alter those conditions so that crime is reduced.

Policymakers have used this knowledge of defensible space, CPTED, and place-based fear to attempt to reduce crime and fear of crime through situational crime prevention. According to Clarke (1997), situational crime prevention consists of approaches that are directed at specific forms of crime where users of that environment manage the environment to make it more difficult for offenders to successfully commit crime in those places. Examples of situational crime prevention measures designed to reduce fear include removing signs of physical incivility such as graffiti and litter (Skogan & Maxfield, 1981), increasing street lighting (Painter, 1996), and using closed-circuit television (CCTV) and security cameras to reduce fear of users in certain areas (Short & Ditton, 1998).

Spinks (2001) suggested that efforts to reduce fear by design can be traced all the way back to Jeremy Bentham's classic panopticon prison design. In the late 18th century, Bentham proposed a model for prison construction whereby inmates were housed in a circular building with an "inspector's lodge" in the middle of the building. This lodge would have windows on all sides of the circular room. The prisoners' cells would be situated around the inspector's lodge. Along with an exterior window to provide natural light into the cells, instead of bars, the cells would have iron gratings facing the inspector's lodge. This would ensure that the inspector could easily see the entire cell for each inmate at the same time (Bozovic, 1995). This design allowed all prisoners to be under constant surveillance, thus reducing the fear of the officers that supervised them. Evaluations of efforts to use defensible space and CPTED in reducing fear of crime suggest that, at least in some situations, these measures successfully reduce the fear of crime among residents living in areas where defensible space and CPTED principles are used (Lab, 2010). Nevertheless, even the strongest advocates of situational crime prevention admit that these measures designed to reduce fear are both (1) likely to be short-lived and (2) difficult to isolate as the only cause of that reduced fear of crime among residents in areas where these principles are used (Pain, 2000).

A number of studies have directly examined the effectiveness of both defensible space and CPTED principles on reducing crime and fear of crime. Almost two decades ago, Fleissner and Heinzelmann (1996) suggested that "... joint police-community efforts to clean up decayed neighborhoods, such as organizing graffiti paint-outs, removing abandoned vehicles, and installing adequate lighting around homes and businesses ..." (p. 2) reduced fear of crime and increased the community's sense of control. They reviewed a number of effective strategies designed to reduce crime and fear, including closing drug houses and using traffic control to promote neighborhood cohesion. They argued that these strategies not only reduce crime, but they increase residents' informal social control and improve their quality of life.

Recently, Lorenc and colleagues (2013) conducted a systematic review of the effectiveness of environmental interventions in reducing fear of crime. They categorized environmental interventions into seven types: home security improvements, installation or improvement of street lighting, installation of CCTV systems, multi-component interventions for crime prevention, housing improvement and relocation, area-based regeneration initiatives, and small-scale improvements in public areas.

The first type of interventions discussed by Lorenc et al. (2013) is better characterized as protective behaviors and is discussed in the protective behaviors section below. The review by Lorenc et al. (2013) concluded the following. First, installation or improvement of street lighting reduced fear of crime in studies that were less rigorous methodologically; in the four studies that used control groups to examine the impact of street lighting on fear of crime, the results were mixed. Second, installation of CCTV systems and urban regeneration programs designed to improve both housing and neighborhoods did not appear to be effective in reducing fear of crime. Next, both small-scale environmental improvements (e.g., cleaning up a park and a bus station) and multi-component interventions for crime prevention (e.g., intervention strategies that use a wide array of security, lighting, and neighborhood design improvements) have a mixed impact on fear of crime; in other words, some studies suggest they reduce fear of crime while others indicate they have no impact on fear of crime. Finally, studies that examined the impact of improvement and/or relocation of dilapidated housing in neighborhoods indicated that doing so appears to reduce fear of crime among residents of those neighborhoods in some studies but has no effect on residents' fear in others.

Other researchers have weighed in on these relationships as well. Foster, Giles-Corti, and Knuiman (2010) examined the impact of physical and social characteristics of neighborhoods on self-reported fear among a sample of 1059 adults living in Western Australia. They operationalized neighborhood design by using a "neighborhood form index" to represent those neighborhood characteristics that would encourage people to use the neighborhood spaces (e.g., public open space and retail land) and encourage movement and guardianship in the neighborhood. They determined that the design of a neighborhood had a strong, statistically significant impact in reducing fear of crime. Specifically, respondents living in those neighborhoods designed to ensure use by the residents were significantly less fearful of crime than their counterparts. This effect persisted even after controlling for a number of demographic and contextual characteristics normally associated with fear of crime.

Nevertheless, Hinkle and Weisburd (2008) revealed that the relationship between design, reducing disorder, and strategies used by police and other social control agents may not be as straightforward as previously believed. Using self-report studies from 733 adult residents of neighborhoods in a U.S. city that experienced increased police presence to reduce disorder in those neighborhoods, Hinkle and Weisburd found that reduced disorder in the neighborhood increased residents' perceptions of safety but their perceptions of safety were decreased by additional police presence in their neighborhoods. Thus, it appears that CPTED works best in reducing fear of crime when it is done in a way that reduces the presence of police in the neighborhood or when the design occurs prior to residents moving into those neighborhoods.

The use of situational crime prevention and defensible space has been one of the strongest reasons that planners have designed neighborhoods to reduce fear of crime among residents in these areas. Despite the wide implementation of defensible space principles, the previous review suggests that limited research has examined the impact of defensible space principles on individuals' fear of crime and, when it is available, these studies indicate that the impact of these design improvements on fear of crime is "mixed" at best. Consequently, this area of research is ripe for fear of crime studies and one that should be considered in the future.

Protective Behaviors

Protective behaviors include active behaviors taken by individuals in hopes of reducing their fear of crime. Examples of protective behaviors include taking self-defense classes, purchasing locks and extra lighting, carrying mace, or obtaining a watch dog. A number of researchers have examined these behaviors and the impact of fear of crime on those behaviors. We begin the discussion of these behaviors by examining the relationship between fear of crime and self-defense training.

Self-Defense Training

A recent area of inquiry in behaviors that result from fear of crime revolves around self-defense training to reduce one's likelihood of criminal victimization. While this is still an emerging line of study, the vast majority of this research examines enrolling in self-defense classes among women. A few of these studies asked women about why they enroll in self-defense classes but, with limited exception (Hollander, 2010), most participants in these studies reported their reasons for enrolling in self-defense classes anecdotally rather than providing a detailed examination of those reasons. For example, when De Welde (2003a) asked 30 women why they enrolled in a self-defense class, the most common response was that they were tired of being afraid. De Welde (2003b), in further analysis of the same data, cited "fear of crime" and "curiosity" as reasons for why the majority of the women enrolled in self-defense classes. McDaniel (1993) also asked a sample of 49 women enrolled in self-defense classes in New Zealand why they had enrolled in the course. She determined that the most common reasons were to defend themselves from attackers and to increase self-confidence.

More recent research has examined this phenomenon as well. Hollander (2010) examined reasons for enrolling in self-defense classes among a sample of 292 female students in a large public university in the Pacific Northwest region of the United States. Of the 292 students under study, 118 were enrolled in a self-defense course. The students enrolled in the self-defense class were asked to indicate why they had enrolled. Although the most popular reason for enrolling in the self-defense class was that the student had heard it was a good class, one in five (18%) students said that they had enrolled in the class because they felt fearful.

To our knowledge, the only published study that has directly examined the impact of self-defense classes on fear of crime is the research from McDaniel (1993). Her analyses indicated that, when comparing pre-test and post-test fear among women enrolled in self-defense courses with those of a control group of women enrolled in a physical fitness course at the Young Women's Christian Association (YWCA), women enrolled in self-defense classes were significantly more likely than the women enrolled in the physical fitness classes to have lower levels of fear at post-test than pre-test. Examining the short- and long-term effects of self-defense training on fear of crime remains a rich area for future research.

Other Defensive Behaviors

A number of other defensive behaviors have also been examined. For example, May, Rader, and Goodrum (2010) asked a sample of Kentucky residents whether they had placed a number of items in their homes in the past 12 months "for security reasons." Although May et al. (2010) did not report the frequency of the behaviors in their article, we estimated frequencies of the behaviors in which individuals engaged using their data. Of the approximately 2,000 respondents to the mail survey, two in three respondents (67.6%) had adopted one or more of the items in their homes in the past 12 months for security reasons. Table 7.2 displays the items (and the proportion of the sample that had them in their house). The most common behavior in which these individuals engaged was installation of outside security lights (40.89% had installed these lights), followed by installation of door bolts (37.90%), and installation of extra door locks (25.62%). One in five respondents had a guard dog for protection (20.19%) or had installed automatic timers (19.74%). Smaller percentages had installed window guards (17.00%), burglar alarms (12.84%), and police department identification stickers (12.43%).

Table 7.2 Protective Measures Used By Kentucky Respondents (N=1971)

Type of Measure	N	Percent of Sample
Outside security lights	806	40.89
Door bolts	747	37.90
Did not engage in any defensive behavior	638	32.4
Extra door locks	505	25.62
Guard dogs	398	20.19
Automatic timers/Electronic timers	389	19.74
Window guards	335	17.00
Burglar alarms	253	12.84
Police Department identification stickers	245	12.43

This table was constructed from data used in May et al. (2010). Results are not reported in this format in the original article.

May et al. (2010) examined the impact of fear of crime, perceptions of risk, and victimization experience on protective behaviors in their sample by creating a dichotomous measure of protective behaviors where those that had engaged in any protective behavior were compared to those who had not engaged in any protective behavior. They determined that neither fear nor perceived risk predicted use of protective behaviors. They cautioned that the nonsignificant findings may have been due to the dichotomous nature of their variable operationalizing protective behaviors and encouraged future researchers to better examine these relationships.

Lorenc et al. (2013) conducted a systematic review of the extant research in environmental interventions to reduce fear of crime. As part of that research, they were able to identify five studies that examined the relationship between fear of crime and home security improvements. All of these studies had been conducted in the United Kingdom. Only one study was narrowly focused on home security improvements; the remaining studies included home security improvement as part of a wider array of security precautions. In three of the five studies reviewed, improvements in home security reduced residents' fear of crime. They suggested that, generally, improvements in home security may be promising ways for individuals to reduce their fear of victimization. Thus, as with avoidance behaviors, the limited research in this area provides mixed support for the relationship between fear of crime and protective behaviors.

Weapons Behaviors

Weapons behaviors are a final dimension of constrained behaviors. As discussed above, weapons have been investigated as a separate type of constrained behaviors because the causes, correlates, and consequences of individuals' weapons use can be different than other types of protective behaviors (e.g., purchasing additional lights and locks for doors, taking a self-defense class, or owning a watch dog) (Rader & Haynes, 2012; Wilcox et al., 2006).

One of the most controversial aspects of reactions to fear of crime is the idea that some individuals purchase, own, and/or carry weapons for self-defense, or due to their fear of criminal victimization. In studies of both adult and adolescent gun carrying, respondents often report that they carry weapons for protection. Over four decades ago, Newton and Zimring (1969) suggested an explanation for gun carrying when they argued that firearm possession was motivated by "fear of crime, violence, and civil disorder" (Newton & Zimring, 1969, p. 21). They called this perspective the "fear and loathing" hypothesis. Proponents of this theory argue that the population is arming itself for protection against a fearful and unfamiliar future (Wright, Rossi, & Daly, 1983).

In support of this argument, Newton and Zimring (1969) determined that self-defense was the most frequently cited reason for owning a handgun. They further found that only 16% of gun owners said that hunting was a good reason for owning a handgun compared to 95% who mentioned hunting as a good reason for owning a rifle or shotgun (Newton and Zimring, 1969). Thus, they argued that handguns were primarily purchased for self-defense while long guns such as rifles and shotguns were primarily used for sporting purposes. In their estimation, the purchase of a gun for self-defense naturally led to firearm ownership for protection; thus, "fear and loathing" was associated with firearms ownership for protection.

Since Newton and Zimring's work appeared in 1969, the idea that people purchase and carry weapons and other firearms to reduce their fear of crime has been one of the pillars of gun control opponents in their fight against restrictive gun control policies. Nevertheless, the evidence supporting the relationship between fear of crime and protective gun ownership is both controversial and tenuous (May & Jarjoura, 2006). Below we review several studies examining these phenomena. We begin that discussion with an examination of the relationship between fear of criminal victimization and firearm ownership among adults then close the discussion by looking at that same evidence among adolescents.

Adult Firearm Possession for Protection

Although the exact number of firearms in the United States is difficult to estimate, Reidel and Welsh (2010) suggest that there were an estimated 258 million firearms in the United States in 1999. Because more than five million firearms are being produced each year (United States Department of Justice Bureau of Alcohol, Tobacco, Firearms, and Explosives, 2011), a conservative estimate would suggest that there are at least 300 million firearms in the United States in 2014.

Americans own 90 to 100 million pistols, 175 to 200 million rifles and shotguns, and a million or more "assault weapons" (ATF, 2011). In practically all national polls compiled to date, between 40% and 50% of respondents indicated they have a firearm in their household (Sourcebook of Criminal Justice Statistics Online, 2012a). In certain parts of the country, the South in particular, the passing down of firearms from father to son is a "rite of passage" into manhood, where boys learn to use weapons from their fathers and pass this knowledge on to their sons (Kaplan, 1981). Thus, the idea of having a gun in the home for "safety" is a deeply ingrained part of the American culture, particularly in rural areas.

Among gun owners in the United States, almost half (47%) felt that the presence of a firearm in the home made them safer (Sourcebook of Criminal

Justice Statistics Online, 2012b). The idea that a gun may protect one from victimization is hotly debated, however. On one hand, data from incarcerated felons suggest that criminals are much less likely to assault a victim that they know is carrying a gun (Wright & Rossi, 1986) and defense against an armed victim was an important reason for carrying a firearm for about half of the prisoners interviewed. Wright and Rossi also found that 56% of their sample agreed that "a criminal is not going to mess around with a victim he knows is armed with a gun" and 57% agreed with the statement "most criminals are more worried about meeting an armed victim than they are about running into the police." These studies suggest that, at least according to inmates who have considered or have already committed violent crime, self-protection is a legitimate reason for owning a gun.

On the other hand, competing evidence suggests that firearms kept for self-protection can be just as deadly to the owner as the would-be attacker. In 2010, 31,672 people were killed by firearms; three in five of these deaths (19,392) were due results of suicides while 11,078 (34%) were results of criminal homicide (Murphy, Xu, & Kochanek, 2013). Gun control opponents argue that guns in homes in the United States dramatically reduce home invasions. Yet, because 90% of all burglaries in the United States are committed when no one is at home, the reality is that for every burglar stopped by a gun by a homeowner, four gun owners or members of their families are killed in firearms accidents (Dolan, 1984). Additionally, each year, 1 in 10 fatal firearm accidents involve victims under the age of 14 (Murphy et al., 2013), many of whom are killed by a sibling or relative that was mishandling a firearm.

Despite the debate around whether firearms kept in the home actually protect one from crime victimization, the perception among many gun owners is that firearms are needed for protection of self, family, and property. Nevertheless, the relationship between fear of crime and firearm ownership among adults appears to be inconclusive at best (Hauser & Kleck, 2013), and researchers generally find no relationship between the two phenomena. These studies are discussed below.

Arthur (1992), after analyzing data obtained from the Black respondents in the General Social Survey (GSS) from the years 1973 to 1990, found that fear of crime does not predict gun ownership. Williams and McGrath (1976) in an analysis of the 1973 GSS found that fear of crime has a negative relationship with gun ownership as did Wright and Marston (1975) in their analysis of all the 1973 GSS respondents. That is, those who were afraid were less likely to own guns. Lizotte and Bordua (1980) found in a telephone study of heads of household in the state of Illinois in the spring of 1977 that violent crime in the county was the only predictor for owning a gun for protection, and that women were as likely to own guns for protection as men. Lizotte, Bordua, and White (1981), using the same data, found that those who were more fearful of crime were more likely to own guns for protection. Smith and Uchida (1988) using data collected from 9,021 interviews with random samples of residents in 59 residential neighborhoods, also found that where respondents believed their chances of being victimized were high, defensive weapons ownership increased markedly with rising income. Hill, Howell, and Driver (1985), in an examination of the 1980 GSS, found that fear was also related to handgun ownership, but only for males. Bankston, Thompson, Jenkins, and Forsyth (1990) and Bankston and Thompson (1989), using a sample of 1,177 White respondents from Louisiana, found little evidence that fear of crime accounted for any differences in the frequency of carrying firearms for protection. In other words, studies find that fear of crime is sometimes related to gun ownership and sometimes not.

Hauser and Kleck (2013) argued that the temporal order of the relationship between fear of crime and gun ownership may not be as clear as it seems. DeFronzo (1979) in his analysis of male respondents from the 1973, 1974, 1976, and 1977 GSS surveys found that handgun ownership reduced fear of crime, indicating the relationship may be reciprocal. More recent research yields similar results. Hauser and Kleck (2013) used two waves of data from 1,331 respondents to the Community, Crime, and Health phone survey of Illinois residents collected in 1995 and 1998. Their findings point to the difficulty of measuring the association between fear of crime and gun ownership. They determined that a higher level of fear of crime at Wave 1 (1995) had a positive but nonsignificant effect on firearm acquisition by Wave 2 (1998) while gun acquisition at Wave 1 had an inconsistent, nonsignificant effect on fear of crime at Wave 2. In other words, people who were afraid in 1995 were a little more likely to have guns by 1998. Additionally, Hauser and Kleck (2013) also identified households in which a firearm was present in Wave 1 but not in Wave 2 and found that respondents from those households that lost a firearm between waves were significantly more fearful than those respondents who either (a) had no firearm in their household in either wave or (b) had a firearm in their household in both waves.

Thus, the available evidence about the relationship between fear of crime and firearm possession suggests that, while many adults report that they own firearms for protection, in those studies where fear of crime is specifically measured, it has no relationship with firearm ownership, although fear may increase when firearms are removed from a household. Given the practical challenges of measuring both firearm possession and fear among adults, better evidence about this relationship may come from adolescents because adolescents often complete self-report surveys about this topics as captive audiences in one of two locations: (1) in-school settings or (2) while incarcerated in a residential facility. In these situations, researchers are better able to use long, detailed questionnaires than could be used with telephone or mail surveys of adults. Below we review that evidence.

Owning/Carrying Weapons for Protection among Adolescents

Although protection is an often cited reason for weapon possession among adolescents and has been for decades (Chandler, Chapman, Rand, & Taylor, 1998; Melde, Esbensen, & Taylor, 2009; Webster et al., 1993), only a limited number of studies examine the relationship between fear of crime and causes of weapon possession for protection. These studies are discussed in detail below.

Durant et al. (1997), using data collected from a sample of 3,054 public high school students in Boston, examined the relationship between weapon possession at school ("During the past 30 days, on how many days did you carry a weapon such as a gun, knife, or club?") and fear of school crime ("During the past 30 days, how many days did you not go to school because you felt you would be unsafe at school or on your way to or from school?") (p. 362). After controlling for a number of other variables previously shown to be related to weapon possession, they determined that students who had not attended school on six or more days in the previous month because of fear were over five times more likely to carry weapons to school (Durant et al., 1997). Harris (1993, p. 15), in an analysis of data collected from 2,508 public and private school students across the United States, further determined that those youth who had carried a gun to school in the past 30 days were twice as likely *not* to be worried "… about being in danger of being attacked physically" as their counterparts who had not carried a gun in the past 30 days. Thus, both Durant et al. (1997) and Harris (1993) found no support for the fear and loathing hypothesis.

Both May (2001) and May and Jarjoura (2006) examined the impact of fear of crime on weapon possession among youths in book-length monographs. May (2001) was the first to explicitly examine the relationship between fear of crime and weapon possession among incarcerated adolescent criminals. May used data from 318 adolescent males incarcerated for serious delinquent offenses in Indiana to examine whether fear of criminal victimization was associated with their weapon possession prior to their incarceration. To measure respondents' fear, May used an eleven-item index asking individuals about their fear of victimization from various forms of crime. May operationalized defensive weapon possession by asking respondents if they had ever carried a weapon other than a gun for protection (61% had) and defensive gun possession by asking whether they had ever carried a gun for protection. Fifty-nine percent (n=187) of the youth admitted to defensive gun possession, indicating that these respondents commonly carried weapons (both firearms and weapons other than firearms) for protection.

The specific nature of the measurement of both the fear and weapons variables overcame many of the obstacles of examining the relationship between fear and weapons possession found in other studies (although May's data were still cross-sectional and were collected from a sample of incarcerated offenders, limiting the generalizability of the findings in its own way). Thus, May distinguished between weapons carrying in general, and weapons carrying for protection. Consequently, if fear of criminal victimization has a relationship with weapons carrying, it should be strongest for weapons carrying for protection.

May (2001) also was able to control for a number of factors mentioned throughout this book that impact both fear of crime and weapons possession (e.g., race, neighborhood disorder, and perceptions of risk). May's findings also did not support the relationship between fear of criminal victimization and weapons possession. May found that, although Whites and youth from disorderly neighborhoods were more likely to carry weapons for protection, the fear of crime index had no relationship with prior weapon carrying for protection. Fear of criminal victimization also was not associated with firearm possession for protection, although youth from disorderly neighborhoods and youth with higher levels of perceived risk were more likely to carry guns for protection. May (2001) thus argued that these youth are carrying these weapons because of their perception that they are likely to be victimized, not necessarily due to their "fear" that they will be victimized.

Findings from May & Jarjoura (2006) also do not support a linkage between fear of crime and weapon possession. May & Jarjoura analyzed data from 828 male and female youths incarcerated in Indiana in January and February 2002. May & Jarjoura (2006) determined that two in five respondents (40.7%) had carried a gun for protection at some point in their lifetime. In a bivariate logistic regression model predicting whether or not the respondent had carried a gun for protection, May and Jarjoura found that males, non-Whites, older adolescents, respondents from disorderly neighborhoods, and respondents that perceived themselves most likely to be victimized by crime were significantly more likely to carry guns for protection than their counterparts. May and Jarjoura suggested that these results provide partial support for the fear of criminal victimization hypothesis.

May and Jarjoura (2006) also extended the examination of the fear of victimization hypothesis by testing whether protective gun carrying had a triggering effect on violence. Their results suggested that protective gun carriers were six times more likely than respondents that had not carried a gun to engage in violent activities in their lifetime. Thus, May and Jarjoura argued against the fear of criminal victimization hypothesis and suggested that:

> If protective gun carrying were due solely to the impact of fear of criminal victimization, it would be counterintuitive to suggest that those youth who carry guns for protection would be more likely to engage in violent activity. In fact, the fear of criminal victimization hypothesis would argue that their fear of being victimized would make them avoid situations that increased their potential for victimization and, as such, fearful youth should be less likely to engage in violence (May & Jarjoura, 2006, pp. 92–93).

Both Wilcox, May, and Roberts (2006) and Melde et al. (2009) used longitudinal data collected from in-school samples of youths to further examine this relationship. Both determined that fear of criminal victimization at Time 1 did not have an association with weapon possession at school at Time 2. Their findings differed around perceptions of risk, however, as Wilcox et al. (2006) found no relationship between perceptions of risk and weapon carrying, while Melde et al. (2009) found that perceived risk was associated with weapons possession for protection. Further analyses in both studies revealed a strong connection between possession of weapons and delinquency.

Thus, empirical research, either among adults or adolescents, does not strongly support the idea that individuals carry weapons for protection because of crime-related fear. If anything, the available research suggests that youth (and probably adults) carry weapons as part of a deviant lifestyle where they realize that they are increasing their likelihood of victimization as part of that lifestyle.

Concluding Remarks

The evidence that fear of crime brings about substantial physiological and psychological consequences is well established in the published research. The social consequences of fear of crime, however, are much more debatable. Fear of crime appears to predict some, but certainly not all, constrained behaviors and its impact often varies by the type of sample under study and the type of behavior under consideration. Additionally, specifying the direction of causality between fear of crime and constrained behaviors is difficult, given that most studies use cross-sectional data.

Consequently, additional research, using longitudinal data and large national samples is needed to further unpack the relationship between fear of crime and all forms of constrained behaviors. Research using qualitative research designs of gun owners, participants in self-defense classes, and homeowners is also needed. Additionally, the relationship between fear of crime and CPTED and defensible space ideas needs further exploration. Consequently, the research reviewed in this chapter certainly did not establish definitive conclusions about the relationship between fear of crime and constrained behaviors; if anything, we leave this chapter with more questions than answers. Box 7.3 provides some recommendations for future research on the consequences of fear.

Box 7.3 Recommendations for Future Research on the Consequences of Fear

1. Use Longitudinal Data to Specify the Relationship between Fear of Crime and Constrained Behaviors among Both Adults and Adolescents.

2. Use Qualitative Research Designs with Gun Owners to:
    - Determine how long they have owned firearms and what type of firearms they own.
    - Determine their reasons for ownership and possession.
    - Examine emotions gun owners experience when carrying firearms.
    - Understand the types of situations where gun owners find firearm possession suitable and unsuitable.
    - Explore the types of situations gun owners would avoid if they did not have their firearm with them.

3. Use Qualitative and Quantitative Research with Participants in Self-Defense Courses to:
    - Understand reasons for participation.
    - Examine differences in behavior patterns and fear levels before and after participation in the classes.

4. Conduct Qualitative and Quantitative Research with Homeowners to:
    - Specify the types of defensive behaviors homeowners prefer.
    - Understand the decision-making process used in choosing to engage in those behaviors.
    - Explore demographic and contextual differences in the types of defensive behaviors in which homeowners choose to engage.

5. Use Quasi-experimental research designs (with control groups) to determine whether CPTED and defensible space principles actually reduce fear of crime after their implementation.

References

Arthur, J.A. (1992). Criminal victimization, fear of crime, and handgun ownership among Blacks: Evidence from national survey data. *American Journal of Criminal Justice, 16*(2), 121–141.

Bankston, W.B., & Thompson, C.Y. (1989). Carrying firearms for protection: A causal model. *Sociological Inquiry, 59*(1), 75–87.

Bankston, W.B., Thompson, C.Y., Jenkins, Q.A., & Forsyth, C.J. (1990). The influence of fear of crime, gender, and southern culture on carrying firearms for protection. *The Sociological Quarterly, 31*(2), 287–305.

Beaulieu, M., Dubé, M., Bergeron, C., & Cousineau, M.M. (2007). Are elderly men worried about crime? *Journal of Aging Studies, 21*(4), 336–346.

Bozovic, M. (ed.). (1995). *The panopticon writings—Jeremy Bentham.* London: Verso. http://cartome.org/panopticon2.htm. Accessed January 4, 2014.

Carroll, J. (2007). *How Americans protect themselves from crime: Most likely to avoid certain areas because crime occurs.* Gallup. http://www.gallup.com/poll/102418/How-Americans-Protect-Themselves-From-Crime.aspx. Accessed October 8, 2013.

Chandler, K.A., Chapman, C.D., Rand, M.R., and Taylor, B.M. (1998). *Students' reports of school crime: 1989 and 1995.* Washington, D.C.: U.S. Departments of Education and Justice.

Chandola, T. (2001). The fear of crime and area differences in health. *Health & Place, 7*(2), 105–116.

Clarke, R.V. (1997). *Situational crime prevention: Successful case studies (2nd ed.).* Albany, NY: Harrow and Heston Publishers.

Cole, L. (1964). *Psychology of adolescence (6th ed.).* New York: Holt, Rinehart, and Winston, Inc.

Conklin, J.E. (1975). *The impact of crime.* New York: Macmillan.

Cossman, J.S., & Rader, N.E. (2011). Fear of crime and personal vulnerability: Examining self-reported health. *Sociological Spectrum, 31*(2), 141–162.

Darwin, C. (1910). *The expression of emotions in men and animals. 1872.* Reprinted by Appleton: New York.

DeFronzo, J. (1979). Fear of crime and handgun ownership. *Criminology, 17*(3), 331–340.

De Welde, K. (2003a). White women beware! Whiteness, fear of crime, and self-defense. *Race, Gender & Class, 10*(4), 75–91.

De Welde, K. (2003b). Getting physical: Subverting gender through self-defense. *Journal of Contemporary Ethnography, 32*(3), 247–278.

Dolan, E.F. Jr. (1984). Three arguments for gun control. In D.L. Bender & B. Leone (Eds.) *Crime and criminals: Opposing viewpoints (2nd ed.)*, (pp. 139–144). St. Paul, MN: Greenhaven Press.

Durant, R.H., Kahn, J., Beckford, P.H., & Woods, E.R. (1997). The association of weapon carrying and fighting on school property and other health risk and problem behaviors among high school students. *Archives of Pediatric Adolescent Medicine, 151*(4), 360–366.

Ferraro, K.F. (1995). *Fear of crime: Interpreting victimization risk.* Albany, NY: State University of New York Press.

Ferraro, K.F., & LaGrange, R. (1987). The measurement of fear of crime. *Sociological Inquiry, 57*(1), 70–101.

Fisher, B.S., & Nasar, J.L. (1992). Fear of crime in relation to three exterior site features: Prospect, refuge, and escape. *Environment and Behavior, 24*(1), 35–65.

Fisher, B.S., & Nasar, J.L. (1995). Fear spots in relation to microlevel physical cues: Exploring the overlooked. *Journal of Research in Crime and Delinquency, 32*(2), 214–239.

Fleissner, D., & Heinzelmann, F. (1996). *Crime prevention through environmental design and community policing.* Washington D.C.: U.S. Department of Justice, National Institute of Justice, NCJ 157308.

Foster, S., Giles-Corti, B., & Knuiman, M. (2010). Neighbourhood design and fear of crime: A social-ecological examination of the correlates of residents' fear in new suburban housing developments. *Health and Place, 16*(6), 1156–1165.

Giblin, M.J., Burrus, G.W., Corsaro, N., & Schafer, J.A. (2012). Self-protection in rural America: A risk interpretation model of household protective measures. *Criminal Justice Policy Review, 23*(4), 493–517.

Gordon, M.T., & Riger, S. (1989). *The female fear: The social cost of rape.* New York: Free Press.

Gray, J. (1971). *The psychology of fear and stress.* (2nd ed.) Cambridge: Cambridge University Press.

Harris, L. (1993). *A survey of experiences, perceptions, and apprehensions about guns among young people in America.* New York: L.H. Research, Inc., Study 930019.

Hauser, W., & Kleck, G. (2013). Guns and fear: A one-way street? *Crime and Delinquency, 59*(2), 271–291.

Hill, G.D., Howell, F.M., & Driver, E.T. (1985). Gender, fear, and protective handgun ownership. *Criminology, 23*(3), 541–552.

Hinkle, J.C., & Weisburd, D. (2008). The irony of broken windows policing: A micro-place study between disorder, focused police crackdowns, and fear of crime. *Journal of Criminal Justice, 36*(6), 503–512.

Hollander, J.A. (2010). Why do women take self-defense classes? *Violence against Women, 16*(4), 459–478.

Hollander, J.A. (2001). Vulnerability and dangerousness: The construction of gender through conversation about violence. *Gender and Society, 15*(1), 83–109.

Izard, C.E. (1977). *Human emotions.* New York: Plenum Press.

Jeffery, C.R. (1971). *Crime prevention through environmental design* (p. 224). Beverly Hills, CA: Sage Publications.

Kaplan, J. (1981). The wisdom of gun prohibition. *Annals of the American Academy of Political and Social Sciences, 455*(1), 11–23.

Keane, C. (1998). Evaluating the influence of fear of crime as an environmental mobility restrictor on women's routine activities. *Environment and Behavior, 30*(1), 60–74.

Kemper, T.D. (1978). *A social interactional theory of emotions.* New York: John Wiley and Sons, Inc.

Kleck, G. (1988). Crime control through the private use of armed force. *Social Problems 35*(1), 1–21.

Lab, S.P. (2010). *Crime prevention: Approaches, practices, and evaluations (7th ed.).* New Providence, NJ: Lexis Nexis Group.

Lane, J. (2009). Perceptions of neighborhood problems, fear of crime, and resulting behavioral precautions: Comparing institutionalized girls and boys in Florida. *Journal of Contemporary Criminal Justice, 25*(3), 264–281.

Liska, A.E., Sanchirico, A., & Reed, M.D. (1988). Fear of crime and constrained behaviors: Specifying and estimating a reciprocal effects model. *Social Forces, 66*(3), 827–837.

Lizotte, A.J., & Bordua, D.J. (1980). Firearms ownership for sport and protection: Two divergent models. *American Sociological Review, 45*(2), 229–244.

Lizotte, A.J., Bordua, D.J., & White, C.S. (1981). Firearms ownership for sport and protection: Two not so divergent models. *American Sociological Review, 46*(4), 499–503.

Lizotte, A.J., Tesoriero, J.M., Thornberry, T.P., & Krohn, M.D. (1994). Patterns of adolescent firearm ownership and use. *Justice Quarterly, 11*(1), 51–74.

Lorenc, T., Petticrew, M., Whitehead, M., Neary, D., Clayton, S., Wright, K., Thomson, H., Cummins, S., Sowden, A., & Renton, A. (2013). Environmental interventions to reduce fear of crime: Systematic review of the effectiveness. *Systematic Review, 2*(30), May 12, 2013. http://www.system aticreviewsjournal.com/content/2/1/30. Accessed November 23, 2013.

Madriz, E.I. (1997). Images of criminals and victims: A study on women's fear and social control. *Gender and Society, 11*(3), 342–356.

Marks, I.M. (1978). *Living with fear: Understanding and Coping with Anxiety.* New York: McGraw Hill Book Company.

May, D.C. (2001). *Adolescent fear of crime, perceptions of risk, and defensive behaviors: An alternative explanation of violent delinquency.* Lewiston, NY: Edwin Mellen Press.

May, D.C., Rader, N.E., & Goodrum, S. (2010). A gendered assessment of the 'threat of victimization': Examining gender differences in fear of crime, perceived risk, avoidance, and defensive behaviors. *Criminal Justice Review 35*(2), 159–182.

May, D.C., & Dunaway, R.G. (2000). Predictors of fear of criminal victimization at school among adolescents. *Sociological Spectrum, 20*(2), 149–168.

May, D.C., & Jarjoura, R.J. (2006). *Illegal guns in the wrong hands: Patterns of gun acquisition and use among serious juvenile delinquents.* Lanham, MD: University Press of America.

McDaniel, P. (1993). Self-defense training and women's fear of crime. *Women's Studies International Forum, 16*(1), 37–45.

McKee, K., & Milner, C. (2000). Health, fear of crime and psychosocial functioning in older people. *Journal of Health Psychology, 5*(4), 473–486

Melde, C., Esbensen, F.A., & Taylor, T.J. (2009). 'May piece be with you': A typological examination of the fear and victimization hypothesis of adolescent weapon carrying. *Justice Quarterly, 26*(2), 348–376.

Murphy, S., Xu, J., & Kochanek, K.D. (2013). *Deaths: Final data for 2010.* Atlanta, GA: Centers for Disease Control.

Nellis, A.M. (2009). Gender differences in fear of terrorism. *Journal of Contemporary Criminal Justice, 25*(3), 322–340.

Newman, O. (1996). *Creating defensible space.* Washington D.C.: US Department of Housing and Urban Development, Office of Policy Development and Research. Institute for Community Design Analysis, Center for Urban Policy Research, Rutgers University.

Newman, O. (1972). *Defensible space: Crime prevention through urban design.* New York: McMillan.

Newton, G.D., & Zimring, F.E. (1969). *Firearms & violence in American life.* Washington, D.C.: National Commission on the Causes and Prevention of Violence.

Pain, R. (2000). Place, social relations, and the fear of crime: A revew. *Progress in Human Geography, 24*(3), 365–387.

Pain, R.H. (1997). 'Old age' and ageism in urban research: The case of fear of crime. *International Journal of Urban and Regional Research, 21*(1), 117–128.

Painter, K. (1996). The influence of street lighting improvements on crime, fear and pedestrian street use, after dark. *Landscape and Urban Planning*, *35*(2), 193–201.

Rader, N.E., & Haynes, S.H. (2012). Avoidance, protective, and weapons behaviors: An examination of constrained behaviors and their impact on concerns about crime. *Journal of Crime and Justice* (online), DOI:10.1080/0735648X.2012.723358.

Rader, N.E., & Cossman, J.S. (2011). Gender differences in U.S. college students' fear for others. *Sex Roles* 64: 568–581.

Rader, N.E., Cossman, J.S., & Allison, M. (2009). Considering the gendered nature of constrained behavior practices among male and female college students. *Journal of Contemporary Criminal Justice 25*(3), 282–299.

Reidel, M., & Welsh, W. (2010). *Criminal Violence: Patterns, Causes, and Prevention (3rd ed.)*. New York: Oxford University Press.

Ricci-Bitti, P., & Scherer, K.R. (1986). Interrelations between antecedents, reactions, and coping responses. In K.R. Scherer, H.G. Wallbott, & A.B. Summerfield (Eds.) *Experiencing emotion: A cross-cultural study* (pp. 129–142). Cambridge, Great Britain: Cambridge University Press.

Rime, B., & Giovannini, D. (1986). The physiological patterns of reported emotional states. In K.R. Scherer, H.G. Wallbott, & A.B. Summerfield (Eds.) *Experiencing emotion: A cross-cultural study* (pp. 84–97). Cambridge, Great Britain: Cambridge University Press.

San-Juan, C., Vozmediano, L., & Vergara, A. (2012). Self-protective behaviours against crime in urban settings: An empirical approach to vulnerability and victimization models. *European Journal of Criminology, 9*(6), 652–667.

Scott, H. (2003). Stranger danger: Explaining women's fear of crime. *Western Criminology Review 4*(3), 203–214.

Scruton, D.L. (1986). The anthropology of an emotion. pp. 7–49 in *Sociophobics: The anthropology of fear*, D.L. Scruton (ed.). Boulder, CO: Westview Press.

Sheley, J.F., McGee, Z.T., & Wright, J.D. (1992). Gun-related violence in and around inner-city schools. *Archives of Pediatrics and Adolescent Medicine, 146*(6), 677–682.

Sheley, J.F., & Wright, J.D. (1993). *Gun acquisition and possession in selected juvenile samples*. Washington, D.C.: National Institute of Justice, Office of Juvenile Justice and Delinquency Prevention Research in Brief, NCJ 145326.

Short, E., & Ditton, J. (1998). Seen and now heard: Talking to the targets of open street CCTV. *British Journal of Criminology, 38*(3), 404–428.

Skogan, W.G., & Maxfield, M.G. (1981). *Coping with crime: Individual and neighborhood reactions*. Beverly Hills, CA: Sage Publications.

Smith, D.A., & Uchida, C.D. (1988). The social organization of self-help: A study of defensive weapon ownership. *American Sociological Review, 53*(1) 94–102.

Sourcebook of Criminal Justice Statistics Online. (2012a). *Respondents reporting having a gun in their home or on property, United States, selected years 1959–2012.* Albany, NY: Author. http://www.albany.edu/sourcebook/pdf/t2592012.pdf. Accessed January 29, 2014.

Sourcebook of Criminal Justice Statistics Online. (2012b). *Attitudes toward whether having a gun in the home makes it safer or more dangerous, United States, 2000, 2004, & 2006.* Albany, NY: Author. http://www.albany.edu/sourcebook/pdf/t200102006.pdf. Accessed January 29, 2014.

Spinks, C. (2001). *A new Apartheid? Urban spatiality, (fear of) crime, and segregation in Capetown, South Africa.* London: Destin Working Paper No. 20, London School of Economics.

Stanko, E. (1997). Safety talk: Conceptualizing women's risk assessment as a technology of the soul. *Theoretical Criminology 1*(4), 479–499.

Warr, M. (2000). Fear of crime in the United States: Avenues for research and policy. *Criminal Justice, 4*(5), 451–489.

Webster, D.W., Gainer, P.S., & Champion, H.R. (1993). Weapon carrying among inner-city junior high school students: Defensive behavior vs aggressive delinquency. *American Journal of Public Health, 83*(11), 1604–1608.

Wilcox, P., May, D.C., & Roberts, S.D. (2006). Student weapon possession and the 'fear of victimization hypothesis': Unraveling the temporal order. *Justice Quarterly, 23*(4), 502–529.

Williams, J.S., & McGrath III, J.H. (1976). Why people own guns. *Journal of Communication 26*(4), 22–30.

Wright, J.D., & Marston, L.L. (1975). The ownership of the means of destruction: Weapons in the United States. *Social Problems, 23*(1), 93–107.

Wright, J.D., & Rossi, P.H. (1986). *Armed and considered dangerous: A survey of felons and their firearms.* New York: Aldine De Gruyter.

Wright, J.D., Rossi, P., & Daly, K. (1983). *Under the gun: Weapons, crime, and violence in America.* New York: Aldine de Gruyter.

Chapter 8

Tying the Findings Together: Suggestions for Policy and Future Research on Fear of Crime

Given the ubiquity of messages about crime in our society and the costs of inaccurate information, it is incumbent on criminal justice officials to provide the public with reliable information about crime, including information about the risk of victimization for different criminal offenses, the sources and likelihood of error in those estimates, the nature of victimization events (including the risk of injury associated with those events), and, where known, the personal, social, and temporal/spatial characteristics that increase or reduce risk.

Warr, 2000, p. 483

[W]hile making people safe is perhaps the most important purpose of government, making them feel safe is nearly as important because fear has such negative ramifications for politics, economics, and social life.

Cordner, 2010, p. ix

This book synthesized the research regarding what scholars understand about the correlates, causes, and consequences of fear of crime. This final chapter has three goals: (1) briefly summarize fear of crime research, (2) suggest what these results might mean for criminal justice practice and policy, and (3) discuss specific areas of research that the authors believe are important for expanding scholars' and policymakers' current understanding of fear of crime.

Summarizing Fear of Crime Research

Fear of crime has been an important topic of scholarly literature for over 50 years, beginning in the 1960s when the President's Commission on Law Enforcement and Administration of Justice (LEAA) issued *The Challenge of Crime in a Free Society* report. This report noted that one of the worst effects of crime was the fear it caused among the public (Katzenbach et al., 1967), and it was a key catalyst prompting academicians to turn their attention to fear of crime.

Studies during the first decade or so after the LEAA report primarily used questions that were developed for the General Social Survey (GSS) and National Crime Survey (NCS), now called the National Crime Victimization Survey (NCVS). These questions were general, did not mention the word "crime," and some scholars argued they confused perceived risk (a thought) with fear (an emotion) (Ferraro, 1995; Ferraro & LaGrange, 1987, 1988; LaGrange & Ferraro, 1987). These early studies primarily described the demographic characteristics (such as gender, age, and race) that were correlated with fear of crime, because there was so little known about the topic. Early results demonstrated that some groups had levels of fear that were disproportionate to their actual risk of victimization (e.g., women and the elderly); thus, researchers began to focus on understanding fear among these specific groups (e.g., women and older people) and began using more specific measures in an attempt to distinguish between perceived risk and fear of crime (e.g., Lee, 1982; Warr, 1984, 1985; Yin, 1982, 1985).

Soon, influential scholars expanded the focus beyond demographic correlates to better understand the fact that many people who appeared more afraid actually faced less real risk of victimization. Specifically, researchers focused on explaining (rather than just describing) the reasons why these groups were most fearful. Some of these researchers focused on explaining women's fear while others focused on fear of crime among the elderly, providing explanations for their fear based on ideas about vulnerability, socialization, patriarchy, hidden victimization, and fear of sexual assault. Others moved beyond personal victimization experience to examine neighborhood characteristics (such as indirect victimization through other people and/or neighborhood diversity, disorder, and decline) that could explain fear (see Box 8.1 for the theoretical explanations about the causes of fear) (e.g., Skogan et al., 1982; see Warr, 1994, for a review). Each of these theoretical explanations received some empirical support and many of these efforts and ideas have developed into parallel lines of research among fear of crime scholars that continue to the present day. Yet, interestingly, research has not yet focused on comparing how gender interacts with neighborhood characteristics to heighten fear.

Box 8.1 Key Theoretical Explanations about the Causes of Fear

1. **Why Women are More Afraid**

    A. *Irrationality:* They are driven by emotion not fact.

    B. *Vulnerability:* They feel weaker and more physically vulnerable than men do.

    C. *Socialization:* They are told by their parents and the media to be extra careful, that they are likely to be victimized, etc.

    D. *Patriarchy:* Men induce fear to oppress women.

    E. *Shadow of sexual assault:* They worry about other crimes, especially violent ones, because they fear they will lead to rape.

    F. *Hidden victimization:* Women are victimized more than official statistics indicate, because much physical and sexual violence happens behind closed doors or is not reported to law enforcement.

    G. *Boys Don't Cry:* Men are taught to be tough and not show weakness.

2. **Why People Who are Not at High Risk for Victimization and Others May Be Afraid**

    A. *Indirect Victimization:* People hear about crime from other people or from the media.

    B. *Subcultural Diversity/Racial Heterogeneity:* People do not understand the mannerisms and behaviors of people who look different and therefore find them scary.

    C. *Disorder/Incivilities:* People interpret evidence of physical (e.g., graffiti, trash, unkempt yards) and social (e.g., loitering, groups of youths) disorder to mean that crime is also a problem.

    D. *Community concern/Decline:* People are worried that the community is in decline, or no longer the way it used to be and therefore feel more at risk from crime.

Another line of fear research that developed in the 1970s expanded the indirect victimization idea to concentrate on media (e.g., television and newspapers) impacts on fear. Early researchers argued that people who watched more television would be more afraid, regardless of their personal characteristics (Gerbner & Gross, 1976; Gerbner et al., 1977, 1978). Later work showed that other personal characteristics affected the relationship between media and fear as well (e.g., gender, age, and race). For example, one study showed that watching more television was correlated with higher fear levels for those who had been victimized and for White women (Chiricos et al., 1997), and another found that it was related to fear for Whites and Blacks, but not Hispanics (Chiricos et al., 2000). In addition, studies have shown that characteristics of the story matter (e.g., those crime stories that portray the criminal incident as random and are closer to the front of the newspaper are scarier) as do the experiences of the reader/watcher (e.g., whether the story resonates with life experience or whether the crime happened locally) (Gerbner et al., 1980; Heath, 1984; Liska & Baccaglini, 1990).

During the 1980s, researchers also began focusing on the importance of improving measures of fear, in part as a criticism of prior measures and in part to explain results showing women and the elderly were more afraid than others. For example, Warr and Stafford (1983) and Warr (1984) reported results from a survey of Seattle residents, asking them about their fears of specific offenses (e.g., being raped, having someone break into their home, being murdered, or having their car stolen). They examined issues such as the importance of perceived risk, perceived crime seriousness, and sensitivity to risk. Ferraro and LaGrange (1987) specifically critiqued the measurement of fear of crime in prior studies and argued for improving the validity and reliability of the measures. LaGrange and Ferraro (1989) soon examined telephone surveys, comparing the NCS measure of fear and 11 questions measuring fear of specific offenses (e.g., car theft, burglary while away, burglary while home, murder, and rape), and including perceived risk. Their study, like most before and following, showed that women were more afraid no matter how fear was measured. Yet, these scholars were some of the first to show that the effects of age depended on how fear was measured. General questions showed that elderly were more afraid, but more specific measures regarding fear of specific crimes showed that they were not (LaGrange & Ferraro, 1989). Later studies using similar measures with greater precision have also determined that younger people are more afraid than older ones (e.g., Ferraro, 1995, 1996; Lane & Meeker, 2003b; see Warr, 1994, for a review).

The results of early studies using improved measures of both perceived risk and fear of specific crimes confirmed that perceived risk was a conceptually distinct phenomenon from fear of crime and that there were important demographic differences in levels of perceived risk. These studies further determined that perceived risk was an important predictor of fear of crime and that people's level of fear of crime varied by both their individual characteristics and the characteristics of the crime in question. This research arguing for improved measurement was the precursor to the now standard practice of measuring fear of multiple offenses, and measuring perceived risk and fear as separate constructs. These calls to create more valid and reliable measures also led to other researchers working to further refine questions. Researchers began to include questions that compare fear of strangers to fear of acquaintances (e.g., Hickman & Muehlenhard, 1997; Wilcox, Jordan, & Pritchard, 2006) or adding particular perpetrators, such as gangs or terrorists (e.g., Barberet, Fisher & Taylor, 2004; Katz et al., 2003; Lane, 2002; Lane & Meeker, 2000, 2003a, 2003b, 2004, 2005, 2011; Nellis, 2009; Nellis & Savage, 2012; Wilcox et al., 2009). In general, these studies have found that predictors of fear of criminal offenses generally also predict fear of crimes by specific offenders (e.g., gangs in Lane & Meeker studies or Katz et al., 2003). Studies also have also examined the importance of location, such as fear on campus, at school, or at work (e.g., Fisher & Sloan, 2003; Gover et al., 2011; Randa & Wilcox, 2011; Wallace & May, 2005), including site-level characteristics, such as the presence of darkness and possible hiding places for offenders (see Fisher & May, 2009; Fisher & Nasar, 1992a, 1992b, 1995). Still other work has focused on explaining and comparing the predictors of fear of crime and perceived risk in a wide variety of samples (e.g., women versus men, young versus old, juveniles, and/or offenders) (e.g., Lane, 2006, 2009; Lane et al., 2009; Lane and Fox, 2012, 2013; May, 2001a, 2001b; Warr, 1984).

As noted in other chapters, findings of these studies typically show that women are more afraid than men, younger people are more afraid than older ones (when more precise measures are used), and racial and ethnic minorities are more afraid than Whites. Contrary to some expectations, offenders tend to be less afraid than their victimization risk would warrant. One explanation is that they may they feel more knowledgeable or protected by their street experience and peer connections. Interestingly, although psychological research on children shows witnessing crime can have a powerful impact on fear of personal victimization (see Warner & Weist, 1996, for a review), fear of crime researchers have not focused on understanding the impact that witnessing crime victimization of others has on one's own personal fear.

As the last chapter discussed, fear of crime also results in consequences, and these results can be physical, psychological, and social. In terms of reactions to fear of crime, these consequences often involve constrained or active behaviors to protect one's self or others. Fear of crime researchers have most often focused on the behavioral consequences of fear. Examples of precautions include installing extra door locks or lighting around one's home, having a guard dog, avoiding certain areas or people, and buying, keeping, or carrying a weapon (e.g., a baseball bat, a knife, or a gun). Research shows that the most common behaviors are avoidance (such as not going to particular parts of the city) or protective (such as installing locks), while the least common response is carrying a gun. Youths most likely to have guns for protection are also those who are more likely to have less money, have friends who own guns, and are involved in crime or drugs themselves (see Lizotte et al., 1994). Some research shows that fear does not necessarily prompt gun ownership for protection among adolescents (e.g., May, 2001a; May & Jarjoura, 2006) and only sometimes does for adults (e.g., Arthur, 1992; Bankston et al., 1990; Lizotte et al., 1981). For a summary of major findings from fear of crime research, see Box 8.2.

Even with all these efforts to understand the causes and consequences of fear of crime, there still is no consensus among scholars regarding the definition of fear of crime. Yet, as noted in Chapter 3, there are similarities across definitions. The research has established that fear of crime is: (1) an emotional reaction, (2) associated with threat from crime, and (3) related to the immediacy of the event. That is, people are afraid when they perceive danger from crime or symbols of crime. While it may be difficult for scholars to decide on a standard definition, it is clear that the majority of researchers believe that fear is emotional rather than cognitive. Furthermore, researchers are also in consensus that many factors impact where or when fear occurs, how intense the feeling is, and how often the feeling arises. Additionally, fear of crime researchers also agree that fear of crime has important impacts on attitudes, behaviors, lifestyle and life quality.

Implications for Policy and Practice

Not all researchers discuss the policy and practical implications of their fear of crime studies for two possible reasons: they are focused on explanation rather than implication and it is unclear how much policymakers want to reduce fear of crime. Fear of crime among the public is an easy rallying cry to promote harsh crime and punishment policies when politicians want reasons to do so. If "criminals" are terrorizing communities, then it is easier to promote tough punishment policies such as Three Strikes and You're Out, Truth in Sentencing (requiring offenders to serve 85% of their sentences), life without parole, or the death penalty (Chevigny, 2003). Still, given the findings discussed in this book, there are some clear policy implications. Box 8.3 provides seven policy and practice implications of the fear of crime findings.

Reduce Crime

For some people, fear of crime is clearly a rational response and based in their environmental context, such as living in a high crime area or a home where violence is common. For these individuals, fear of crime may be healthy if it prompts them to engage in activities that lower their risk of victimization (e.g., putting bars on their windows, alarms on their cars or homes, or staying out of dangerous areas in the neighborhood at night) (see Warr, 2000). For that subset of the population, part of the answer may be the obvious one. It makes

---

Box 8.2 Major Findings from Fear Research

1. **Fear is an emotional response to danger related to crime or crime victimization.**

2. **How fear is measured matters. Better studies:**
   A. Use words that refer to fear (e.g., fear, afraid, worry) rather than perceived risk (e.g., likely).
   B. Refer to specific crimes (e.g., murder, robbery, rape) rather than the general feeling (e.g., fear of walking alone at night).
   C. Specify perpetrator (e.g., stranger, acquaintance, friend or family member, gang member, terrorist).
   D. Specify time of day (e.g., day or night) and place (e.g., neighborhood, work, or school).
   E. Use multiple measures.
   F. Examine both level and intensity of fear.

3. **Certain groups of people are more afraid than others.**
   A. Women are consistently more afraid than men.
   B. Younger people are more afraid than older people, when using precise measures.
   C. Racial and ethnic minorities are more afraid than Whites.

4. **Personal experience with crime can impact fear.**
   A. Personal victimization can increase or decrease fear depending on the person's reaction to the experience.
   B. Witnessing victimization of others can increase fear.
   C. Participating in crime apparently decreases fear, possibly because offenders feel more knowledgeable or experienced regarding crime.

5. **Contextual factors affect fear of crime.**
   A. Neighborhood factors such as diversity, neighborhood disorder, and negatively changing environments generally increase fear.
   B. Situational cues such as darkness, shrubbery, lack of escape options, and area novelty increase fear.
   C. Media consumption affects some people more than others.
   D. Hearing about crime from others (e.g., friends, neighbors, or community police officers) can increase fear.

6. **Fear levels vary in frequency and intensity.**
   A. People fear some crimes more than others (e.g., rape and murder).
   B. Fear can be episodic rather than continuous.
   C. Some people are more prone to fear than others.

7. **Fear has consequences, affecting both lives and crime policy.**
   A. Consequences can be physical, psychological, and/or social.
   B. People are more likely to avoid places or protect their homes and belongings than to carry a weapon, especially a gun.
   C. Research is mixed on whether gun owners own them for self-protection or not.

Box 8.3 Policy and Practice Implications

1. Reduce crime.
2. Educate the public on local crime.
3. Target some educational efforts to specific groups (e.g., men, women, the elderly).
4. Teach people about other racial, ethnic, and cultural groups.
5. Reduce opportunities for victimization.
6. Reduce neighborhood disorder and reverse community decline.
7. Consider restricting media and violent video game content.

---

sense for practitioners to engage in common but active efforts to reduce crime and improve safety in those neighborhoods and homes. There is a separate literature designed to determine the best approaches to reduce crime, and these efforts cannot be addressed in detail here (see Weisburd & Eck, 2004, for a review of police practices). There is not much evidence that people know when crime statistics show a decrease (see Roberts, 1992); yet, in some areas, differences may be obvious to residents every day. For example, in areas plagued with violence, it will make a difference if there is less disorder in the area and fewer known or obvious criminals around. People may start to believe that they can walk down the street without fear of personal harm (e.g., being mugged or harassed by people hanging out or caught in the crossfire of a gang shooting).

Research shows that community policing, or at least some components of it, may be one way to lower fear levels while indirectly reducing crime (by reducing disorder) (e.g., Dammert & Malone, 2006; Kelling et al., 1981; Pate et al., 1986; Weisburd & Eck, 2004; Xu, Fiedler, & Flaming, 2005). One approach that might also reduce fear of crime is to reduce opportunities for violent crime (or the lethality of it) by reducing the availability of firearms to criminal individuals (see Piehl, Kennedy, & Braga, 2000). In the wake of the Newtown, Connecticut, school shootings, lawmakers have focused on this issue with renewed vigor. For example, in January 2013, President Obama published his plan to reduce gun violence, including requiring background checks on all gun sales, strengthening the background check system, and banning military-style assault weapons and high capacity magazines (The White House, 2013).

Educate the Public on Crime and Their Personal Risk

Educate People on Local Crime

For those individuals who have a higher level of fear of crime than their victimization risk should warrant, reducing crime itself will not be enough. Educational efforts to increase their knowledge of crime risk may be useful if educators and journalists present the information carefully without sensationalizing it. Such efforts could be accomplished through making information about local crime rates or hot spots available via neighborhood newsletters or community police officer visits to neighborhood meetings or events. Newspapers also could publish comparative crime statistics, showing local neighborhood variation in crime or comparing the city of interest to neighboring or similar cities. If crime rates look low in comparison to other places, people might start to feel relatively safe (e.g., Liska & Baccaglini, 1990).

Along those lines, it may also be useful to share information about the most common types of crime people may face. That is, these educational efforts would be most useful if they clearly delineate risk from different types of crime (violent, property, public nuisance, etc.). The public often overestimates the amount of crime and assumes that the crime problem is getting worse, even when it actually is not (see Roberts, 1992). Because of the way crime is portrayed in the media—e.g., the "if it bleeds, it leads" approach to reporting news, and the focus on violent crime in television dramas—people may believe that violent crime is much more common than it is. In fact, the majority of crime is nonviolent (Federal Bureau of Investigation, 2013). It may help to share the incident characteristics of the most common crimes in the local area, so that people can make better judgments about their real risk levels. If they realize that violent crime is rare and therefore unlikely to happen to them, they may be less fearful. As this book has discussed, perceived risk is a strong predictor of fear of crime.

Another important piece of information that could be shared in informational venues is that violent crime is much more likely to be perpetrated by someone the victim knows rather than by a stranger (Lauritsen & Rezey, 2013). Scholars typically measure fears about crime that occur outside the home, or "street crime." The idea of random crime (e.g., being shot in a drive-by gang shooting) can be scary, but in truth these types of crimes are rare. Only about a third of violent crimes reported in the National Crime Victimization Survey (NCVS) were perpetrated by strangers. The remainder were committed by intimate partners, relatives, or people the victim knew. For women, the proportion of violent victimizers who were known to them was even higher than it was for men (Lauritsen & Rezey, 2013). For example, a recent report by the Violence Policy Center (2013) showed that in 2011, 94% of women killed by homicide knew the offender (when examining cases where the relationship was indicated). If the public could be given this information—that their risk of victimization from someone they know is much higher than by someone they do not—it might ease their fears when they are out in public without any reason to be in a high-risk situation.

Target Some Educational Efforts

Educational information may also be tailored to a specific group of the population. For example, because young men, and especially those who are offenders, are at the highest risk from violent crime, it might be prudent to share information both about their heightened risk and ways of preventing it, including changing or being aware of their routine activities and choosing prosocial peers (see Chen, 2009; Planty & Truman, 2013; Sampson & Lauritsen, 1990). Research has shown that fear of crime is one reason that teenagers carry guns and, not coincidentally, a reason that weapons are readily available when conflicts arise, which means disputes quickly can turn lethal (see Piehl, Kennedy, & Braga, 2000). It would be useful to teach children, especially those residing in higher crime neighborhoods, prosocial tactics for addressing their fear of crime so that they are aware of choices other than guns or gang membership to protect themselves (e.g., avoiding unsafe areas, walking with friends when out, talking to trusted adults, or contacting the police when facing threats). This information about risk and protection could be conveyed through information sessions at schools, universities, fraternities, social clubs, juvenile offender programs, probation offices, and other similar venues where youth congregate. To reinforce these messages, it would help to include parents in these educational sessions. Separate programming may also be delivered to parents, to teach them about how to talk to their children about crime, safety, and management of their fears.

Another focus of education for men, in particular, arises from the theoretical arguments designed to explain fear of crime among women. Both the shadow of sexual assault thesis and the patriarchy argument focus specifically on women's fear of men. The former discusses women's greater fear of sexual assault while the latter focuses on the imbalance of power between men and women. The core of the patriarchy argument is that men act purposely to control women, including scary things that involve threat and fear as their instruments. This would include the threat of rape, which is at the core of women's fear according to the sexual assault thesis. Stanko (1998) has argued that one of the reasons women are more afraid than men are is because society and practitioners put the responsibility for women's victimization on them (e.g., telling them not to wear revealing clothes, to avoid places, and not to drink at parties) rather than focusing our efforts on reducing the behavior of men that victimizes and terrorizes women (e.g., sexual harassment, rape, and domestic abuse). Men could be encouraged to participate in activities and behaviors that reduce women's fear of sexual assault rather than increase it. For example, they could be taught to intervene when women are drunk at parties and around potential offenders, use positive peer pressure to reduce rape myths among other men, and vocalize opposition to sexist attitudes when their friends do not appear to understand that "no means no." From this perspective, programs that focus on changing men's attitudes, expectations, and behaviors toward women are sorely needed.

There are already some programs in place that focus on efforts to change men's behavior. For example, Foubert and his colleagues (2004, 2010, and 2007) have shown that rape prevention programs focused on males (not females) can teach men to think differently about women and rape. In addition, these researchers have shown that such programs can improve male behavior—for example, leading them to stop telling jokes about rape, prompt them to intervene when someone else is doing something that implies a rape might occur, and being cautious when sexual encounters occur while a woman is drinking (e.g., Foubert & Cowell, 2004, Foubert, Godin, & Tatum, 2010; Foubert & Perry, 2007).

Women could also benefit from education about crime and their own victimization risk, yet this issue is complicated because of their already heightened fear levels compared to men. The vulnerability theory, which focuses on women's self-perceived lack of strength and ability to fend off attackers, would easily translate into teaching women self-defense to help build their confidence or teaching them how to target harden by having a companion when out, carrying pepper spray, or avoiding places that make them feel uneasy. Yet, as noted above, Stanko (1998), who subscribes to the patriarchy argument, asserts that these efforts to teach women to protect themselves actually increase women's fear levels by putting the onus for crime prevention on them. Still, Hollander (2004) has shown that women who take self-defense classes feel more confident and assertive when doing things like walking by a man or being confronted by one on the street. She also found that women who completed self-defense classes felt better about their bodies and stronger when comparing themselves to men (see Lane, 2013).

Although the elderly are not necessarily as fearful as the early research with weak measures of fear indicated, many of them feel vulnerable due to their reduced physical strength, poor health, or frailty (Akers et al., 1987; McCoy et al., 1996; McKee & Milner, 2000). Some fear they could not recover if they were violently victimized (Greve, 1998; Yin, 1980), others are more afraid because they are also not happy with their life or living conditions (McCoy et al., 1996). Some elderly have reduced their own victimization risk by moving to communities designed to house residents over the age of 55, or cities where the people around them are similar in age and also less threatening due to their similar long term physical decline. Some cities are designed primarily for the elderly and, consequently, most of their establishments also cater to older customers (e.g., The Villages, Florida, or Sun City, Arizona). This design limits the risk of victimization and likely fear of crime even when older residents are out of their neighborhoods. Yet, many of those in isolated retirement neighborhoods within larger cities still feel vulnerable when they venture out to shopping malls, restaurants, or other parts of town where they mingle with people who are younger, who look different (racially or culturally), or who have different lifestyles.

Older people could also be the focus of educational efforts specifically designed to reduce their fear of crime. These efforts could both make older people aware of their objective risk of victimization and teach them ways to avoid victimization and therefore feel safer (e.g., shopping during the day, parking under a light pole at night, going out with companions, keeping doors locked). The American Association for Retired Persons (AARP) sometimes publishes tips for avoiding victimization. These tips include strategies designed to reduce victimization while shopping online (e.g., Kirchheimer, 2011), while dealing with current cyber threats (Kirchheimer, 2013b), while answering automated solicitation calls (Kirchheimer, 2013a), and when staying in hotels (Greenberg, 2011). At this point, there is no research on the impact of these types of information on the elderly's fear of crime. Articles such as these have the potential to increase fear if they make people aware of risks they never considered, but they also have the power to help older citizens feel empowered if they believe they can take active measures to ward off any real threats of victimization.

Teach People about Other Racial and Ethnic Groups and Other Cultures

Research shows that people are often afraid of others who look and act differently than they do because they do not understand the behaviors and mannerisms of the other group. This could include racial and ethnic differences (e.g., Whites being afraid of African-Americans or Hispanics) or cultural differences (e.g., Americans being afraid of foreigners) (see Merry, 1981), but it could also include fear of people who simply dress or approach the world differently (e.g., some people might be afraid of others covered in tattoos or wearing piercings). Another scary group can include groups of teenagers hanging out in the neighborhood (Skogan, 1990).

One way to reduce fear might be to increase opportunities for different socio-demographic groups to interact in comfortable, non-threatening situations, so they can learn more about each other. For example, people spearheading efforts designed to improve the community (e.g., reduce disorder or decline) could actively pursue the participation of people from different racial, ethnic, cultural, and/or age groups to work together. This could also be an element of community policing efforts, especially in racially or ethnically diverse areas. In addition, programs to increase cultural competency could be incorporated into grants aimed at increasing collective efficacy and increasing cohesiveness of neighborhoods (see Lane & Meeker, 2003b). As Taylor (1996) noted, when people know others in their neighborhood, they feel more invested in the community, which makes them feel less vulnerable and more empowered to do something about local social problems there. One hurdle practitioners will face, though, will be how to get people to actively engage in such efforts when they already feel overwhelmed with their daily family and work activities. Given current technology, one approach might be to have interactive internet-based meetings that reduce the need for all parties to be in one room to work together.

Reduce Opportunities for Victimization

Years ago, Cohen and Felson (1979) argued that predatory crime requires three elements: a motivated offender, a suitable crime target, and the absence of a capable guardian. In other words, when predatory crimes occur, someone must want to commit a contact crime, have a suitable person or property to victimize, and there must not be anyone watching or protecting the intended target or place. If any one of those elements were removed from a particular situation, then most types of crime could not happen. The focus of their work was on crime itself, but this argument has important implications for reducing fear of crime as well. Specifically, as a way to reduce crime, police officers have often tried to show community members how to protect themselves and their property. For example, they teach people how to make their home seem protected (e.g., putting a large breed dog bowl on the front porch or leaving lights on at night), keep their home from being a suitable target (e.g., cutting

shrubbery away from windows and doors to reduce hiding places), and to protect themselves (e.g., to go out at night with companions rather than alone) (National Sheriff's Association, N.D.). Although there is not specific research on
whether teaching these crime-reduction methods actually reduce fear, it is possible that people who learn and use them will feel more able to fend off criminal victimization and therefore will be less afraid.

The responsibility to reduce opportunities for victimization does not fall
solely on individuals but can be shared by governments and urban and suburban
planners. For example, Stanko (1989) enumerated other ways to specifically reduce women's victimization and fear of victimization by men. Some of her
more practical solutions—for example, allowing women to design public
areas—have real potential for reducing both crime and fear of crime (see Lane,
2013). In addition, architects and engineers could be instrumental in designing areas with women's perceptions of the safety of the environment in mind.
To strengthen these efforts, architectural design companies or scholars could
survey women before building open-areas (such as parks) and parking garage
features that would make them feel safer.

In addition, it might be useful to require local governments, urban planners,
people asking for new building permits, and schools to present plans for addressing fear of crime to earn or keep federal funding. For example, planners
might be required to indicate how their blueprints address situational crime prevention and defensible space issues. Schools, including K–12 institutions and
colleges and universities, might also be required to demonstrate how they will
reduce fear of crime on their campuses. For example, elementary and secondary schools might be able to show plans for developing toll-free numbers
to report bullying or victimization, bullying prevention programs (including
information about how it will attempt to reduce student fear), and programs
that ensure equity of discipline across teachers and administrators (see Sampson, 2009). In the wake of school shootings from outsiders (most recently, the
Newtown, Connecticut, mass shootings), schools might also focus not only
on how to make their campuses safer but also how to make students and school
employees *feel* safer while on campus (see Nance, 2013). For example, after
Newtown, many school districts had police on campus for a few weeks after-
ward. We would argue this approach was more symbolic than protective, because many of these police did not remain at campuses permanently. It would
take more funding to keep police on campus in areas where there are no school
resource officers. The United States Department of Justice (DOJ) recently an-
nounced that they were providing about $45 million to hire 356 school safety
officers nationwide, including in Newtown, Connecticut, where the December 2012 massacre of elementary school occurred (DOJ, 2013). Where officers

are on campus, schools might work with police to ensure their presence and availability is more obvious while at the same time taking care to ensure the open, caring environment typical of schools remains. Evaluation programs of school resource officer programs are sparse, though, so it is unclear whether these programs actually decrease crime or whether they increase or decrease fear.

Colleges and universities might also utilize a number of strategies to increase perceptions of safety among their students. These measures could include providing transportation home from late night classes, making available free call phones that dial directly to safety personnel, and providing counseling and other services where women and other vulnerable groups feel free to share their concerns. Teaching smart safety behavior in residence halls and sorority/fraternity houses is another possibility. Campuses across the country already are working toward these efforts, in part due to the provisions of the 1990 Jeanne Clery Disclosure of Campus Security Policy and Campus Crime Statistics Act (commonly called the Clery Act) (20 USC § 1092; see also Ball, 2012).

Similarly, police departments receiving federal funds for crime prevention activities could be required not only to demonstrate how their strategies will reduce crime, but also how they will reduce fear of crime. As reported in Chapter 6, some of their community policing efforts generally have been shown to reduce fear of crime, although the specific details about why or how they make the difference are not well-understood. Still, community policing and similar efforts are a good place for police to start attempting to address community fear levels as an important goal (not just as a side effect).

Finally, given the possible impact of target hardening on fear reduction, it might be useful for insurance companies to consider expanding their discounts for the installation of home security systems on homeowner's policies to apply to renter's policies. Crime is more likely to occur in areas with higher proportion of renters because of increased community mobility and lower levels of collective efficacy found in those areas (see Sampson, Raudenbush & Earls, 1997). Giving people an incentive to protect themselves and their property by reducing the cost may have some impact on both crime victimization and fear of crime levels.

Reduce Neighborhood Disorder and Reverse Community Decline

Gentrification—or renewing communities, rebuilding run down areas, and moving middle- and upper-income people into poorer neighborhoods—has been criticized because it often displaces poorer residents from their home neighborhoods (see Betancur, 2011). Yet, it has the potential to reduce fear of crime because it focuses on reducing neighborhood decline. Some research indicates that it may not completely eradicate fear (e.g., McDonald, 1986), but when people feel there are positive aspects to a community, including development efforts, they are less likely to worry about crime (Skogan, 1986).

Gentrification is a major undertaking, but it is only one approach to reducing disorder and reversing community decline. Many community policing efforts include strategies to reduce neighborhood problems beyond crime, and research shows that they can reduce fear of crime by reducing disorder (Pate et al., 1987; Skogan, 1990). Consequently, in congruence with Wilson and Kelling's (1982) broken windows theory, code enforcement and community improvement efforts—whether driven by police departments or not—show real promise as a way of reducing fear of crime.

Community mobilizers may also be able to reduce community disorder and decline if they are successful in helping community groups to work together. Lane (2002) found, for example, that long-term residents, who were mostly White, felt that "illegal" immigrants were causing the disorder, decline and gang problems in their communities. Finding ways to help groups like these to work together to solve community problems has the potential to reduce fear of crime while also improving the community through reduced disorder and decline and increased collective efficacy.

Consider Restricting Media and Video Game Violence Content

One of the "hot button" issues with regard to crime is how violence on television, and especially in video games, affects criminal behavior (see Grim & Wilkie, 2013). Although there is no published research on the effects of violent video games on fear of crime, research is pretty clear that "violent video games increase aggressive thoughts, angry feelings, physiological arousal (e.g., heart rate, blood pressure), and aggressive behavior ... [and] decrease helping behavior" and empathy (National Science Foundation, 2013). It is not far-fetched to expect that violence on television and in video games also increases fear of crime. Research shows that seeing crime on television news or crime dramas or reading about it in the newspaper can increase fear of crime for certain groups of people (see Chapter 6).

Consequently, it might be a good idea to consider restricting the type and availability of violence in mass media and video games. The Federal Communications Commission (FCC) enforces laws that ban media depiction of nudity, obscenity, vulgarity, etc. According to the FCC, "It is a violation of federal law to air obscene programming at any time. It is also a violation of federal law to broadcast indecent or profane programming during certain hours." The FCC primarily focuses on restricting indecent programming between 6 a.m. and 10 p.m., when children are most likely to be awake (FCC, N.D., paragraph 1). Policymakers might consider expanding these provisions to include the amount and type of violence on television during these hours. In addition, it might be prudent to consider regulating the development and dissemination of violent video games, beyond the current approach of simply attaching labels that indicate they are for mature groups or adults only (Entertainment Software Ratings Board, N.D.).

Some lawmakers, such as U.S. Representative Frank Wolf, are leading this charge already and have recently called for legal efforts to reduce violent video games and their effects (see Gerstein, 2013). After the Newtown shootings, President Obama also called for more research on the effects of violent video games on children (The White House, 2013). In September 2013, the U.S. House of Representatives planned a hearing on the topic, after the Washington Navy Yard shootings that killed 12 people, and congressmen learned that the shooter had played up to 16 hours of violent video games a day (Grim & Wilkie, 2013). However, when these topics are considered, First Amendment concerns related to freedom of the press often arise and must be considered and addressed (see Gerstein, 2013).

Implications for Future Research

One of the realities of fear of crime research is that despite over 40 years of research, there is still much to learn. This section will focus on some of the key questions that we believe should be addressed in new research studies. Because there are so many ideas and topics that could be explored, this section will discuss them by topic area. Box 8.4 provides a summary of the implications for future research discussed here.

Continue to Improve and Expand Measurement

We believe that the long-term use of the same fear of crime questions by the General Social Survey (GSS) and National Crime Victimization Survey (NCVS) allows us to understand trends in fear over decades. Nevertheless, the particular questions used in those surveys provide little understanding of fear itself. We suggest that the American Society of Criminology (ASC) and the Academy of Criminal Justice Sciences (ACJS) work with the Bureau of Justice

---

Box 8.4 Implications for Future Research

1. Continue to improve and expand measurement of fear of crime.
2. Continue to compare the causes and consequences of fear across different subpopulations.
3. Conduct more qualitative studies to expand on fear of crime theory.
4. Evaluate the impact of crime prevention programs on fear.
5. Conduct more research on understudied factors.
   a. Personal victimization
   b. Witnessing victimization of others
   c. Seeing live crime events on television/internet
   d. Social networks
   e. Urban legends
   f. Different routes to community concern
   g. Reciprocal effects of fear and precautionary behaviors
6. Examine altruistic fear in more detailed studies.

Statistics (BJS, which administers the NCVS) and the National Opinion Research Center (NORC, which administers the GSS) to add better measures of crime fear as well as perceived risk of victimization measures to the annual surveys. The old questions could remain on the surveys to allow trend comparison with decades past, but scholars have known for years that the current measures are problematic. Expert focus and federal funding to improve these surveys are both sorely needed, and a working group of fear of crime scholars to create new measures would be a good first step. In the absence of better measures in these national surveys, researchers might conduct more national surveys of their own, which would require large grants from the federal government or private foundations. These data could then be shared with other scholars through the Interuniversity Consortium for Political and Social Research (ICPSR), a data repository where researchers gain access to data sets.

Studies also should continue to add more detail to the measures now generally used by fear of crime scholars, as a way to allow a better understanding of the causes and consequences of crime-related fear. To date, these studies have focused on separating perceived risk from fear, specifying particular offenses (e.g., murder, rape, burglary, assault), and adding perpetrator characteristics (e.g., gang member, terrorist, stalker, or stranger v. acquaintance v. intimate partner). Some studies have also measured fear in specific locations, such as work and school. These studies should continue and expand, for example, by including new types of offenses (e.g., cybercrimes or being swindled by retailers or contractors) or offenders (e.g., family members or mass shooters). In addition, researchers would learn more by studying how fear of specific perpetrators varies by context. For example, are people more afraid of strangers, gangs, or terrorism when they are in specific places (such as specific neighborhoods, large urban areas, or on commercial airplanes)? Similarly, are people more afraid of acquaintances, friends, or family when they are in particular contexts (e.g., when another person has been drinking or people are in private places rather than public ones)?

We also recommend that researchers expand their work and find new ways to gauge the causes and consequences of fear. That is, there should be more research specifically on the best way to measure fear of crime. For example, researchers do not yet know enough about the intricacies of men's fear of crime. Lane (2013) suggested finding new ways to measure men's fear of crime, under the socialization theory's assumption that men are socialized to believe that admitting fear shows weakness and therefore is not "masculine." She recommended asking questions that allow men to discuss how they show strength, why and how often they do so, and in what types of situations they feel the need to do so, rather than asking them questions that expect them to admit they are afraid (i.e., show weakness).

In addition, to examine the patriarchy argument more fully, Lane (2013) recommended asking questions of both men and women that allow them to discuss their feelings about their own power. For example, researchers might ask both groups if they feel capable of physically defending themselves against a potential attacker. Both groups could also be asked questions about their socialization experiences, including whether their parents or others (1) taught them to be strong or submissive or (2) told them they were at greater risk of victimization because of their gender, size, sexual orientation, etc. Researchers might also ask males and females about their own beliefs regarding whether society is patriarchal and about their behavioral precautions, specifically related to these issues (rather than the general questions used now). For example, does having a weapon make them feel less vulnerable and more able to fight someone (Lane, 2013)?

Longitudinal studies could also examine how fear changes as individuals age, move to different areas (e.g., change the types of areas where he/she works or lives), or face life's turning points (such as moving out of parents' homes, going to college, getting married or divorced, having children, or experiencing physical and mental declines due to age or illness). Such studies would require not only long-term funding sources but also a long-term career commitment on the part of researchers.

Future studies should also continue to add measures that help tease out the details regarding the intensity of fear (how much people have) and the frequency (how often it occurs). This would involve including additional survey questions to gauge these aspects of fear (see Farrall, Jackson, & Gray, 2009). Another way to do this is to move beyond attitudinal and emotional measures to examine physiological responses to situations that incite fear of crime. Researchers could use heat sensors, heart monitors, and other mechanisms to determine reactions and could determine if there are physical differences across gender, age, and racial groups in the physical experience of fear. These studies could occur in controlled settings (such as research laboratories) or in daily life (people could wear monitors as they go about their days and log their activities and experiences in journals). These studies might shed light on the differential impact of certain stimuli on the length and intensity of fear for different groups. Yet, because monitoring equipment is expensive, researchers would need government or private funding to do this type of study well. In addition, they would need to move beyond their disciplinary confines to collaborate with experts in the area of physical reactions to stimuli.

Continue to Compare Causes and Consequences of Fear across Subpopulations

More recent research has continued to separate samples by demographic group to help unpack the relationship between personal characteristics and the other factors that predict fear of crime. For example, studies have compared men and women, minorities (or specific minority groups, such as African-Americans, Hispanics, or Asians) and Whites, or older versus younger people (see Chapters 2 & 6). New studies might further separate the groups (e.g., women and men of color compared to White men and women or older and younger people of color versus White people in these groups). Only a few studies have examined the intersections of race or ethnicity, gender, age, and community factors, because such comparisons require large enough samples to disaggregate into groups and still have the power to discern differences if they exist. In this vein, as immigrant populations increase, it would be helpful to know how culture shock and language barriers impact fear of crime. Another key group that has yet to receive much attention is the homeless (but see Coston & Finckenauer, 1993).

In addition, to date, there are only a few studies that examine fear of crime among adolescents, and almost none of younger children's fear of crime. Consequently, we know almost nothing about very young (e.g., elementary) children's fear of crime. Learning about their fear levels, as well as what they are told about what they should fear and how they should protect themselves from victimization, may add important information to our theoretical ideas about how socialization works to increase or decrease fear of crime among different groups. It would also be useful to know how socialization experiences vary by race and ethnicity, gender and context (e.g., by neighborhood levels of crime and social disorganization) and over time as children become teenagers and then adults (see Lane, 2013).

It is also important to better understand the role of crime, delinquency, and victimization in fear of crime, especially among young men. Studies to date generally show that offenders are not afraid of crime, even though they face much higher risk of victimization than the general population. Studies should further examine why. For example, do they feel emboldened by their street knowledge, peer group or gang membership, or believe they can handle anything? Or, is it that being "tough" means one cannot admit fear even when they experience it? Could asking questions in different ways (without the word "afraid") help them express any fear they might feel? New studies might also examine differential fear levels among male and female offenders as well as among older versus younger ones. Research could also increase knowledge about fear among different types of offenders (e.g., violent versus property or drug offenders, gang members versus non-gang members, or offenders not engaged in typical street crime, such as terrorists or white-collar criminals) or by length of prior record or level of immersion in a delinquent group. Other important factors that might affect fear levels include race and ethnicity and geographical location (e.g., urban or rural or socioeconomic or social disorganization status of area).

In addition, there is limited information about how fear varies among these groups when they are on the street and when they are locked up in penal institutions. Early research on prisons showed that safety is a major concern for inmates (e.g., Sykes, 1958; Toch, 1992), but fear researchers have not yet fully examined the experiences of inmates and the factors that increase or decrease their fear while inside. Additionally, fear of crime researchers have not examined how fear in these situations affects individuals' behavior, including criminal behavior, such as gang membership or the use or carrying of "homemade" weapons. As the prison population ages due to long-term prison sentences, the dynamics of fear may change there also. For example, researchers do not know how (or even if) fear of crime levels change when older inmates (who experience physical problems that are likely heightened due to hard living and lack of self-care) are mixed with younger, stronger inmates or whether fear is still present among older inmates when they are housed in prisons specifically designed for geriatric inmates. Hence, it would be useful to understand how fear in prison changes based on the characteristics of the population itself (e.g., juvenile versus adult facility or ages, crimes, and affiliations of offenders housed there).

Conduct More Qualitative Studies to Expand and Build upon Theory

As Lane (2013) noted, qualitative studies have the potential to build and expand theory beyond current ideas. For example, letting men and women or people of color and Whites speak for themselves may open up new approaches to understanding sources and consequences of fear among different groups. In addition, studies of juvenile and adult offenders may allow them to discuss their fears of crime in ways that will help researchers understand their reported lack of fear in the face of heightened objective risk. That is, they may describe their feelings in ways that indicate fear without using the terms researchers choose in their typical survey measures or they may indicate how they manage their greater perceived risk to lessen their fear. As new ideas are generated, larger, quantitative studies could survey new samples to determine if the new ideas apply to individuals beyond the original group of subjects.

Evaluate the Impact of Crime Prevention Measures on Fear of Crime

After researchers determine exactly who is afraid and why, it will be important not only to recommend policies to reduce fear, but also to see if they actually work. Specifically, there is not enough information on what measures actually reduce fear and why. There is some research on how police (e.g., community policing efforts and police crackdowns) impact fear. Nevertheless, most of this research used the weaker measures of fear (or measures of that were actually designed to measures levels of perceived risk) or was conducted by policing scholars, not fear of crime scholars who might have more expertise in the particular area of interest (e.g., Dietz, 1997; Hinkle & Weisburd, 2008; Kelling et al., 1981; Roh & Olive, 2005). In addition, there has not been much published research in recent years about how police patrol, school resource officers, or other police strategies (such as Closed-Circuit Television, CCTV, in neighborhoods) affect fear in their locales.

The government-supported website, www.crimesolutions.gov, lists a number of programs and practices that are considered effective, primarily at reducing crime. Some of these programs are focused on policing efforts, such as hot spots policing, Operation Cease Fire in Boston, and closed-circuit television (CCTV). Others include crime prevention through environmental design (CPTED) measures. Examples include gating-off neighborhoods to prevent burglary or installing traffic barriers to reduce drive-by shootings and other killings in high-crime neighborhoods. There is almost no published research on how these programs that are considered "effective" at reducing crime impact fear of crime. We recommend including measures of fear in surveys that evaluate the effects of these programs on community outcomes. Specifically, we suggest that programs be judged not just on their ability to prevent crime or reduce recidivism, but also on their ability to reduce fear of crime and improve quality of life. Measuring fear both before and after the measures are instituted would be most useful, because it would allow researchers to understand how fear changed, if at all, after the programs were implemented.

Especially following the school massacre in Newtown, Connecticut in December 2012 and well-publicized suicides of schoolchildren after they were bullied, there has been a renewed focus on ensuring a safe and comfortable environment in schools. Adding school resource officers has been one focus, including the earlier-mentioned funding from the federal government (see DOJ, 2013). Another recent focus of schools has been on bullying prevention and the federal government notes that some of these programs are either effective at reducing bullying (e.g., *Steps to Respect* and *Positive Action* programs) or show promising results in stopping bullying behavior (e.g., *Success in Stages Program* and *KiVa Antibullying Program*) (www.crimesolutions.gov). Yet, there is little information available regarding effects on students' fear of bullying or feelings of safety in school when these programs are in place. More research is needed on the impact of school-based crime prevention programs and their effects on feelings of safety among students.

Conduct Studies That Examine the Impact of Understudied Factors on Fear

Despite the large quantity of research on fear, there are still a number of predictive factors that have yet to be explored in depth or at all. Each of these factors could be measured through survey research or qualitative methods and could be examined in both the general population and specific subpopulations (e.g., by gender, race, ethnicity, age, and/or neighborhood context). This section will list some of these variables and mention some of the important questions that remain unanswered.

Personal Victimization

As mentioned in Chapter 6, studies are inconsistent regarding the impact of prior crime victimization on current levels of fear of crime. Therefore, better and more detailed measures of victimization may help tease out the intricacies of these inconsistent results. For example, new studies might examine: what types of victimization provoke higher fear levels and more frequent fear episodes and why; what types of victimization are more likely to prompt people to change their behaviors and routines, and whether or not these changes actually reduce individuals' fear levels; and, finally, whether how recent the victimization is and number of times it happened matters in predicting fear levels.

Witnessing Crime against Others

There are few published studies that examine the impact of witnessing crime on personal fear, except for studies with children that have been conducted by psychologists. Consequently, this area of research is wide open for exploration. Important questions include: how does witnessing violence affect different groups of people (e.g., young versus old, women versus men, racial and ethnic minorities versus Whites); what are the effects of witnessing different types of violence (e.g., a fight versus domestic violence versus murder); what are the differential effects of witnessing one event (e.g., a murder) versus sustained violence over time (e.g., in a community or in a home); and what are the effects of witnessing crimes other than violence, such as drug dealing, blatant weapon carrying, or property crime? As with violent crimes, does it matter whether the crime is witnessed once or over time or if multiple crimes are witnessed or if it occurs in a rural versus suburban versus urban area?

Witnessing Crime Events on Television (or Internet Feed)

There is also little information on how the increased availability of immediate information about crime events (e.g., the Boston marathon bombing, the Newtown, Connecticut mass school shooting, the Aurora, Colorado theatre mass shooting) affects fear of crime among people near or far from the crime scene. There is also little information on constant repetition of news stories about these events (and subsequent constant exposure to those stories) affects fear. For example, video footage of airplanes flying into the World Trade Center on September 11, 2011 has been played regularly on television since the event, especially around the time of the event anniversary each year. Research questions that might be addressed include: how does watching a real crime event affect fear of crime? And, what is the difference in effects on fear of hearing about a story on the television news versus seeing the actual events on television? Additional questions that might be asked include (1) whether fear of crime diminishes as the physical and temporal distance from a criminal event increases or (2) whether viewing a violent crime once impacts fear differently than viewing the same event multiple times or viewing stories on the aftermath (e.g., victim experiences and recovery or first responders' stories). Moreover, how does seeing such events multiple times affect general levels of anxiety about safety not necessarily attributed to particular crimes—that is, feelings of urban, neighborhood, or travel "unease"? (Garofalo & Laub, 1978). All of these questions remain unanswered and ripe for researchers to begin exploring.

The Impact of the Internet

The Internet has become widely available in recent decades, and people are increasingly using it as their primary news source (Pew, 2012). In addition, it is now much easier to gain access to newspapers from across the country or world via their Internet sites. Yet, there is almost no research on the impact of the use of the Internet for crime news and its effect individuals' on fear of crime (but see Higgins et al., 2008). For example, it remains unclear if access to newspapers or other news sources that one would not see otherwise increases the amount, type, and immediacy of crime news that people receive. Moreover, if the amount of crime news increases, then what is the impact on one's fear of crime? Do people feel safer by comparison (see Heath, 1984) or does the overwhelming amount of information available on the Internet have other effects, such as increasing fear in geographical areas where crime and concern about it has historically been low? These questions remain currently unanswered and ripe for future research.

The Impact of Social Networks

Studies in the 1980s (e.g., Skogan, 1986; Tyler, 1980, 1984) discussed the importance of social networks (e.g., friends, family, and coworkers) on fear of crime, indicating that they had the power to increase fear of crime. Yet, there is much to learn about how these social networks increase or decrease fear. For example, when community police officers hold meetings in neighborhoods to share crime information, does that increase or decrease fear of crime? Has the tremendous expansion of Internet availability and communication with social networks, through applications such as Facebook and Twitter (e.g., friends vary in how close they are emotionally and geographically) increased or decreased fear of crime. Other examples of unanswered questions include: How do discussions with others, including family, friends, coworkers, and community policing officers, affect fear? How much do people talk about crime with others and how do those conversations affect their fear levels and why? How do the frequency and content of communication between police officers and the community affect fear of crime? How much detail do community policing officers actually share with the community regarding crimes, offenders, victims, etc. and how do different amounts of crime detail impact fear? How does this information vary by context and how does it affect different groups of people (by race, gender, age, etc.)? Answers to such questions would inform the role, if any, that social networks play in generating fear of crime.

Effects of Urban Legends

There is almost no research on how the diffusion of urban legends affects fear of crime, such as the old rumor (now often promulgated via email) that people put razor blades in apples or candy to give children at Halloween (see Best & Horiuchi, 1985) or that gangs drive with their headlights out and then follow and kill people who flash their lights to warn them (see Best & Hutchinson, 1996). There has been no research that examines how these types of emails and shared stories affect fear of crime. That is, do people believe these rumors? If so, how does it affect their fears or behaviors (e.g., do they check all Halloween candy before allowing their children to eat it or let other cars drive in the dark without their headlights for fear of harm)? If people do not believe the rumors, why do they forward the information to other people's email accounts? The topic of how urban legends affect fear of crime remains practically unexplored.

Different Routes to "Community Concern"

Many of the studies that empirically examine the effects of community concern on fear of crime examine the theory without other theoretical constructs in the model or consider it a result of concern about disorder and incivilities that then leads to fear (e.g., Garofalo & Laub, 1978; Skogan, 1990; Skogan & Maxfield, 1981; Taylor & Hale, 1986). New research on this theoretical perspective might expand these ideas by examining different ways that people become concerned about community decline and, therefore, more afraid. For example, does increasing urbanization, changing local businesses, and/or more diversity increase concern about decline and therefore fear, even if obvious signs of disorder do not increase? Or, are broader societal changes, such as economic changes and real estate market declines, causing community concern in areas where there are no outward signs of disorder? That is, as Farrall et al. (2009, p. 242) argue, are fears about crime really a manifestation of broader societal concerns ("expressive") and not necessarily about real community decline?

Reciprocal Effects of Behavioral Precautions and Fear of Crime

Scholars have long wondered whether people who are more afraid and take more behavioral precautions (like buying more locks for their homes, leaving lights on, or carrying pepper spray) are actually reducing or increasing their own fear of crime levels. One way to examine this question would be to conduct qualitative research to ask people to explain the thought process they had when they bought or started to carry weapons or installed additional locks on their homes, and then ask them to discuss how their thought processes and feelings have changed since they engaged in the avoidance or constrained behaviors. Another approach would be to conduct longitudinal research using surveys to examine the reciprocal effects of fear and behavioral precautions on each other, as well as the temporal ordering of behavioral precautions and fear of crime (see Wilcox, May, & Roberts, 2006, for an example with adolescent weapon possession at school). For example, are people first fearful, then buy guns, and then subsequently have increased or decreased fear? Or, do people have guns available and then fear increases? If people have a security system installed or put bars on the windows, why do they do so? And, once these obvious signs of "protection" are there, does it make residents feel more or less safe?

Conduct More Studies on Altruistic Fear

Warr (1992) first studied fear for others, such as children and spouses, looking specifically at one's fear for others in the household. He found that about half of his respondents feared for others, especially children and spouses. Warr and Ellison (2000) later examined altruistic fear in family households, finding that people worry as much about others as for themselves. They found that husbands were more likely to worry about their wives than vice versa, that mothers were slightly more likely to worry about their children than fathers were, and that parents were more likely to fear for their daughters than their sons. While a few others (e.g., De Vaus & Wise, 1996; Rader, 2010; Snedker, 2006, Tulloch, 2004) have studied people's fear for other people they care about, there have been relatively few studies on this topic. Consequently, future researchers have the potential to add significantly to the knowledge base about altruistic fear.

Specifically, there is little theoretical consideration of this topic, except for socialization arguments that women are more involved in caretaking responsibilities (e.g., for children or older or ill family members) and are socialized to be more emotionally connected while men are socialized to be protectors of those who are not as physically strong as they are (see Snedker, 2006; Warr & Ellison, 2000). New research could explore other possibilities, such as workload imbalance in families (e.g., women being expected to do caretaking and therefore feeling more responsible for others, even if they prefer egalitarian family approaches) or the attitudes and behaviors of the person for whom the individual is fearful (e.g., does the spouse or child make bad choices or take risks that might prompt more fear for their safety among parents or other family members?). Along those lines, are there specific reasons that mothers might fear more for their children than fathers do, such as having more intimate knowledge of the daily activities and experiences of their children (e.g., at school or with friends or acquaintances?). In addition, the importance of context might be critical to explaining heightened fear for others in some cases. For example, context might be especially relevant in problematic and high crime neighborhoods or schools or in jobs that include high risk of harm, such as policing, correctional institutions, or the military. Or, one might fear for an elderly family member when the person must be released to the care of others, either in home or in an assisted living or nursing home situation.

More research on the personal factors other than gender that predict altruistic fear would also be useful. For example, how does altruistic fear vary by the age, race, or prior personal victimization experiences of the one who is afraid or of the one for whom someone is afraid? If a child has been victimized before (e.g., by bullying, harassment, or violence), does this heighten a parent's fear level about their general safety or for specific types of victimization? How do these characteristics and other factors interact? For example, research has shown that parents are often more likely to fear for daughters than sons (see De Vaus & Wise, 1996), but is this true in urban neighborhood contexts where gang activity and violence are common? These are just some ideas about where research on this topic might go, but the larger point is that there is much room for theoretical and empirical development in explaining fear for others being victimized.

Synthesize Theoretical Ideas into a Comprehensive Model

Although some studies have examined theoretical models about fear of crime in connection with others (e.g., Lane, 2002; Lane & Meeker, 2003b, 2011; Taylor & Hale, 1986), there have been few attempts to incorporate the current theoretical models about the causes of crime-related fear into a comprehensive theoretical model. A major contribution to the current fear of crime field of study would be if scholars could synthesize the "competing" ideas into one integrated model that theorizes how and when the factors come together to increase fear of crime levels and how and when these fears lead to constrained or avoidance behaviors. For example, how do all the models about contextual effects (e.g., indirect victimization, subcultural diversity/racial heterogeneity, disorder/incivilities, and community concern/decline) (see Chapter 6) jell with other theoretical models regarding gender and fear (e.g., the shadow of sexual assault hypothesis, socialization, or patriarchy) (see Chapter 4)? Which of these perspectives better predict different types of fear and behavioral reactions? While this effort to pull different theoretical ideas together may be a large undertaking, the potential to expand knowledge about the causes and consequences of fear cannot be denied.

Final Words

In this book, we have provided a detailed examination of the research on fear of crime with the hope that this synthesis will prove useful to fear of crime researchers, students, policymakers, and others interested in reducing both crime and fear of crime. We have discussed several avenues for future research, each deserving further scientific scrutiny. Thus, we close with a challenge to those interested in examining fear of crime in research settings. Use the foundation of knowledge provided here to inform your research. Find those gaps in the research that we have identified and use them to inform your research agenda. Push the envelope of knowledge about fear of crime as discussed in this chapter and throughout this book. Seize the opportunity!

References

Akers, R.L., La Greca, A.J., Sellers, C., & Cochran, J. (1987). Fear of crime and victimization among the elderly in different types of communities. *Criminology, 25*(3), 487–505.

Arthur, J.A. (1992). Criminal victimization, fear of crime, and handgun ownership among Blacks: Evidence from national survey data. *American Journal of Criminal Justice 16*(2), 121–141.

Baldassare, M. (1986). The elderly and fear of crime. *Sociology and Social Research. 70*(3). 218–221.

Ball, A.L. (2012). Staying safe on campus. *The New York Times* (July 20). Accessed October 7, 2013. http://www.nytimes.com/2012/07/20/education/edlife/students-fear-venturing-out-alone-at-night-on-campus.html?pagewanted=all&_r=0.

Bankston, W.B., Thompson, C.Y., Jenkins, Q.A.L., & Forsyth, C.J. (1990). The influence of fear of crime, gender, and Southern culture of carrying firearms for protection. *The Sociological Quarterly, 31*(2), 287–305.

Barberet, R., Fisher, B.S., & Taylor, H. (2004). *University student safety in the East Midlands*. United Kingdom: Home Office.

Berk, R.A., Campbell, A., Klap, R., & Western, B. (1992). The deterrent effect of arrest in incidents of domestic violence: A Bayesian analysis of four field experiments. *American Sociological Review, 57*(5), 698–708.

Best, J., & Horiuchi, G.T. (1985). The razor blade in the apple: The social construction of urban legends. *Social Problems, 32*(5), 488–499.

Best, J, & Hutchinson, M.M. (1996). The gang initiation rite as a motif of contemporary crime discourse. *Justice Quarterly, 13*(3), 383–404.

Betancur, J. (2011). Gentrification and community fabric in Chicago. *Urban Studies, 48*(2), 383–406.

Chen, X. (2009). The link between juvenile offending and victimization: The influence of risky lifestyles, social bonding, and individual characteristics. *Youth Violence and Juvenile Justice, 7*(2), 119–135.

Chevigny, P. (2003). The populism of fear: Politics of crime in the Americas. *Punishment & Society, 5*(1), 77–96.

Chiricos, T., Eschholz, S., & Gertz, M. (1997). Crime, news, and fear of crime: Toward an identification of audience effects. *Social Problems, 44*(3), 342–357.

Chiricos, T., Padgett, K., & Gertz, M. (2000). Fear, TV news, and the reality of crime. *Criminology, 38*(3), 755–785.

Cohen, L.E., & Felson, M. (1979). Social change and crime rate trends: A routine activity approach. *American Sociological Review, 44*(1), 588–608.

Cordner, G. (2010). *Reducing Fear of Crime: Strategies for Police.* Washington D.C.: Office of Community Oriented Policing Services. Accessed December 23, 2013. http://www.cops.usdoj.gov/files/RIC/Publications/e110913242-ReducingFear.pdf.

Coston, C.T.M., & Finckenauer, J.O. (1993). Fear of crime among vulnerable populations: Homeless women. *Journal of Social Distress and the Homeless, 2*(1), 1–21.

Dammert, L., & Malone, M.F.T. (2006). Does it take a village? Policing strategies and fear of crime in Latin America. *Latin American Politics and Society, 48*(4), 27–51.

De Vaus, D. & Wise, S. (1996). The fear of attack: Parents' concerns for the safety of their children. *Family Matters, 43*, 34–38.

Dietz, A.S. (1997). Evaluating community policing: Quality of police service and fear of crime. *Policing: An International Journal of Police Strategy and Management, 20*(1), 83–100.

Entertainment Software Ratings Board. (N.D.). ERSB Ratings Guide. Accessed September 25, 2013. http://www.esrb.org/ratings/ratings_guide.jsp.

Farrall, S., Jackson, J., & Gray, E. (2009). *Social order and the fear of crime in contemporary times.* Oxford: Oxford University Press.

Federal Bureau of Investigation. (2013). Crime in the United States, 2012. Accessed October 2, 2013. http://www.fbi.gov/about-us/cjis/ucr/crime-in-the-u.s/2012/crime-in-the-u.s.-2012.

Federal Communications Commission. (N.D.) Regulation of Obscenity, Indecency, and Profanity. Accessed September 25, 2013. http://www.fcc.gov/encyclopedia/regulation-obscenity-indecency-and-profanity.

Felson, R.B., Ackerman, J.M., & Gallagher, C.A. (2005). Police intervention and the repeat of domestic assault. *Criminology, 43*(3), 563–588.

Ferraro, K.F. (1995). *Fear of Crime: Interpreting victimization risk.* New York: State University of New York Press.

Ferraro, K.F. (1996). Women's fear of victimization: Shadow of sexual assault? *Social Forces, 75*(2), 667–690.

Ferraro, Kenneth F., & LaGrange, R.L. (1987). The measurement of fear of crime. *Sociological Inquiry, 57*(1), 70–101.

Ferraro, K.F., & LaGrange, R.L. (1988). Are older people afraid of crime? *Journal of Aging Studies, 2*(3), 277–287.

Fisher, B.S., & May, D. (2009). College students' crime-related fears on campus: Are fear provoking cues gendered? *Journal of Contemporary Criminal Justice, 25*(3), 300–321.

Fisher, B., & Nasar, J.L. (1992a). Fear of crime in relation to three exterior site features: Prospect, refuge and escape. *Environment & Behavior, 24*(1), 35–65.

Fisher, B., & Nasar, J.L. (1992b). Students' fear of crime and its relation to physical features of the campus. *Journal of Security Administration, 15*(2), 65–75.

Fisher, B., & Nasar, J.L. (1995). Fear spots in relation to microlevel physical cues: Exploring the overlooked. *Journal of Research in Crime and Delinquency, 32*(2), 214–239.

Fisher, B.S., & Sloan, J.J., III. (2003). Unraveling the fear of victimization among college women: Is the 'shadow of sexual assault hypothesis' supported? *Justice Quarterly, 20*(3), 633–659.

Foubert, J.D., & Cowell, E.A. (2004). Perceptions of a rape prevention program by fraternity men and male student-athletes: Powerful effects and implications for changing behavior. *NASPA Journal, 42*(1), 1–20.

Foubert, J.D., Godin, E.E., & Tatum, J.L. (2010). In their own words: Sophomore college men describe attitude and behavior changes resulting from a rape prevention program 2 years after their participation. *Journal of Interpersonal Violence, 25*(12), 2237–2257.

Foubert, J.D., & Perry, B.C. (2007). Creating lasting attitude and behavior change in fraternity members and male student-athletes: The qualitative impact of an empathy-based rape prevention program. *Violence Against Women, 13*(1), 70–86.

Garofalo, J., & Laub, J. (1978). The fear of crime: Broadening our perspective. *Victimology, 3*(3–4), 242–253.

Gerbner, G., & Gross, L. (1976). Living with television: The violence profile. *Journal of Communication, 26*(2), 172–194.

Gerbner, G., Gross, L., Elcey, M.F., Jackson-Beeck, M., Jeffries-Fox, S., & Signorielli, N. (1977). "TV violence profile No. 8: The highlights." *Journal of Communication, 27*(2), 171–180.

Gerbner, G., Gross, L., Jackson-Beeck, M., Jeffries-Fox, S., & Signorielli, N. (1978). Cultural indicators: Violence profile no. 9. *Journal of Communication, 28*(3), 176–207.

Gerbner, G., Gross, L., Morgan, M., & Signorielli, N. (1980). The 'mainstreaming' of America: Violence profile no. 11. *Journal of Communication, 30*(3), 10–29.

Gerstein, J. (2013). Wolf lashes out at violent video games. *Politico.* Accessed September 25, 2013. http://www.politico.com/blogs/under-the-radar/2013/03/wolf-lashes-out-at-violent-video-games-159312.html.

Gover, A.R, Tomsich, E.A., Jennings, W.G, & Higgins, G.E. (2011). An exploratory study on perceptions of safety, fear of crime, and victimization experiences among faculty and staff at an urban university: A focus on gender. *Criminal Justice Studies, 24*(1), 37–55.

Greenberg, P. (2011). Hotel room safety: Don't take your security for granted. AARP, January 12. Accessed September 20, 2013. http://www.aarp.org/travel/travel-tips/info-01-2011/greenberg_video_hotel_safety.html.

Greve, W. (1998). Fear of crime among the elderly: Foresight, not fright. *International Review of Victimology, 5*(3–4), 277–309.

Grim, R., & Wilkie, C. (2013). House set to examine link between video games, culture of violence in wake of navy yard shooting. *Huffington Post* (September 20). Accessed October 7, 2013. http://www.huffingtonpost.com/2013/09/20/video-game-lobby_n_3957441.html?view=print&comm_ref=false.

Heath, L. (1984). Impact of newspaper crime reports on fear of crime: Multimethodological investigation. *Journal of Personality and Social Psychology, 47*(2), 263–276.

Hickman, S.E. & Muehlenhard, C.L. (1997). College women's fears and precautionary behaviors relating to acquaintance rape and stranger rape. *Psychology of Women Quarterly, 21*(4), 527–547.

Higgins, G.E., Ricketts, M.L., & Vegh, D.T. (2008). The role of self-control in college student's perceived risk and fear of online victimization. *American Journal of Criminal Justice, 33*(2), 223–233.

Hinkle, J.C., & Weisburd, D. (2008). The irony of broken windows policing: A micro-place study of the relationship between disorder, focused police crackdowns, and fear of crime. *Journal of Criminal Justice, 36*(6), 503–512.

Hollander, J.A. (2004). "I can take care of myself": The impact of self-defense training on women's lives. *Violence Against Women, 10*(3), 205–235.

Katz, C.M., Webb, V.J., & Armstrong, T.A. (2003). Fear of gangs: A test of alternative theoretical models. *Justice Quarterly, 20,* 95–130.

Katzenbach, N., Blatt, G., Breitel, C.D., Brewster, K., Byrne, G.H., Cahill, T.J., & Youngdahl, L.W. (1967). *The challenge of crime in a free society.* Washington, D.C.: United States Government Printing Office.

Kelling, G.L., Pate, A., Ferrara, A., Utne, M., and Brown, C.E. (1981). *The Newark foot patrol experiment.* Washington D.C.: The Police Foundation.

Kirchheimer, S. (2011). Online shopping crimes and misdemeanors: 7 ways to avoid being a victim in cyberspace. AARP Bulletin, June 13. Accessed September 20, 2013, http://www.aarp.org/money/scams-fraud/info-06-2011/shop-online-safely-scam-alert.html.

Kirchheimer, S. (2013a). Avoiding illegal robocalls: Protect your money from automated telemarketing scams. AARP, February 26. Accessed September 23, 2013. http://www.aarp.org/money/scams-fraud/info-02-2013/avoiding-illegal-robocalls.print.html?intcmp=AE-ENDART1-BOS.

Kirchheimer, S. (2013b). Cyber-threat trends of 2013: Experts predict a surge in computer and cellphone scams. AARP, January 24. Accessed September 23, 2013. http://www.aarp.org/money/scams-fraud/info-01-2013/2013-cyber-threats.print.html.

LaGrange, R.L., & Ferraro, K.F. (1987). The elderly's fear of crime: A critical examination of the research. *Research on Aging, 9*(3), 372–391.

LaGrange, R.L., & Ferraro, K.F. (1989). Assessing age and gender differences in perceived risk and fear of crime. *Criminology, 27*(4), 697–719.

Lane, J. (2002). Fear of gang crime: A qualitative examination of the four perspectives. *Journal of Research in Crime and Delinquency, 39*(4), 437–471.

Lane, J. (2006). Exploring fear of general and gang crimes among juveniles on probation: The impacts of delinquent behaviors. *Youth Violence and Juvenile Justice, 4*(1), 34–54.

Lane, J. (2009). Perceptions of neighborhood problems, fear of crime and resulting behavioral precautions: Comparing institutionalized girls and boys in Florida. *Journal of Contemporary Criminal Justice, 25*(3), 264–281.

Lane, J. (2013). Theoretical explanations for gender differences in fear of crime: Research and prospects." pp. 57–67 In *Routledge International Handbook of Crime and Gender Studies,* edited by C.M. Renzetti, S.L. Miller, and A.R. Gover. New York: Routledge.

Lane, J., & Fox, K.A. (2012). Fear of crime among gang and non-gang offenders: Comparing the effects of perpetration, victimization, and neighborhood factors. *Justice Quarterly, 29*(4), 491–523.

Lane, J, & Fox, K.A. (2013). Fear of property, violent, and gang crime: Examining the shadow of sexual assault thesis among male and female offenders. *Criminal Justice and Behavior, 40*(5), 472–496.

Lane, J., Gover, A., & Dahod, S. (2009) Fear of violent crime among men and women on campus: The impact of perceived risk and fear of sexual assault. *Violence & Victims, 24*(2), 172–192.

Lane, J., & Meeker, J.W. (2000). Subcultural diversity and the fear of crime and gangs. *Crime & Delinquency, 46*(4), 497–521.

Lane, J. & Meeker, J.W. (2003a). Ethnicity, information sources, and fear of crime. *Deviant Behavior, 24*(1), 1–26.

Lane, J. & Meeker, J.W. (2003b). Fear of gang crime: A look at three theoretical models. *Law & Society Review, 37*(2), 425–456.

Lane, J., & Meeker, J.W. (2004). Social disorganization perceptions, fear of gang crime, and behavioral precautions among Whites, Latinos, and Vietnamese. *Journal of Criminal Justice, 32*(1), 49–62.

Lane, J. & Meeker, J.W. (2005). Theories and fear of gang crime among Whites and Latinos: A replication and extension of prior research. *Journal of Criminal Justice, 33*(6), 627–641.

Lane, J. & Meeker, J.W. (2011). Combining theoretical models of perceived risk and fear of gang crime among Whites and Latinos. *Victims and Offenders, 6*(1), 64–92.

Lauritsen, J.L., & Rezey, M.L. (2013). *Measuring the Prevalence of Crime with the National Crime Victimization Survey.* Washington D.C.: Bureau of Justice Statistics.

Lee, G.R. (1982). Sex differences in fear of crime among older people. *Research on Aging, 4*(3), 284–298.

Liska, A.E., & Baccaglini, W. (1990). Feeling safe by comparison: Crime in the newspapers. *Social Problems, 37*(3), 360–374.

Lizotte, A.J., Bordua, D.J., & White, C.S. (1981). Firearms ownership for sport and protection: Two not so divergent models. *American Sociological Review, 46*(2), 499–503.

Lizotte, A.J., Tesoriero, J.M., Thornberry, T.P., & Krohn, M.D. (1994). Patterns of adolescent firearms ownership and use. *Justice Quarterly, 11*(1), 51–74.

May, D.C. (2001a). *Adolescent fear of crime, perceptions of risk, and defensive behaviors: An alternative explanation of violent delinquency.* Lewiston, NY: Edwin Mellen Press.

May, D.C. (2001b). The effect of fear of sexual victimization on adolescent fear of crime. *Sociological Spectrum, 21*(2), 141–174.

May, D. & Jarjoura, G.R. (2006). *Illegal Guns in the Wrong Hands: Patterns of Gun Acquisition and Use among Serious Juvenile Delinquents.* Lanham, MD: University Press of America.

McCoy, H.V., Wooldredge, J.D., Cullen, F.T., Dubeck, P., & Browning, S.L. (1996). Lifestyles of the old and not so fearful: Life situation and older persons' fear of crime. *Journal of Criminal Justice, 24*(3), 191–205.

McDonald, S.C. (1986). Does gentrification affect crime rates? In A.J. Reiss, Jr. & M. Tonry, (Eds.). *Communities and crime.* pp. 163–201. Chicago: University of Chicago Press.

McKee, K.J., & Milner, C. (2000). Health, fear of crime and psychological functioning in older people. *Journal of Health Psychology, 5*(4), 473–486.

Merry, S.E. (1981). *Urban danger: Life in a neighborhood of strangers.* Philadelphia: Temple University Press.

Nance, J.P. (2013). School security considerations after Newtown. *Stanford Law Review Online, 65*, 103–110.

National Science Foundation. (2013). *Youth violence: What we need to know; report of the subcommittee on youth violence of the advisory committee to the social, behavioral and economic sciences directorate, national science foundation.* (February 1 and 2). Accessed September 25, 2013. http://wolf.house.gov/uploads/Violence_Report_Long_v4.pdf.

National Sheriff's Association. (n.d.). *Neighborhood watch manual: USAonWatch—national neighborhood watch program.* Alexandra, VA: National Sheriff's Association. Accessed September 29, 2013. https://www.bja.gov/Publications/NSA_NW_Manual.pdf.

Nellis, A.M. (2009). Fear of terrorism. In K. Borgeson & R. Valeri (eds.), *Terrorism in America* pp. 117–144. Boston: Jones and Bartlett Press.

Nellis, A.M., & Savage, J. (2012). Does watching the news affect fear of terrorism? The importance of media exposure on terrorism fear. *Crime & Delinquency, 58*(5), 748–768.

Pate, A.M., Wycoff, M.A., Skogan, W.G., & Sherman, L.W. (1986). *Reducing fear of crime in Houston and Newark.* Washington D.C.: Police Foundation.

Pew Research Center for the People and the Press. (2012). *Trends in news consumption: 1991–2012; In changing news landscape, even television is vulnerable.* Washington D.C. Pew Research Center.

Piehl, A.M., Kennedy, D.M., & Braga, A.A. (2000). Problem solving and youth violence: an evaluation of the Boston Gun Project. *American Law and Economics Review, 2*(1), 58–106.

Planty, M., & Truman, J.L. (2013). *Firearm violence, 1993–2011.* Washington D.C.: Bureau of Justice Statistics.

Rader, N.E. (2010). Until death do us part? Husband perceptions and responses to fear of crime. *Deviant Behavior, 31*(1), 33–59.

Randa, R. & Wilcox, P. (2012). Avoidance at school: Further specifying the influence of disorder, victimization, and fear. *Youth Violence and Juvenile Justice, 10*(2), 190–204.

Roberts, J.V. (1992). Public opinion, crime, and criminal justice. *Crime and Justice, 16,* 99–180.

Roh, S., & Oliver, W.M. (2005). Effects of community policing upon fear of crime: Understanding the causal linkage. *Policing: An International Journal of Police Strategies &Management, 28*(4), 670–683.

Sampson, R. (2009). *Bullying in Schools.* Washington D.C.: Center for Problem-Oriented Policing. Accessed October 2, 2013. https://www.ncjrs.gov/pdffiles1/Archive/227422NCJRS.pdf.

Sampson, R.J., & Lauritsen, J.L. (1990). Deviant lifestyles, proximity to crime, and the offender-victim link in personal violence. *Journal of Research in Crime and Delinquency, 27*(2), 110–139.

Sampson, R.J., Raudenbush, S.W., & Earls, F. (1997). Neighborhoods and violent crime: A multilevel study of collective efficacy. *Science, 277*(5328), 918–924.

Skogan, W. (1986). Fear of crime and neighborhood change. In A.J. Reiss, Jr. & M. Tonry, (Eds.). *Communities and crime,* pp. 203–229. Chicago: University of Chicago Press.

Skogan, W.G. (1990). *Disorder and decline: Crime and the spiral of decay in American neighborhoods.* New York: The Free Press.

Skogan, W.G., Lewis, D.A., Podolefsky, A., DuBow, F., Gordon, M.T., Hunter, A., Maxfield, M.G., & Salem, G. (1982). *Reactions to crime project: Executive summary.* Washington, D.C.: U.S. Department of Justice, National Institute of Justice.

Skogan, W.G. & Maxfield, M.G. (1981). *Coping with crime: Individual and neighborhood reactions.* Beverly Hills: Sage.

Snedker, K.A. (2006). Altruistic and vicarious fear of crime: Fear for others and gendered social roles. *Sociological Forum, 21*(2), 163–195.

Stanko, E.A. (1989). Missing the mark? Policing battering. In J. Hanmer, J. Radford & E.A. Stanko (Eds.). *Women, policing, and male violence: International perspectives.* pp. 46–69. London: Routledge.

Stanko, E.A. (1998). Warnings to women: Police advice and women's safety in Britain. In S.L. Miller (Ed.), *Crime control and women: Feminist implications of criminal justice policy.* pp. 52–71. Thousand Oaks: Sage.

Sykes, G.M. (1958). *The society of captives: A study of a maximum security prison.* Princeton, N.J.: Princeton University Press.

Taylor, R.B. (1996). Neighborhood responses to disorder and local attachments: The systemic model of attachment, social disorganization, and neighborhood use value. *Sociological Forum, 11*(1), 41–74.

Taylor, R.B., & Hale, M. (1986). Testing alternative models of fear of crime. *The Journal of Criminal Law & Criminology, 77*(1), 151–189.

Toch, H. (1992). *Living in prison: The ecology of survival.* Washington D.C.: American Psychological Association.

Tulloch, M.I. (2004). Parental fear of crime: A discursive analysis. *Journal of Sociology, 40*(4), 362–377.

Tyler, T.R. (1980). Impact of directly and indirectly experienced events: The origin of crime-related judgments and behaviors. *Journal of Personality and Social Psychology, 39*(1), 13–28.

Tyler, T.R. (1984). Assessing the risk of crime victimization: The integration of personal victimization experience and socially transmitted information. *Journal of Social Issues, 40*(1), 27–38.

United States Department of Justice. (2013). *Department of justice awards hiring grants for law enforcement and school safety officers.* Accessed September 27, 2013. http://www.justice.gov/opa/pr/2013/September/13-ag-1088.html.

Violence Policy Center. (2013). *When men murder women: An analysis of 2011 homicide data.* Washington D.C. Violence Policy Center. Accessed October 1, 2013. http://www.vpc.org/studies/wmmw2013.pdf.

Wallace, L.H. & May, D.C. (2005). The impact of parental attachment and feelings of isolation on adolescent fear of crime at school. *Adolescence, 40*(159), 457–474.

Warner, B.S., & Weist, M.D. (1996). Urban youth as witnesses to violence: Beginning assessment and treatment efforts. *Journal of Youth and Adolescence, 25*(3), 361–377.

Warr, M. (1984). Fear of victimization: Why are women and the elderly more afraid? *Social Science Quarterly, 65*(3), 681–702.

Warr, M. (1985). Fear of rape among urban women. *Social Problems, 32*(3), 238–250.

Warr, M. (1992). Altruistic fear of victimization in households. *Social Science Quarterly, 73*(4), 723–736.

Warr, M. (1994). Public perceptions and reactions to violent offending and victimization. In A.J. Reiss, Jr. & J.A. Roth, (Eds.). *Understanding and preventing violence: Consequences and control,* Vol 4. pp. 1–66. Washington D.C.: National Academy Press.

Warr, M. (2000). Fear of crime in the United States: Avenues for research and policy. In D. Duffee (Ed.), *Crime and Justice 2000: Vol. 4,* pp. 451–489.

Measurement and Analysis of Criminal Justice. Washington D.C.: National Institute of Justice.

Warr, M., & Ellison, C.G. (2000). Rethinking social reactions to crime: Personal and altruistic fear in family households. *American Journal of Sociology, 106*(3), 551–578.

Warr, M., & Stafford, M. (1983). Fear of victimization: A look at the proximate causes. *Social Forces, 61*(4), 1033–1043.

Weisburd, D., & Eck, J.E. (2004). What can police do to reduce crime, disorder, and fear? *ANNALS, 593*(1), 42–65.

White House, The. (2013). *Now is the time: The president's plan to protect our children and our communities by reducing gun violence.* Accessed September 25, 2013. http://www.whitehouse.gov/sites/default/files/docs/wh_now_is_the_time_full.pdf.

Wilcox, P., Jordan, C.E., & Pritchard, A.J. (2006). Fear of acquaintance versus stranger rape as a "master status": Towards refinement of the "shadow of sexual assault." *Violence and Victims, 21*(3), 355–370.

Wilcox, P., May, D.C., & Roberts, S.D. (2006). Student weapon possession and the 'fear and victimization hypothesis': Unraveling the temporal order. *Justice Quarterly, 23*(4), 502–529.

Wilcox, P., Ozer, M.M., Gunbeyi, M., & Gundogdu, T. (2009). Gender and fear of terrorism in Turkey. *Journal of Contemporary Criminal Justice, 25*(3), 341–357.

Wilson, James Q., & Kelling, G.L. (1982). Broken windows: The police and neighborhood safety. *Atlantic Monthly* (March): 29–38.

Xu, Y., Fiedler, M.L., & Flaming, K.H. (2005). Discovering the impact of community policing: The broken windows thesis, collective efficacy, and citizen's judgment. *Journal of Research in Crime and Delinquency, 42*(2), 147–186.

Yin, P.P. (1980). Fear of crime among the elderly: Some issues and suggestions. *Social Problems, 27*(4), 492–504.

Yin, P. (1982). Fear of crime as a problem for the elderly. *Social Problems, 30*(2), 240–245.

Yin, P. (1985). *Victimization and the aged.* Springfield, Ill: Charles C. Thomas.

Index

Pages with boxes, tables and diagrams are indicated with **B**, **T** and **D**, respectively.